CONTRIBUTIONS BY STUDENTS AT
THE SCHOOL OF BUSINESS,
TRINITY WESTERN UNIVERSITY

perspectives

On Christianity, Society & The Law

Volume II

Richard J. Goossen, Editor

Perspectives
On Christianity, Society & The Law
A COLLECTION OF UNDERGRADUATE
STUDENT ESSAYS

Published August 2004

EDITOR
Richard J. Goossen
Assistant Professor
School of Business
Trinity Western University

CONTRIBUTORS
Students
School of Business
Trinity Western University

GUIDE TO CITATION
MLA handbook for writers of research papers, 6th ed. (primary)
Canadian guide to uniform legal citation, 5th ed. (secondary)

DIRECT INQUIRES TO
School of Business, Trinity Western University
7600 Glover Road, Langley BC Canada, V2Y 1Y1
Tel: 604.513.2035
Fax: 604.513.2042
Web: www.twu.ca/business

Designed by University Communications © 2004 TWU/UComm
To request this book in alternate formats: call 604.888.7511 ext. 3384
Printed in Canada

CONTENTS

ACKNOWLEDGEMENTS

This book was a team effort. First and foremost I commend the student contributors for their sustained effort over a two-semester period in the midst of a variety of other commitments. In addition to student contributors, several others provided valuable assistance. Thanks to Ms. Suzanne Staryk, Administrative Assistant, for providing support services; Mr. Rod Ross, Corporate Programs Manager, for organizing initiatives for the distribution and marketing of the book; Ms. Debbie Dutka, a student at TWU, for her editorial assistance; Ms. Joy Pecknold and Ms. Michelle Sourisseau, at the TWU University Communications office, for providing excellent input on the design and format of the book; Mr. Kevin Sawatsky, Dean, for facilitating the use of the School of Business resources to complete this project. I thank all of them for their contributions to Volume II of *Perspectives On Christianity, Society & The Law*.

What is the basis for the custom of "sanctuary," whereby churches safeguard refugee claimants from the Canadian legal system while they remain on church property? How do Hutterite communities attempt to preserve their unique way of life while still being subject to the laws of the land? Are churches flouting the copyright laws of Canada by photocopying song sheets and educational materials? Is the download-ing and sharing of music and movie files over the internet a practice that Christians should be concerned with? These issues, and others, are discussed in Vol. II of *Perspectives On Christianity, Society & The Law.*

As society and technology evolve, so does the concept of conventional be-haviour. Much of what was deemed acceptable a mere generation ago is unthinkable today. At their core, laws reflect the current mores of the particular society. Up until a generation ago, Canada had in force a piece of legislation called the Lord's Day Act. The purpose of this Act, quite plainly, was to prohibit commercial outlets from being open on Sunday. Growing up in the late 1960s and early 1970s in Vancouver, I recall how uncommon it was to see a store opened on Sunday. On my way to church, it was even striking to see some one mowing their lawn.

But times change. The Lord's Day Act was challenged in 1982 by Big M Drug Mart under the newly-enacted Canadian Charter of Rights and Freedoms. The Charter was enacted in 1982 along with the repatriation of the Canadian constitu-tion. In their hearing, the Supreme Court of Canada focused on the purpose of the Lord's Day Act, which was to protect the sanctity of the Christian Sabbath. The Su-preme Court held that the multicultural heritage of Canada was recognized in s. 27 of the Charter and that non-Christians should not be prohibited from carrying out otherwise legal activities on Sundays. As a result, the Lord's Day Act was declared invalid. Now a generation later, most Canadians in their 20s would hardly believe that such a law could have ever existed in Canada.

The Big M Drug Mart case is simply one example of how laws that were based on certain presuppositions of legitimacy, such as the historical role of Christian values in Canada and their acceptance by the majority of the population, are being routinely overturned. When I was in high school in the early and mid-1970s, we had a Bible reading and the Lord's Prayer read weekly over the intercom during home-room. All students had to stand for the Lord's Prayer, regardless of how unchristian or disinterested they were. Today, the pendulum has swung dramatically and such a practice would be a flagrant violation of the Charter. Christian groups often struggle to gain permission to meet on a school's premises. In the current environment of "freedom of religion" there cannot be the promotion or the primacy of one religion. Within one generation, the legal system's view of Christianity has devolved from privileged status to simply being one of a number of similar religions.

Christians need to understand the changing societal dynamics that take root in the legal system. I hope that *Perspectives* will help make readers aware of some of these issues.

The first volume of *Perspectives* was so well-received by students, parents and the wider community that we've decided to publish *Perspectives* annually as a way of highlighting the interrelationship between Christianity, society and the law. This volume, the outgrowth of a year's effort, is a collection of essays written by students of the School of Business at Trinity Western University as a product of the upper level class, "An Introduction to Business Law."

For our student contributors, the benefits of writing these essays were two-fold. They discovered that a concentrated effort over a two-semester period and successive re-writing can produce the best work of their university experience. They also found that prospective employers were rightly impressed with their quality of work, clarity of thought, and level of analysis—sought-after skills in any business sector.

Parents, who are often a fiscal partner in a student's education, have also recognized the value of this book project. "It's wonderful that young people are encouraged to look at these moral and ethical dilemmas that we are faced with in today's society. They are our future. They will be facing tough times as Christians and thinking through their response is an important factor," said a parent of one of our student contributors to Vol. I, "We feel that TWU is sending them out very cognizant of these issues."

A book for those trying to understand how the changing legal landscape affects their rights and those of their fellow citizens, the benefits of *Perspectives* extend to churches, ministry organizations, and their leadership. Youth pastors have a starting point to counsel their charges on the legal and ethical issues surrounding the downloading, uploading, and distribution of music and movies over the internet. Pastors have some food for thought regarding the potential legal liability of their actions.

These essays are not intended to be groundbreaking scholarship, but rather a primer for the discussion of relevant topics facing Christians. They provide thoughtful commentary for readers who may not be familiar with how their Christian-based beliefs are affected by the evolving legal system. Each volume will inevitably address a different collection of issues, because as society changes, new issues arise and old ones are reconsidered. *Perspectives*, I trust, will continue to be a current resource on issues that need to be discussed.

Using the Law to Combat Mandatory Union Dues

Aaron Barber

Presently, many unions require employees of unionised organisations to be mandatory members in the union and force all employees to pay obligatory union dues. I
believe that this is an injustice to democracy and to individuals' rights. The point
that I will convey is that Christians should have the right to not be forced to align
themselves with a group that may support political or social activities that are against
Christian beliefs. First, I will give a brief background on unions, explain the basic
policies of unions, and why they are and were important to workers in the business
world. I will also include what society currently says about unions and the issues involving unions. Secondly, I will present the laws and legislation that define workers'
rights locally, nationally, and internationally. I will use these laws in order to argue
that Christians should be exempt from paying mandatory union dues to activities that
they do not believe in. I will also look at present-day issues without the law and focus
on how they relate with the unions. Finally, I will provide a Christian perspective of
how an employee should work in the business world and deal with unions or other
organisations so that the lifestyle of a Christian can reflect Christ's life. In attempting
to be "a light" in the world, Christians need to look at present-day law, using godly
wisdom, in order to decline the obligation to pay mandatory union dues.

Unions were originally formed to protect the workers and to give them a
voice along with some bargaining power in order to have collective negotiations with
the employer. The union was set up to act as the workers' representative in negotiating deals, terms, and conditions of work with the employer. The need for unions

became apparent during the industrial age where harsh working conditions, long hours, and low wages led to many employee injustices. Many Canadian companies and industries were owned or financed by American owners so the workers did not even meet or ever see their employer that set the rules and paid their wages. Unions needed to step in to protect the workers' rights and to bring attention to the employers' injustices. The unions helped to organise the workers so that as a group they could stand up, negotiate properly, and fight against these injustices. Also, the unions would lobby to the government so that the government would begin to make laws that would ensure minimum employment standards. Article V of the CLC Code of Union Citizenship emphasised that one of the many objectives of their union is "to press for such legislation changes as are necessary to protect and enhance the welfare and rights of their members" (McQuarrie 133). The members of the union vote on what actions the union should be taking, how the union dues are spent, and who were to represent them at the local levels. Unions were established with a democratic vote in order to democratically and legally change the workplace.

However, the importance of unions has diminished due to the Employment Standards Act, Charter of Rights and Freedoms (Charter) and other legislation. Unions have had to try and adopt and gain power so that they survive and still have a place in the business world. I see that unions cause a major dilemma to the average Christian worker. Many places of employment are "closed shops," which means that the only way that a person can be employed by the company is if he or she joins the union. The employee must then pay mandatory union dues to the union. Even if the job is not a "closed shop," but there is a union that represents the majority of workers, the employee still has to pay union dues whether they are in the union or not. This is because the union work and influence often provides benefits for every employee in the company, not just the union members.

Furthermore, unions can then participate in social or political activities. The unions can donate a portion of those union dues to make presentations to local government bodies, to participate in events that support other organisations that are facing difficulties, and to participate in charities. Occasionally, union members are able to vote on which events they wish the union to participate and support, but more often the discretion is up to the executives of the union. I believe that this is contrary to Christians' rights of freedom. The reason that Christians would want to fight mandatory union membership and mandatory payment of union dues is because some unions spend a proportion of the union dues on organisations and non-union activities. These organisations and activities may support homosexual marriages, the freedom to choose to have an abortion, political parties that are more liberal, and many other beliefs that Christians are strongly opposed to on a religious basis. Thus, through donating to these groups while making union membership mandatory, the unions have violated Christians' rights of freedom, religion and the freedom to not support and associate.

The law provides rules of conduct that change as society changes. Therefore, it is a good idea to look at how society views the issue of unions, mandatory membership, and how union dues are spent. Dr. Reginald W. Bibby from the Department of Sociology at the University of Lethbridge conducted a study on Canadians and Unions. In this study, he found that "ninety percent of Canadians do not believe that workers should be required to join unions" (Bibby 3). This means that Canadians believe that there should be no "closed-shop" places of employment and that the ultimate decision of joining the union should rest with that individual. Evidence found that with respect to unions spending their dues on non-union activities, "eighty percent of Canadians continue to indicate that such contributions should be voluntary—a level that has remained very steady since the late eighties" (Bibby 5). Furthermore, "The survey found that just over two in ten Canadians favour the involvement of unions in political activities, while more than seven-in-ten are opposed" (Bibby 6). Ultimately, most Canadians believe that unions should not be involved in political activities that are outside of the workplace. Thus, I believe that new laws should be enacted to allow people who pay the union dues to have the freedom to decide whether or not to pay union dues and where and when their contributions are being spent.

Since we have touched lightly on the issue and on the background of unions and union dues, it is best to look at the law and the present-day issues. The Canadian Labour Congress (CLC) was formed in 1956 and became the first to form a national Canadian labour federation. The idea was that this labour federation would be able to focus on only Canadian industrial relations. This is because before the CLC there were too many influences from American investors and American international unions. Currently, it is the largest labour body in Canada. It is best to begin with the CLC Code of Ethical Practices Article VII which begins:

> The record of union democracy, like the record of our country's democracy, is not perfect. A few unions do not adequately, in their constitutions, provide for the basic elements of democratic practice. A few unions do not practice or implement the principles of set forth in their constitutions. Finally, while the overwhelming majority of unions both preach and practice the principles of democracy, in all too many instances the membership, by apathy and indifference, have forfeited the rights of union citizenship. (McQuarrie 134)

I see this as an injustice and even though social democracy is not a law when dealing with unions, but rather a code of conduct, it is still difficult to see that democracy is jeopardised by organisations of vast power. The Merriam-Webster Dictionary defines democracy as being a "government by the people; especially: rule of the majority 1: a government in which the supreme power is vested in the people and exercised by them directly or indirectly through a system of representation usually involving periodically held free elections 2: a political unit that has a democratic government" (Merriam-Webster, "Democracy"). There is obviously a conflict of interest if the majority of people in Canada believe that unions should not be involved in politics, that contributions of union dues to non-union activities should be voluntary, and that workers should have the choice whether or not to be in a union. It is appalling that the largest labour body in Canada publicly denies that they are always democratic and that they do not always give their members the ability to vote for issues that concern them. The CLC publicly states that it takes away from a person's individual rights and freedoms.

Another problem for unions relates to the so-called "Rand Formula." In 1945 workers at a Ford Motor plant in Windsor went to arbitration over the fact of being in a "closed shop" workplace where the employees had to become union members as a condition of employment. The dispute went to the Justice Ivan Rand and he settled the dispute by stating that union dues would be automatically deducted from every worker's paycheque. Workers that did not want to be part of the union could opt out of their obligation to be a union member. However, everyone still had to pay the union dues whether the worker was a union member or not because Justice Rand believed that the union still represented the interests of all workers to management (McQuarrie 92). The union was negotiating to the employer for the benefit of all employees regardless of whether or not the individual was a member in the union. Thus, the "Rand Formula" was created and many people presently see the "Rand Formula" as a way to compensate Christians for the lack of laws in provinces that do not have provisions for religious exemption. The supporters of the "Rand Formula" argue that employees can use the "Rand Formula" to get out of mandatory union memberships. However, I see the formula as sort of an injustice to those people that do not want to be associated with the union. Also, some public opinion is that the law has bypassed citizens that have made a stand against the union and the decisions made by the union that supports activities that those workers do not agree with. The workers are still forced to help pay for those activities that made them want to not participate in the union in the first place.

Originally, the union used the Charter in order to battle the employers and owners of companies. The Charter is part of the Constitution Act that was established as law in 1982 (McQuarrie 18). The unions argued that they were organising workers in order to have a strong voice so that they could be involved in collective bargaining that would further the benefits of workers. The union said that they had the right to organise because of the Charter's rights and freedom to associate, freedom of peaceful assembly, and freedom of thought, belief, opinion and expression. However, I see that the union has in turn violated the Christian's rights under the Charter. If a Christian has the right of freedom of association, then he or she also has the freedom and right to not associate themselves with a particular group that they believe violates their religion or viewpoints. Christians are also justified in having their own thought, belief, opinion, or expression, which includes their support and input to associate with a certain religion or viewpoint. A case in Ontario directly relates to this thought.

In 1991 the case of Lavigne v. Ontario Public Service Employees Union directly relates to the Charter and the freedoms involved. In this case, a professor claimed that the mandatory union dues that he had to pay violated the Charter, more specifically, his freedom of association. The professor was upset that the union dues that he was paying were going to organisations and non-union activities that he personally didn't agree with. Lavigne argued that he would not voluntarily donate any amount of money to these organisations. He continued that the freedom of association also meant the freedom to not associate (McQuarrie 20). The Supreme Court came back with a narrow decision that the donations of mandatory union dues did not violate the Charter. The Supreme Court said that, "all individuals in the workplace benefited from the union's representation and that unions had the right to spend union dues in support of political and social causes" (McQuarrie 20). I find that this violates an individual's rights, freedoms of association, and potentially the freedom of religion. What if the man was part of a "closed shop" company that forced him to join the union and pay mandatory union dues? Thus, he would be forced to be part of a group that he didn't want to be a part of, pay dues to a group he did not agree with, and support organisations and non-union activities that he would not normally support or that are blatantly contrary to his beliefs.

Furthermore, one author states that "none of the rights set out in the Charter is absolute: section one states they are all subject 'to such reasonable limits prescribed by law as can be demonstrably justified in a free and democratic society'" (Smyth, Soberman, and Easson 13). This proclamation protects the viewpoints and rights of the Christians and I believe that this helped to change the Canadian Labour Code and a couple of provinces to change their provincial labour codes. British Columbia, Saskatchewan, Manitoba, and Ontario all allow religious exemption to "employees that object to belonging to a union for reasons associated with their religious affiliation" (McQuarrie 233).

A Christian who relies upon a religious exemption can request that the proportion of the union dues that would have gone to the organisation that the union supports be directed to a charity that the Christian employee and the union agree upon. However, the employee that uses religious exemption must show their religious beliefs definitely conflicts with the general idea of being a member within the specific union. A person cannot simply use religious exemption in order to protest a union that they disagree with or do not support the actions of. The employee has the onus, the responsibility, to prove beyond a reasonable doubt that he or she has a sincere belief in a particular religion, whether they be Catholic, Sikh, Protestant, or any other religion ("Religious Objectors"). The particular individual must show that he or she and their religion lives by a non-union philosophy. The employee must go farther than just being a member of that religion, but must also prove that he or she has a strong belief against the objectives of the union. "The objections to the union cannot be based on social, economic, political, ethical or philosophical grounds" ("Religious Objectors"). The objections must also be to any or all unions, and not based on a particular union or a specific action done by a union. If the employee applying for religious exemption has been a union member in the past, the possibility is very unlikely that he or she will be granted religious exemption. The exemption will also have more support and be more appropriate if the applicant has witnesses that show his or her strong convictions to a religion. The witnesses may have to provide a letter of support for the applicant.

An employee does not have to apply to the labour board if the union agrees to let the employee go free from paying union dues, but this is highly unlikely because unions generally want as much money and support as they can get. Legal advice is not required, but it may be of some assistance. The labour board will then question the employee, but not question the thoughts or beliefs of the religion as a whole. The employees that use religious exemption are usually not allowed to participate in voting done by the union, but the union does still represent all employees in the workplace so the employee still receives benefits from the collective bargaining and agreements. I believe that the provinces that have passed religious exemption provisions in their labour codes see that Christians' rights and freedoms have been violated when they are forced to pay union dues to organisations that they oppose. I congratulate these provinces for making adjustments to accommodate everyone and to give Christians their individual freedoms in this democratic society. Important insight and precedent that would be helpful by taking a look at law in the United States to see if Americans have any laws or provisions that can be related to similar situations.

Since Canada and the United States are both nations that have legal systems under the common law, it is useful to look at the laws of the United States because many laws that Canada and America pass influence the laws of the other country (Smyth, Soberman, and Easson 21). In the United States there is one foundation called the National Right to Work Legal Defense Foundation that has been set up that defends workers in the United States from joining mandatory memberships and paying mandatory union dues ("National Right To Work"). The foundation provides vast amounts of information to the American worker so that the average person is aware of their rights.

According to this foundation, American workers that are employed by the federal government are not required to be a member of a union nor do the employees have to pay mandatory union dues. Employees in private sectors, railway or airline industries, state or local government, or teachers also have the freedom to choose whether or not to become members of a union. However, if a union represents their place of employment, the employee will still have to pay a small union fee that is called an agency fee. This agency fee is the equivalent of the amount that the union can prove is its cost for collective bargaining, administration fees, and grievances. The employee has to pay for the agency because of the case of Abood v. Detroit Board of Education, 431 U.S. 209 (1977) where a judge ruled that the union does represent all of the employees in the workplace whether they are unionised or not. Therefore, the employee must pay for this representation by the union, but does not have to pay the full amount of the union dues that would be contributed to political parties or social activities ("National Right To Work").

The American worker does not have to use religious exemption as an excuse to bypass the union dues. Every worker has the freedom to choose what group or charity he or she would like to support or desires to be affiliated with. The employee also has the freedom to choose his or her association and other rights based on Title VII of the Civil Rights Act of 1964. Title forty-two, Chapter twenty-one, Subchapter VI (C,1), states that "It shall be unlawful employment practice for a labour organisation to exclude or to expel from its membership, or otherwise to discriminate against, any individual because of his race, colour, religion, sex, or national origin" ("Ontario Labour Relations Board"). Therefore, this is evidence that the United States is more lenient when it comes to paying union dues and there is more freedom for employees in these circumstances.

Christian principles have been prominent and referenced throughout this paper, but the citation of relevant Bible verses will assist in understanding a Christian perspective on the issue of unions. The Bible does not specifically speak about unions, but there are many references of how a person is suppose to work in order to set them apart and reflect Jesus Christ in their lives. Ephesians 6:5-9 (NIV) speaks about slaves and masters. It reads:

> Slaves, obey your earthly masters with respect and fear, and with sincerity of heart, just as you would obey Christ. Obey them not only to win their favour when their eye is on you, but like slaves of Christ, doing the will of God from your heart. Serve wholeheartedly as if you were serving the Lord, not men, because you know that the Lord will reward everyone for whatever good he does, whether he is slave or free. And masters, treat your slaves in the same way. Do not threaten them, since you know that he who is both their Master and yours is in Heaven, and there is no favouritism with him.

I believe that this passage represents employees, employers, and unions. Many times employees feel like they are slaves or feel like there is a lack of justice in the workplace with regards to paying the union dues. However, God tells us that we need to obey those people that He placed in charge of us and to show these people the same respect and sincerity that we would show Jesus. We should obey our "masters," whether they be employers or unions, not only win their favour, but also to show Christ through our lives. We can be a light to this world and show our love for our neighbour and for Christ by living a life that reflects hard work and equality to all. God will reward those that do good deeds. I am not saying that people should not use the law and religious exemption to show people their faith. I think that this can be a good witness to others in the workplace and the union executives, especially when done with gentleness and respect. However, I think that Christians need to also show humility and respect if they are not able to prove that they need to bypass the paying of union dues. Christians have other options like playing a bigger role in the unions so that they bind together and can impact the union's decisions on where the union dues are contributed. Christians can do this by being active in union votes and maybe even by being representatives in the union so that they can work to influence, and correct the issues and injustices from the inside.

Colossians 3:23-24 (NIV) also says, "Whatever you do, work at it with all of your heart, as working for the Lord, not for men, since you know that you will receive an inheritance from the Lord as a reward. It is the Lord Christ you are serving." This goes hand in hand with the previous verse. We need to work with a passion for God that others can see our dedication to a better lifestyle that God has blessed us with. The "better life" may not be through riches and a high social standing, but rather God blesses us with accomplishments and the satisfaction to know that we are building treasures in heaven through our actions on Earth. Christians need to remember that this life is only temporary and that we have the best part waiting for us for all of eternity. Therefore, we cannot be consumed with fighting over petty stuff or small amounts of money. We need to live a life that is an example for non-believers and believers alike. People will see that we follow Christ through our actions and they will want to know what we live for and that is Christ. Therefore, I encourage workers to challenge the laws and the union dues that prevent Christians from leading a more pure life. However, it is important that we are near flawless in our deeds so that people do not say that we are using religion as an excuse for anything, which includes saving money from not having to pay union dues. Christians need to "be real" and people full of integrity that recognise their weaknesses and imperfections, but find strength and completion in Christ. If it comes down to it, act like Christ and "give to Caesar's what is Caesar's, and to God what is God's" (Matt. 22:21 NIV). I am saying give the taxes, union dues and the money to the union

Perspectives On Christianity, Society & The Law

because it is just a small amount of money, but remember to give the Lord God your life. Be blameless so that no one falls because of the sin or aggravation that you cause.

In conclusion, there is great importance and instructions as Christians to be a light in the world. Christians need to look at present-day law and religious exemption in order to decline the obligation to pay mandatory union dues. Christians would not support a proportion of their union dues being directed to specific political parties and activities as well as social and non-union activities. In review, I have discussed the background and the uses of unions and what society currently thinks about them. We can determine that there needs to be laws and provisions in place because the majority of society does not believe in unions supporting political parties. The majority of people also believe that contributions and union membership should be voluntary by the individual. Next, I looked at the law and saw that religious exemption is a way for Christians to bypass the payment of union dues. I discussed past cases, labour boards and their codes, the Charter of Rights and Freedoms, and United States law to assist in determining that all employees should not pay out mandatory union dues. Finally, I looked at the Christian perspective and decided that Christians should use the law to their benefit in order to be a light in the world, but if the Christian cannot avoid paying union dues than they must live a life that Christ would be proud of. I understand that there are sometimes hassles and many "hoops to jump through" in order to get religious exemption with regards to the union. If more Christians go through these "hoops," then there will be a voice of people that the government will have to recognise. Hopefully, new laws will be made to allow for religious exemption to be more convenient. However, if a Christian does not wish to go through the struggles of fighting unions, then he or she should build relationships and become active in the union and the voting in order to work with the union and change the union from the inside.

WORKS CITED

Agreement Between British Columbia Hydro and Power Authority and Local Union 258 of the International Brotherhood of Electrical Workers. Expiry Date 31 Mar. 2005.

Anderson, John. Morley Guderson, and Allen M. Ponak. Union-Management.Relations in Canada. Don Mills, Ont.: Addison-Wesley, 1989. A greement Between British Columbia Hydro and Power Authority and Office and Professional Employees' International Union, Local 378. Effective Date 1 April 2002, Expiry Date 31 Mar. 2005.

Brown, Steven Preston. Trumping Religion: The New Christian Right, the Free Speech Clause, and the Courts. Tuscaloosa, Al.: University of Alabama Press, 2002.

Christenson, Sandra. Unions and the Public Interest: Collective Bargaining in the Government Sector. Vancouver, BC: Fraser Institute, 1980.

CNS News Monday, Sept. 5, 2000. 18 Oct. 2003 <http://www.newsmax.com/articles/?a=2000/9/25/80126>.

European Industrial Relations Observatory On-Line. <http://www.eiro.eurofound.ie/2001/04/inbrief/seo10419.html>.

Labour Canada and Human Resource Development Canada. Industrial Relation Legislation in Canada. Ottawa: Labour Canada, 1989.

Lens, Sydney. Unions, and What They Do. New York: Putnam, 1968.

MacDowell, Laurel Setton, and Ian Walker Radforth. Canadian Working Class History. Toronto: Canadian Scholars' Press, 2000.

McQuarrie, Fiona A.E.. Industrial Relations in Canada. John Wiley and Sons Canada, Ltd., 2003.

Menendez, Albert J., and Edd Poerr. Great Quotations on Religious Freedom. Amherst, NY.: Prometheus Books, 2002.

National Right to Work Legal Defense Foundation, Inc. 1996-2000. 24 Sept. 2003 <http://www.nrtw.org/a/a_3_5.html>.

Nissen, Bruce, eds. Unions and Workplace Reorganization. Detroit MI.: Wayne State Press, 1997.

Ontario Labour Relations Board. 18 Oct. 2003 <http://www.gov.on.ca.lab/olrb/eng/infbul/infbul18.html>.

Sutherland, John R. Us and Them: Building a Just Workplace Community. Mississauga, ON: Work Research Foundation, 1999.

The Associated Press. "Unions Want Non-members to Pay Fees." The Cincinnati Enquirer. 17 June 2002. <http://www.enquirer.com/editions/2002/06/17/loc_unions_want.html>.

The Centre for Cultural Renewal. 18 Oct. 2003 <http://www.culturalrenewal.ca>.

Union Dues Check-off-Chapter 11. 18 Oct. 2003 <http://www.tbs-sct.gc.ca/pubs_pol/hrpubs/tbm_11b/aal11-2_e.asp>.

Williams, Jack. The Story of Unions in Canada. Don Mills, Ont.: J.M. Dent, 1975.

OF CHURCH AND STATE:
The Custom of Sanctuary

Rachel deRuiter

II

To most individuals in Canada, playing a role in Canadian history would likely evoke feelings of pride and patriotism. For Mohammed Cherfi, who on March 5,2004 became the first person in the history of Canada to be arrested, handcuffed, and dragged from a religious establishment where he had sought sanctuary, the experience was wracked with fear and foreboding. Cherfi is a civil rights activist who played a significant role in protesting the government's deportation of fellow Algerians due to the pervasive violence and government corruption his home country. Upon receiving his own deportation order, Cherfi believed he had found safety in the age-old tradition of sanctuary. However, that ancient tradition was "broken" when police removed Cherfi from the basement of Quebec City's Eglise Unie St. Pierre were he had been hiding for nearly a month (Hanes 1).

For decades, the "new world" of the United States and Canada has been a beacon of a free society welcoming the marginalized and persecuted from other nations. Millions of immigrants, like Cherfi, have flocked to Canada and the United States with visions of attaining such personal liberties inaccessible in their home countries. Those fortunate enough to be born on Canadian soil are heirs to wealth, opportunity, and a stable future. By contrast, those born into violent and corrupt regimes prize Canadian citizenship for such fundamental rights as freedom of person, freedom of religion, and freedom of speech.

For Alvaro Vega-Ulloha and Menen Ayele, Canada is a safe haven from violence and persecution. They are among a dozen known refugees who, like Cherfi, have been evading Canadian deportation officials by claiming sanctuary in a church building. Vega-Ulloha escaped Columbia where the university professor had been abducted, tortured, and made a target of attempted murder—the penalty paid for speaking openly about human rights and environmental laws in a country identified by humanitarian agencies as one of the most violent places in the world. The professor arrived in Canada with his wife and daughter and claimed refugee status in October 2001 but was denied citizenship due to mistranslation by an immigration consultant. Contrary to the Canadian Charter of Rights and Freedoms, Vega-Ulloha was deprived of the right of appeal and sought refuge in a church in the Ville St. Laurent area of Montreal as a last resort.

Ethiopian mother Menen Ayele and her three children are also claiming sanctuary in a Montreal church. Because of her membership in the All Amhara People's Organisation (AAPO), Ayele was tortured, beaten and imprisoned. She was released only after the actions of the government gained the attention of Amnesty International and the Human Rights Watch. Her husband, who was associated with the Ethiopian Human Rights Council, also disappeared while several of his colleagues were arrested. Ayele's story is supported by human rights reports compiled by Amnesty International, Human Rights Watch, and the U.S. Department of State which document the atrocious human rights abuses that occur in Ethiopia at the hands of law enforcement officials (U.S. Bureau of Democracy, Human Rights, and Labour 2-3). Given that Ms. Ayele's scars are no longer visible and that she was unable to provide previous medical records from Ethiopia which would prove the torture took place, the Immigration and Refugee Board rejected Ayele's claim as "implausible" (Interfaith Sanctuary Coalition 3).

The circumstances surrounding the Vega-Ulloha and Ayele cases are appalling—one cannot argue in good conscience that these individuals should be deported to face further anguish and possible death—yet the integrity of the law demands obedience; should the churches of Canada be held culpable for blatantly superseding the law? My thesis is that sanctuary is not an act of civil disobedience but a viable principle with a basis in law and custom. However, sanctuary carries grave consequences and should be reserved for extreme cases in order to preserve the integrity of Canadian law.

According to Gunther W. Plaut, author of Asylum—A Moral Dilemma, the meaning of "sanctuary" has changed dramatically over the course of history. The earliest recorded occurrence of the tradition stems from the Hebrew translation of miqdash 'holy place' in which sanctuary referred to the Jewish Tabernacle. Consequently, Hebrew custom commanded that those who grasped the horns of the altar were granted temporary asylum (Plaut 129-30).

The term is most often referred to in a medieval context when it became associated with churches and monasteries. Outlaws who were able to escape arrest fled to the Church where they were allowed forty days to exercise their right to call for a coroner and confess their crimes. This accomplished, they were granted safe conduct to a port and passage on a ship never again to return to their native country (Plucknett 431). In doing so, the outlaw abandoned his oath to the King thereby forfeiting his property to the monarch, leaving his wife the status of a widow and his children fatherless. In England, sanctuary was abolished from English common law while in France the Revolution brought the practice to an abrupt close. The most common modern understanding of sanctuary now denotes the practice of diplomatic asylum under international laws.

A Canadian movement reminiscent of the medieval form of sanctuary surfaced as the "Ontario Sanctuary Coalition" in 1992—its aim was not to commit civil disobedience but to participate in a 'civil initiative.' Plaut suggests:

> The Canadian government was seen as breaking its international commitments, and therefore law-abiding, religiously motivated persons felt it was their responsibility to protect the unprotected... There would be no repetition of the situation that the Jews of Germany experienced in the 1930s, when everyone looked away while they were being deported to their deaths. (135)

In the decade since the dawning of the Ontario Sanctuary Movement, the form and function of the act has moved from the church supporting private individuals in hiding refugees, to church buildings themselves becoming havens for persons facing deportation. By August of 2003, over a dozen refugees had sought asylum in Canadian churches in order to evade Immigration and Refugee Board officials (Kinda 2).

Churches that allow sanctuary to refugees are in an awkward position; in a sense, though they are not in alignment with the intentions of government and immigration officials, they are not technically perpetrators of civil disobedience. To be precise, civil disobedience occurs when the law is broken in a non-violent manner in order to bring attention to an injustice. Though an act of protest in the face of what churches believe is unjust, sanctuary is neither sanctioned nor prohibited by Canadian law and consequently is not an illegal act of civil disobedience. In an article of defence stating that the practice acts as a check on the refugee system, Henry Aubin writes, "Sanctuary is not authorised in law. Indeed, it's a kind of loophole in the law. It's based on the idea secular authorities can sometimes be excessively zealous in enforcing the law" (Aubin 1).

The absence of legislation therefore requires an examination of the laws of custom to fully understand the legal basis for providing sanctuary in a church. There is no documentation as to the first instance of sanctuary in Canada but it is commonly believed that the arrest of Cherfi marks the first occasion of police officers removing a sanctuary-seeker from a church. Historically, Canadian authorities have honoured the tradition of sanctuary when granted within a church but the convention was broken when Cherfi was taken from the basement of Quebec City's Eglise Unie St. Pierre (Hanes 1). The local police maintain that his prior arrest during a political protest required that he advise the court of any change of address; his failure to do so was a violation of a bail condition and the cause of his arrest. The spokesman for the Canadian Border Services Agency who escorted Cherfi to American authorities claims that Cherfi's arrest was due to the criminal charges, not an immigration warrant (Vancouver Indymedia 1-2). The agency works with its American counterparts to patrol the borders as well as to remove illegal immigrants to their country of entrance. Cherfi, like most refugees, gained access to Canada via the United States where the possibility of citizenship is dismal due to severe detention policies. Unlike the Canadian system, refugees in America may be subject to confinement with sentenced criminals for indefinite periods of time (Wichert 1).

Both churches and secular defenders of sanctuary can argue the value of the tradition on legal bases grounded in the current ineffectiveness of the refugee determination process, principles of equity, and natural law. According to Section seven of the Canadian Charter of Rights and Freedoms, legal rights should be granted not only to citizens, but to all individuals within Canadian borders. Inclusive is the fundamental right of appeal, a process which is no longer part of the refugee determination process. Portions of the Immigration and Refugee Protection Act (IRPA) received Parliamentary assent on June 28, 2002 yet the sections addressing the Refugee Appeal Division have yet to be implemented. For this reason, refugees are denied citizenship by authority of a single member of the Immigration and Refugee Board (IRB) without the possibility of appeal (Canadian Council for Refugees 1). This governing body is responsible for determining refugee claims. December 2002 promises of Canada's former Minister of Citizenship and Immigration—the Honourable Denis Coderre—to reassess the delayed implementation of the Refugee Appeal Division as endorsed by the complete IRPA, have failed to materialise (Citizenship and Immigration Canada 30).

Law is not only founded on rulings, clauses and codes but a belief that self-evident principles of justice should prevail in a free society. Few people would argue that compassion is one such principle. The reports of the Human Rights Watch, a respected humanitarian organisation, have consistently echoed the sentiments of Canada's current sanctuary claimants; the social conditions of Kosovo, Bangladesh, Columbia, Algeria, and Ethiopia (the countries of origin for current sanctuary-seekers) are unstable at best, often worsened by misuse of government authority. Deporting claimants to face execution—as the Immigration and Refugee Board have consciously done in the case of former North Korean Trade official Song Dae Ri—violates the most intrinsic principles of justice, principles that are not of any cultural or national origin, but of the rational, human logic that innocents should not be punished and the instinct to protect the persecuted (Canadian Council for Refugees 1).

Beyond the scope of our embedded values, the 1951 Convention relating to the Status of Refugees and the 1984 UN Convention against Torture champion non-refoulement whereby Canada is under the obligation of international law to grant stays to refugees certain to face physical persecution. The 1984 Convention against Torture and Other Cruel, Inhuman or Degrading Treatment or Punishment reads,

> [N]o State Party shall expel, return or extradite a person to another State where there are substantial grounds for believing that he would be in danger of being subjected to torture. 2. For the purpose of determining whether there are such grounds, the competent authorities shall take into account all relevant considerations including where applicable, the existence in the State concerned of a consistent pattern of gross, flagrant or mass violations of human rights. (Danieli 177)

Similarly, Article 33 of the 1951 Convention states:

> [N]o contracting State shall expel or return ('refouler') a refugee in any manner whatsoever to the frontiers of territories where his life or freedom would be threatened on account of his race, religion, nationality, membership of a particular social group or political opinion. (Danieli 176-77)

Non-refoulement is seldom enforced by the United Nations and would require ratification in Canadian law to command credibility with immigration officials, however, as a matter of principle, Canada's position as a signatory of these covenants implies a duty to defend and endorse the policies they contain. Those who condone sanctuary often claim that Canada has neglected its international responsibilities by returning claimants—such as Song Dae Ri—to a violent country.

While it is a long-established custom that nations do not always abide by United Nations' conventions, Canadians themselves are subject to time-honoured customs and practices of the land. Until the recent arrest of Cherfi, churches found protection in the knowledge that in the course of Canadian history and dozens if not hundreds of instances of sanctuary, Canadian officials have respectfully abstained from arresting refugees within the walls of a church. The customs and traditions of

Canada are a factor in the common law and the unwritten constitution of Canada. Common law, developed in England and a source of Canadian law, adheres to the system of "precedent," giving significance to previous decisions made by judges in court (Canadian Department of Justice 1). This very principle suggests that the Immigration and Refugee Board's habit of turning a blind eye to the granting of sanctuary and abstaining from judicial action is the foundation of the concept of sanctuary in Canadian custom.

In recent years, sanctuary has been openly discussed by churches who grant it, yet the Citizenship and Immigration Department has created a legal precedent of ignorance to the practice. This implies that unless legislation is passed barring churches from offering this protection, they are not committing civil disobedience and should not be charged for interfering with deportation orders. Furthermore, customs and traditions are recognised as a source of law in Canada; as part of the unwritten portion of the Canadian Constitution, citizens and governing bodies are accountable to customs as they contribute to law (Canadiana 2). In essence, this means that were the Eglise Unie St. Pierre to be charged for protecting Cherfi, their counter arguments would merit serious consideration.

While providing sanctuary is not illegal, allowing churches to impart sanctuary has serious repercussions that could significantly affect Canada on many levels: administrative chaos, church/state relations, the possibility of abuses, and credibility issues have the potential to cripple government processes. These are the factors that generate uneasiness among Citizenship and Immigration officials.

The sheer administrative burden caused by a lenient refugee determination system is illustrated by the situation which arose as a result of the ruling Re Singh and the Minister of Employment and Immigration and 6 other appeals (Singh 1985); the case conceded that the term "everyone" as used in Section 7 of the Canadian Charter of Rights and Freedoms applied to all those on Canadian soil as well as anyone 'seeking admission at a port of entry.' According to Michael Mandel who authored "The Charter of Rights and the Legalisation of Politics in Canada," the administrative disaster that ensued as a result of the flood of refugee claimants "turned out to be an immense bureaucratic knot that would take millions of dollars and years of labour to untie" (Mandel 243). At this time, Canada was flooded with such an abundance of claims from overseas that those awaiting citizenship in Canada were lost in the chaos and confusion of an overburdened system (243). The central truth is that comparatively speaking, Canada is a wealthy nation in a world teeming with poverty and injustice; if immigration to Canada is significantly relaxed we will have more claimants than we can realistically process and legitimate claims will take longer to complete. A difficult and time-consuming procedure encourages fewer applicants, allowing for claims to be processed more expediently.

Apart from creating conflict within the workings of the Immigration and Refugee Board, permitting sanctuary by churches undermines government authority, bringing tension to a relationship beset with conflict since the birth of Christianity. In a recent article on the Cherfi incident, a human rights lawyer commented, "I think this [Cherfi's arrest] is an indication that there is a growing impatience in the [Immigration] Department with arguments of moral suasion" (Hanes 1). Indeed, former Citizenship and Immigration Minister Denis Coderre has asserted in the past that he would not enter into negotiations with refugees hiding in churches (Dawes 3).

Churches have been employing media tactics to further their cause and create a public relations nightmare for immigration officials; an easy task in the wake of Cherfi's arrest. Professor at the University of Windsor, Randy Lippert, has investigated each of the thirty-three cases of sanctuary in Canada that have occurred since 1983. The increasing number of sanctuary-seekers in Eastern Canada caused him to predict–prior to the arrest of Mohammed Cherfi—that Immigration Canada would continue to abstain from removals:

> It's really the spectacle that would be created… People are claiming to be persecuted by authorities in the countries they fled, and here are Canadian authorities using heavy-handed tactics to drag them out of a church. It would look so bad that they have never done it and never will. Their strategy is to wait them out. (Solyom 12)

Church leaders effectively spout the historical importance of sanctuary in English common law but do not divulge that the practice was abolished in the seventeenth century nor that our American counterparts have already broken sanctuary traditions due to the barrage of refugees whose sheer numbers rendered the American immigration system helpless. In order for sanctuary to be a viable option, the church and government have to recognise the validity of each other's arguments and seek to open the channels of communication.

Though the concerns of the churches regarding the efficacy of the Immigration and Refugee Board (IRB) are valid, they have yet to acknowledge that Immigration officials have admitted their defects and are working to implement change. In a recent news release, newly appointed Citizenship and Immigration Minister Judy Sgro promised changes to be made within the Immigration and Refugee Board selection procedure; these modifications include an intensive screening process involving a large advisory panel of experts including lawyers, academics, members of organisations that assist refugees, and human resource experts (Citizenship and Immigration Canada News Release 1-2). Sgro promises changes will be in effect within ninety days and reviewed by the Standing Committee on Citizenship and Immigration within one year. The aim of these alterations is to "eliminate political patronage, strengthen the criteria for the Board and increase parliamentary review." Churches have not acknowledged the proposed changes to the Immigration and Refugee Board but it must be noted that the activities of the churches may have been a catalyst in the IRB changes and perhaps sanctuary has served its purpose.

In addition to the organisational and relational difficulties of offering sanctuary, churches must realise the government is once again dealing with the proverbial "slippery slope" situation. Lines must be drawn to separate sanctuary seekers in crisis from those who merely see Canada as a vehicle for opportunity. Furthermore, if sanctuary were to be established as a sanctioned Canadian practice, officials would need to distinguish whether the custom were reserved for Christian churches or open to religious institutions or non-profit organisations of all faiths and causes.

The case of Leticia Cables illustrates the potential for abuses within the system. Saint Anthony's Church in Edmonton granted sanctuary to the Filipino nanny from July 1999 to February 2000 when Cables decided to return to the Philippines. While Father Emmett Crough believed that the church was lawful in granting refuge, Cables was under no threat of persecution and chose to immigrate for financial reasons. The nanny was working as a care-giver but was denied permanent residency when it was found that she violated the Live-In Care-givers Program by working for more than one employer (Hoang 2). While Cables deportation was unfortunate for such a minor offence, the church had no reason to believe that return to the Philippines would threaten her safety. If churches are willing to manipulate rules for the sake of Cables, the potential for abuse is enormous.

Another form of abuse comes in the form of the institutions that can grant protection to refugees. Who should be allowed the right to grant sanctuary? The practice developed under government systems of old that allowed the Christian Church to play a major role in the judicial system but contemporary Canada—as the cultural mosaic of the world—is brimming with religions. Distinguishing between them would not only be cumbersome, but inevitably require the support of the Canadian Constitution, especially relating to section 15 of the Charter of Rights and Freedoms (Smythe 14). Allowing churches to discriminate between potential candidates would also put them at risk for legal action from other groups wishing to provide sanctuary and could open the door for 'less desirable' groups—cults, for example—to demand the right to grant asylum.

Finally, sanctuary undermines the credibility of the law. The integrity of the law is subject to the perception of those who are governed by it. Law is tangible in the sense that actions result from disobedience to it yet it is intangible as it has no presence except that which we as a nation grant it. In part, law is a mental framework that allows us to understand our country; the ability of churches to use ambiguities and tradition to circumvent penalties for interfering with government processes casts uncertainty on the legal system as a whole. Without legal certainties no legislation can be upheld, for the authority of law rests not on the shoulders of those who enforce the law, but those who abide by it. Without legislation, Canadian citizenship does not afford the safety and chance of prosperity that refugees desire.

The case for churches that have chosen to override the actions of deportation officials also have a biblical defence. From a distinctly Christian perspective, churches are recognising the supremacy of God above the government by showing compassion to the persecuted much as the disciples honoured the Lord by disobeying the laws of the Sadducees, preaching the Gospel of Jesus in Acts 5:17-42 (NIV). By showing Christian love to the refugees, churches view their work with sanctuary-seekers as fulfilment of the Greatest Commandments as cited in Mark 12:29-31(NIV).

The biblical argument against sanctuary is equally sound; though granting sanctuary may not be tantamount to civil disobedience; neither is it acting in obedience to the government as instituted by God. In the book of Romans, the Apostle Paul emphasises that all governing authorities are established by God and submission to them is in its very nature, an act of obedience to God (Rom. 13:1-13 NIV). There is a hierarchy to the primary commandments of Jesus; he commands that our love for God surpass our love for fellow man (Matt.22:36-9 NIV). In this sense, if obedience to authority is an expression of our love for God—as we read in 1 John 5:3 (NIV)—and we work against God-implemented powers by harbouring refugees, interrupting a government process, we are placing man above God and sacrificing the Greatest Commandment of Jesus for the second.

Generally speaking, Canadian churches have been diligent in their selection of sanctuary seekers; claimants are by and large those who pose no threat to Canadian society and have reasonable fear of death or violence upon re-entrance to their birth country. Unfortunately, the concept of sanctuary in Canada is riddled with consequence. Though not an act of civil disobedience, sanctuary should only be undertaken by churches willing to accept the legal responsibility for claimants. Priority should be placed on encouraging the enactment of the complete Immigration and Refugee Protection Act. In its entirety, this portion of Canadian law allows for appeals to be made by refugees who feel their claims were ignored yet the sections regarding such appeals have not yet been implemented. Once ratified, the complete act will be in accordance with the Canadian Charter of Rights and Freedoms.

Churches must seek effective communication and become involved in the Immigration and Refugee Board appointment process. If Christian churches are to make an impact on the lives of refugees such as Cherfi, Vega-Ulloha, and Ayele, they must actively encourage changes in the Citizenship and Immigration Department by encouraging Parliament to (1) enact legislation protecting their right to provide sanctuary and (2) improve the refugee determination process rather than disobey its authority.

Compliance with God-ordained government authority is an underlying biblical principle. If churches disagree with government policy, change must be achieved through legal means to properly claim biblical consistency and to represent Christians not as a hindrance to government by offering the questionable practice of sanctuary, but as a body of citizens willing to offer support in endorsing positive change. Returning victims to violence will certainly continue to cause debate in a country that preaches humanitarian action and egalitarianism, but to preserve the rights and privileges that make this country the envy of so many, government and religious institutions must work with one another to give credence to the laws of the land, a feat that cannot be accomplished under the shield of sanctuary.

WORKS CITED

Aubin, Henry. "Sanctuary Provides Check on Refugee System." The Gazette (Montreal). 9 Mar. 2004. 11 Mar. 2004 <http://web.lexisnexis.com/universe>.

Barker, Kenneth, ed. The NIV Study Bible. Grand Rapids: Zondervan, 1995.

Danieli, Yael., ed., et al. The Universal Declaration of Human Rights: Fifty Years and Beyond. New York: Baywood, 1999.

Dawes, David F. "Five Churches Giving Sanctuary to Refugee Claimants." Canadian Christianity.com. 16 Oct. 2003. 22 Mar. 2004 <http://www.canadianchristianity.com/cgi-bin/na.cgi?nationalupdates031016sanctuary>.

Duhaime, Lloyd. "Sanctuary." Duhaime's Law Dictionary. <http://www.duhaime.org>.

"Ethiopia: Country Reports on Human Rights Practices—2003." Bureau of Democracy, Human Rights, and Labour. U.S. Department of State. 31 Mar. 2003. 8 April 2004.

Hanes, Allison. "Cherfi Arrest Called Warning to Sanctuary Seekers." The Gazette (Montreal). 11 Mar. 2004. 11 Mar. 2004 <http://web.lexis-nexis.com/universe>. —"Sanctuary Seeker's Fate in Trio's Hands of 3." The Gazette (Montreal). 10 Mar. 2004. 11 Mar. 2004 <http://web.lexis-nexis.com/universe>.

Hoang, Anh. "Pastor Defends Right to Offer Sanctuary." Western Catholic Reporter. 21 Feb. 2000. 4 Feb. 2004 <http://www.wcr.ab.ca/news/2000/0221/nannysanctuary022100.html>.

Human Rights News. Human Rights Watch. 18 Mar. 2004. 22 Mar. 2004 <http://hrw.org/english>.

Jayoush, Kinda. "Ethiopian Mother, Kids Seek Sanctuary in Church: Bid for Refugee Status Rejected." The Gazette (Montreal). 7 Aug. 2003. 31 Jan. 2004 <http://web.lexis-nexis.com>.

Mandel, Michael. The Charter of Rights and the Legalization of Politics in Canada. Toronto: Thompson Educational, 1994.

"Minister Sgro Announces Reform of the Appointment Process for Immigration and Refugee Board Members." Citizenship and Immigration Canada. Mar. 2004. 23 Mar. 2004
<http://www.cic.gc.ca/english/press/04/0403-pre.html>.

Plaut, W. Gunther. Asylum: A Moral Dilemma. Westport: Praeger, 1995.

Plucknett, Theodore. A Concise History of the Common Law. 5th ed. Boston: Little, Brown & Co, 1956.

"Protesters Angry Refugee Arrested in a Church." Vancouver.Indymedia.org. 9 Mar. 2004. 22 Mar. 2004
<http://www.vancouver.indymedia.org/news/2004/03/114480.php>.

"Refugee Appeal Division Implementation Delayed." Citizenship and Immigration Canada. 29 April 2002. 27 Jan. 2004
<http://www.cic.gc.ca/english/press/02/0212-pre.html>.

"Refugee Rights in Canada, 4 April 2003: 'Two Steps Forward, Six Steps Back.'" Canadian Council For Refugees. 3 April 2003. 31 Jan. 2004
<http://www.web.net/~ccr/april4.pdf>.

Smyth, J.E., et al. The Law and Business Administration in Canada. 10th ed. Toronto: Prentice Hall, 2002.

Solyom, Catherine. "Desperately Seeking Sanctuary: An Ancient Concept is Becoming a Trend Among Canada's Frightened Refugees." The Halifax Daily News. 4 Aug. 2003: 12.

"Sources of Canadian Law." The Canadian Department of Justice. 24 April 2003. 23 Mar. 2004
<http://canada.justice.gc.ca/en/dept/pub/just/CSJ_page7.html>.

"The Written and the Unwritten Constitution." Canada in the Making. 23 Mar. 2004
<http://www.canadiana.org/citm/specifique/written_e.html>.

"What Does it Take to Win Protection? Lessons From the Song Dae Ri Case." Canadian Council For Refugees. 25 Feb. 2004. 22 Mar. 2004
<http://www.web.net/~ccr/ri.htm>.

"Why Do People Turn to Sanctuary?" The Interfaith Sanctuary Coalition. 9 Oct.
2003. 28 Jan. 2004
<http://www.web.net/~ccr/whysanctuary.htm>.

Wichert, Tim. "No Room at the Inn? Take the Underground Railroad." Ottawa
Comment. 12 Dec. 2002. 23 Mar. 2004 <http://www.mcc.org/canada/refugees/
articles/Ottawa_comment_Dec02.html>.

THE RIGHT TO SING:
Is the Church Breaking the Law?
Carlos Ekkert

III

In 1996 a variety of girl scouts, boy scouts, and inner city campers in the US were breaking the law, namely the Copyright Act, and many of them did not even know it. They were taken a back by a lawsuit demanding that artists be reimbursed for songs that were sung at camps (Christianity Today). Today, many churches in Canada are likewise breaching some provisions of the Copyright Act. As technology plays an increasingly more prominent role in communicating the Christian gospel, churches in North America are beginning to enter an age where the Copyright Act will play a big role in the way churches go about their activities. In the past the Copyright Act primarily applied to issues such as the copying of choral music. However, today it applies mostly to the unauthorized use of worship music, songs that are usually sung on a weekly basis in the majority of contemporary churches. While most administrators of North American churches plead ignorance, they are still liable to a standard of care that includes being informed about the licensing arrangements in their churches (Carters). Churches cannot allow themselves to conform to standards that are not in line with the laws and regulations of the government, otherwise, the churches themselves will come across as hypocritical when they try to correct and give suggestions to other organizations. Obeying copyright law is not only an issue of compliance, but also an issue of integrity. Consequently, Christian organizations need to take more proactive action in obeying the Copyright Act of Canada, because if they fail to obey copyright laws their members will be encouraged to do likewise. And collectively they will taint the reputation of evangelical churches.

This paper will examine the different applications of the Copyright Act, where North American churches (the "Church") have failed to obey the Copyright Act, and what our response ought to be as the Church. The Church and its connections with the Copyright Act is not something that will go away, but only increase as the Church tries to continually become more integrated with the community and modern society.

The Law of Canada gives specific rights to the copyright holders, and methods of reimbursement if rights have been infringed. These rights include:

1) The exclusive right to copy music, art or other copyrighted material.
2) The exclusive right to reproduce intellectual property.
3) The exclusive right to perform property (Copyright Act).

In Canada, the law suggests that each person's intellectual property is copyrighted automatically whether or not they have applied for copyright protection. However, in most cases the law will require a copyright seal to prove that one's intellectual property has actually been infringed upon. Once copyrighted the copyrighted property is protected for fifty years after its owner's death. A good example of this is Elvis Presley who still today, many years after his death, is one of entertainment's top money earners as his estate collects dues for performance of his music. Fifty years after the owner of the copyrighted material has died, the property is considered public domain (United Church), meaning anyone has the authorization to use the material. Other reasons originally copyrighted material might be public domain is that the term of the copyright may have expired, the owner assigned the copyright to the public, or the work is not signed to a treaty in which the copyright laws apply in Canada (United Church). Furthermore, the Copyright Act of Canada gives an author the right to collect $500 - $200,000 for each infringement of his/her property. Therefore, if a church were to be taken to court for copyright violations, the outcome could result in significant monetary damages. Additionally should be noted that all material, art or music produced by ministers employed by the church during working hours belongs to the church (Christian Activities). This includes Music Pastors who may naturally consider music written by them as their private property. These copyright laws are increasingly coming into play as Music Pastors, employed full-time by their churches produce worship CD's and choral productions.

The Copyright Act applies the same to non-profit organizations as it does to corporations (Carters). Administrators of churches need to know the applications of the law in regard to their organizations. The law holds the Pastor or administrator liable to a minimum "standard of care" in which the "reasonably prudent person" would have known what the law stated. People with specialized knowledge or experience (like Music Pastors who hold music degrees) are held to a higher standard than others, depending on their background and experience. The Copyright Act not only affects the future liability of the church, but also the future liability and careers of church volunteers and pastors. 1 Corinthians 6:1 says, "If any of you has a dispute with another, dare he take it before the ungodly for judgment instead of before the saints?" (NIV) This verse, in the past, has probably deterred Christian recording companies from suing Christians and Christian organizations. However, it does not give Christians a right to continue being negligent about copyright law. We need to inform ourselves about the implications of the law and abide by them.

Churches have in the past routinely violated the Copyright Act, often without knowledge of copyright law, while other times blatantly. For many churches the church office has ironically become a hub of illegal, and possibly, even criminal activity. Some of the more obvious ways churches are breaking the Copyright Act are the following:

1) Music ministers producing rehearsal tracks for their worship teams by burning (copying) CDs they have purchased and handing them out to worship team members in order for them to learn songs that they want to play in the future (Church CA).
2) Choral ministers only buying one copy of sheet music and photocopying it for their choir members.
3) Singing, printing, and displaying (LCD projectors) worship music without the appropriate licensing agreements (CCLI).

Regrettably, the excuses that Christian organizations use to defend themselves for breaking the law (in regard to the Copyright Act) are unacceptable. Some of these include the following:

1) Licensing takes too much time and too much effort.
2) We lack the resources (in other words, compliance is too costly)
3) Licensing costs too much.
4) People do it all the time (the implication is that the behaviour is socially acceptable).
5) We do it for the ministry / it's for a good purpose (the ends, which are positive, therefore justify the means) (Agape Press).

These are only a few of the arguments used to justify such actions. One cannot say that these are appropriate reasons for breaking the Copyright Act. The Gospel Music Association (GMA) President was quoted as saying, "It's not about business or ministry; it's about ministry or theft" (Agape Press). His point being that one cannot decipher whether to steal for business purposes or for ministry purposes. The Copyright Act makes no differentiation between a for-profit corporation and a non-profit organization. Therefore, as a Christian organization, one should be held to at least the same standard than those around us.

There are some specific infringements of the Copyright Act that do not pertain to music, that are not so easily identified, or may not have been considered by church administrators. First, some of these include showing videos and news broadcasts at Bible studies or youth groups. These movies, videos and broadcasts need public licenses in order to be shown, even if they are only shown in small groups. Most movies that are released in public theaters need a "public license" to be shown in church. The following celebrated movies; The Ten Commandments and Jesus of Nazareth need public licenses in order to be viewed in churches (ECLA). These are only several of the movies that are often shown in churches without a public license. Secondly, website images that are being copied from other websites to create your own website also constitute a copyright infringement. Thirdly, backgrounds displayed in "PowerPoint" presentations need to have to be owned by the church or

Perspectives On Christianity, Society & The Law

at least have permission to be used. As well, background music played during services needs to be owned by the church. Do you at least have the compact disk on hand that you are playing? With MP3 technology (a technology that compresses music into a format in which it is easier to transport) it is becoming easier for people to transport music, play it in multiple places, and play music that they do not own. These are all aspects that need to be carefully looked at because they so often escape the administrator's supervision.

The Church needs to respond in a way that reflects the values and faith it holds. The response needs to be in the education of its members, the buying of blanket licenses to cover licensing agreements, teaching respect for government law, and setting guidelines for obeying copyright law.

The Church needs to take a clear step in educating its members. In educating the regular church member about church copyright, one rule to go by is "when in doubt don't use it" (Christianity Today). It is important that members not take a careless approach to the resources they use. In general, one can assume that everything that is of value is copyrighted. If it can be determined that there is no commercial duplicate of the product you are using (for example there is no company selling the software you are using for profit purposes) one can then safely assume that there is no copyright. The first vital step is to educate church members about copyright law and to take copyright law seriously.

Further, blanket licenses give the Church an important way of making sure they are obeying copyright law and are legally using the property of others. Probably the most evident blanket license comes in the form of the Church Copyright License (CCLI). By purchasing the CCLI license one purchases the right to:

1) Record your worship service on tape, create audio and video-
tapes of services, weddings, or camps.
2) Project your songs onto overhead or LCD.
3) Copy lyrics into bulletins, handouts, or songbooks.
4) Maintain a database of songs on a computer (CCLI).

What the CCLI license does not cover is the following:

1) Making rehearsal tracks (for choirs or for worship teams).
2) Making custom arrangements.
3) Duplicating choral music.
4) Concerts and performances that are not part of religious performances.
5) The ability to show videos / DVD's in presentations (CCLI).

The CCLI license is used in over 140,000 churches in North America and over 170,000 worldwide. The license itself includes over 150,000 songs which can be used for worship, choirs and performances (Christian Activities). It is almost a must today that churches own a CCLI license for their corporate worship. Licenses are adequately priced and range anywhere from fifty-five dollars a year for a small church up to $1,110 a year for a church over twenty thousand members (CCLI). The license provides an affordable and legal solution to copyright infringements. Unfortunately, the CCLI license does not give churches permission to show movies in public places. Youth groups, Bible studies or churches that watch videos need to acquire the adequate licenses to show these movies. The best approach for getting a license to present movies in public places is to obtain a Christian Video License (CVLI). The CVLI license is a recently established agreement between CCLI and Motion Picture Licensing Corporation to allow churches to show movies in their premises. If the church refuses or cannot buy a CVLI license the next best approach is to ask people to watch the video or movie at home before attending Bible study or youth group. Blanket licenses are an essential and easy way to administer copyright in a church.

In order to respond correctly to the education of its members with respect to the provisions of the Copyright Act, churches need to teach its members to obey and respect the government. Romans 13 explicitly gives us instruction on how to cooperate with our government when it says, "Obey the rulers who have authority over you. Only God can give authority to anyone, and he puts these rulers in their places of power. People who oppose the authorities are opposing what God has done, and they will be punished" (NIV). It is for this reason that churches need to inform

Perspectives On Christianity, Society & The Law

its members about copyright law. First, educating people about the importance of respecting government regulations must come from the pulpit. Members of churches must be made aware that Christians ought to be held to a higher standard than the rest of society, which often disregards copyright laws as something which does not really need to be obeyed. Secondly, the example of respecting the Copyright Act needs to come from the elders/leadership of the church. If the Music Pastor in the church does not respect the Copyright Act and freely hands out "rehearsal tracks" produced on the church office CD writer, how can a church expect its members to go home and not download music illegally off the Internet? Members' first justification will be that the Music Pastor at church copies music illegally and if he does it then it must be an acceptable thing to do. Even if not consciously, then subconsciously this will be a members' reasoning. If Pastors readily disregard purchasing licenses needed to stay in compliance with the Copyright Act, it will filter through to their members that the Pastor has a low standard of respect for the law. A student is never above his teacher (Matt. 10:24), and therefore, church members will follow the examples of their leaders. Thirdly, we need to equip leaders with the tools and knowledge to obey government regulations. It is important to make sure that Music Pastors are properly educated and have the proper resources to keep track of copyright infringements. An overworked Music Pastor will be more likely to disregard a copyright infringement in order to meet expectations that he cannot otherwise reach. Subsequently, the administration in a church needs to show leadership on copyright law and teach and promote obedience to the Copyright Act.

The following are some suggested guidelines for keeping churches in compliance with the Copyright Act. First, the most important step for churches is that they commit themselves to buying a CCLI license. The CCLI license gives them the authority to reprint and copy material needed for regular praise and worship on Sunday mornings and other occasions where corporate worship might exist. While the majorities of churches have committed themselves to a CCLI license there are still some churches that refuse to commit themselves to the blanket license format. Secondly, it is very important to establish a "Copyright Administrator." Having a "Copyright Administrator" is important because it makes someone responsible for the compliance and infringements of the church's activities. One can assume that this person would also have some knowledge about the copyright laws and if not, will learn what they are through out the course of their term as copyright administrator in the church. Recommended is for larger churches that this position is a separate position from that of a full-time Music Pastor. Copyright administration can entail keeping track of a lot of the obligations the church has in regard to copyright law, which may easily be sidelined if a Pastor becomes too busy with their other responsibilities. The responsibility of copyright administration could be delegated to the secretary, but would need a clear outlining of the responsibility involved. As well, the copyright administrator will likely not end up administering only musical copyright and therefore the position may not be suitable for the Music Pastor. Some of the responsibilities of the copyright administrator should include:

1) Being responsible for the appropriate buying of blanket licenses in order for church to be in compliance with the Copyright Act.
2) Being the "go to" person for worship leaders, choir directors, Sunday School teachers or anyone else to ask for permission in order to copy materials.
3) Being responsible for checking that all music in the church being played over the sound system is properly accounted for and is owned by the church.
4) Being responsible for the installation of software licenses on computers.
5) Being responsible for reviewing the church website and PowerPoint, and making sure that no images or materials are being used without permission.

A third recommendation is that churches establish a library of music which would consist mostly of Christian CD's. This library of music is necessary in the church, so that worship leaders can use the library as a resource for teaching their peers music, as this is a very common method used today. The church's library of music CD's could be used to play the background music played before and after services. It is also important that churches implement some kind of guidelines to keep track of their list of compliance with the Copyright Act.

Perspectives On Christianity, Society & The Law

A question that we need to ask is what are the consequences of not obeying the Copyright Act as a church? The first consequence will be seen in the members of the church as they assimilate to the standards set around them. It is widely known that many Christians (especially younger generations) participate in downloading music "for free" in peer-to-peer networks (CRIA). The "free music myth" has penetrated deep into the average Christian church member. Maranatha Music (a Christian recording company) stated that in 2003 music sales have dropped ten to fifteen percent largely due to illegal downloads (Rachel, Warren). In 2003, pirated sites offering illegal music doubled in only four months and in the same time global music sales dropped by seven percent. Churches need to set a precedent as to how to act in times of uncertainty and set an example for its younger generation in regard to how to respect the Copyright Act.

If the church does not obey the Copyright Act it will ultimately affect its integrity. The church that wants to be a church that makes an impact in the new millennium needs to be a church that respects the laws of the new millennium. Trying to stay modern is no excuse for the church to disobey the Copyright Act. If the church undermines its integrity it will lose a lot more then just being up to date with the latest technologies and resources. It will lose the trust of the government and citizens alike. Additionally, if churches are to be blessing to other public organizations it will need to obey not only human standards, but also God's standards. The church is the form of Jesus Christ here on earth and for those who do not know Jesus Christ the church is what they judge their perception of the gospel on. The integrity of the church is also what the government bases its trust of the Church on. Once the Church has lost its ability to be trusted to obey the laws of the country, the government will be even less likely to hear it out on other issues, and end up giving the church less responsibility for caring for the citizens of its country. It is the integrity of churches that is at stake by not obeying the Copyright Act.

In conclusion, the Church must take a tough stance on obeying the copyright law otherwise the reputation of the Church will be affected by it. The Church must make itself aware of the different laws of the Copyright Act. The Copyright Act gives the author the sole right to copy, the sole right to reproduce, and the sole right to performance. The church must therefore inspect itself to see where it's failed the Copyright Act. For many churches, their failures to respect copyright law may come in the form of making rehearsal tracks for worship teams, photocopying choral music illegally, or not acquiring the proper licensing. Excuses churches use, like licensing takes too much time and "we do it for the ministry" are unacceptable. The Church's response must be clear and concise in order to save its integrity and to influence its members in the right direction. Some suggestions given for copyright compliance are purchasing an annual CCLI license and instating a copyright administrator who oversees compliance with the Copyright Act. A copyright administrator would be responsible for overseeing licensing agreements and giving permission for copying of materials owned by the Church. A consequence of not obeying the Copyright Act will be that church members assimilate to society's standards. The consequences of not obeying the Copyright Act will affect more then just the compliance of a law by the Church's members though. At stake for the Church by not complying with copyright law is its integrity, the integrity of its members, and the integrity of its faith.

"About the Licenses." CCLI. 2000. 24 Sept. 2003 <http://www.ccli.com>.

"Access Copyright > resources." Cancopy. 24 Sept. 2003
    <http://www.accesscopyright.ca/resources.asp?a=35>.

"Applying for a US Copyright License through Integrity Music." Copyright License
    Application. 22 Oct. 2003
    <http://www.integritymusic.com/contact/copyright/body.html>.

"Are You Breaking the Law?" Enrichment Journal. 22 Oct. 2003
    <http://www.ag.org/enrichmentjournal/200303/200303_042_break_lawa_
    sb.cfm>.

"CCLI's Church Copyright License." Ray Watson's Secret Place. 22 Oct. 2003
    <http://www.christianactivites.com/church/story.asp?ID=3192>.

"CCLI Release List of Top Songs Sung by US Churches." Christian Activities
    Online. 22 Oct. 2003
    <http://www.christianactivities.com/ church/story.asp?ID=3192>.

"Charity Law." Carters. 7 Nov. 2002. 22 Oct.2003 <http://www.carters.ca>.

"Church Copyright Administration." CCA. 2003. 24 Sept. 2003
    <http://www.churchca.com/core.html>.

Copyright Act (R.S. 1985, c. C-42) "Copyright Act." 30 April 2003. 24 Sept. 2003
    <http://laws.justice.gc.ca/en/C-42>.

"Copyright Guide for Congregations." United Church. 24 June 2003. 24 Sept. 2003
    <http://www.united-church.ca/copyright/congregations.html>.

"Copyright How to Avoid Infringement." The First Amendment Handbook. 22
    Oct.2003 <http://www.rcfp.org/handbook/c10p06.html>.

"Copyright: Laws." South Indian Conference. 22 Oct.2003
    <http://www.sicumc.org/media/copyright.asp>.

"Do we need a License to Show Videos in Our Congregation?" ELCA. 22 Oct. 2003
    <http://www.elca.org/co/faq/videos.html>.

"FAQ." Kansas West Conference of the United Methodist Church. 22 Oct. 2003 <http://www.kswestumc.org/faq2.htm#does>.

"1 Corinthians 6:1." Bible: New International Version. 15 Nov. 2003. Zondervan, 1985.

Martin, Allie. "GMA Blames Illegal Downloading for Christian Music Sales Slump." Agape Press. 10 July 2003. 24 Sept. 2003 <http://headlines.agapepress.org/arc hive/7/102003f.asp>.

McIntyre, Dean. "FQ News and Notes." 2003. 24 Sept. 2003 <http://www.gbod.org/fqnews/nov01/page3.html>.

Normand Tamaro. "The Annotated Copyright Act 1992." 22 Oct. 2003. Scarborough Ontario: Carswell, 1992.

"Re: a CCLI Question." Forum for Discussing CCLI licensing. 22 Oct. 2003 <http://www.fni.com/worship/200305/msg00133.html>.

Robertson, Brian. "Don't Torch Musician's Income Burn Media Piracy." Vancouver Sun. 17 Oct. 2003. 14 Oct. 2003.

Smyth, Soberman, Easson. "The Law and Business Administration in Canada." Toronto, Ontario: Pearson Education Canada, 2004.

"Society of Composers, Authors and Music Publishers of Canada." Socan Society. 24 Sept. 2003 <http://www.socan.ca/jsp/en/index.jsp>.

Stockton, Train. "Christian Copyright License International." Government of UK. 22 Oct. 2003 <http://www.train.stockton.gov.uk/pages/viewpage.asp?uniqid=2401>.

"The Church and the Law." Alliance Resources. 22 Oct. 2003 <http://www.cmalliance.org/resources/churchrisk/law/copyright.htm>.

"The Church Musician and the Copyright Law." MPA Document Library. 24 Sept. 2003 <http://www.mpa.org/church.html>.

"The Copyright Guide." Oxford Anglican. 22 Oct. 2003 <http://www.oxford.anglican.org/info/copyright.html>.

"The 'Free Music' Myth." CRIA. 2000. 24 Sept. 2003 <http:www.cria.ca/fmm.html>.

Throop, John R.. "Finance and Law: Right Those Copyright Wrongs." Christianity Today. May/June 1999. 24 Sept. 2003 <http://www.christianitytoday.com/yc/9y 3/9y3038.html>.

Warren, Rachel. "Re: losses of music industry." Email to Sales Department. 3 Oct. 2003.

Hate Crime vs. Free Speech:
The Effects of Bill C-250 on Religion in Canada

Joshua Frankamp

IV

Wherever there is a right to speak, there is someone who wants that right controlled. The right to speak and the right not to hear someone else speak are constantly in tension because speech is the means by which we as a free and open society communicate ideas, ideals and values. Canadians face an interesting challenge to the freedom of speech, especially religious speech, in the introduction of Bill C-250 and its passing in Parliament (Bowman). Proponents of the Bill envision a protection of citizens that will ensure greater peace and safety for all Canadians. While the Bill has not yet passed through the Senate, those who are against it are concerned about a future where religious discussion and statements of disapproval of lifestyle choices would amount to criminal offences thereby stifling free speech.

In this paper I will argue that hate crime laws, including the recent amendment by Bill C-250, do not directly hinder religious expression, however, they may reduce constructive speech in the attempt to deter hate-inciting speech. I intend to support this argument by first laying out the background of free speech and the development of hate crime law. Second, I will look at current freedom of speech and freedom of religion rights and how religious expression is negated in the public sphere. Last, I will explore current hate propaganda law and using a case I will draw conclusions as to the effect that Bill C-250 would have on religious expression in the public arena.

BACKGROUND

In this section I will present some of the philosophical foundations and background of free speech law in order to facilitate a discussion of hate speech. Second I will show from a Christian standpoint why freedom of speech is an important value to uphold. Third, I will show how in Canada the idea of group protection versus individual protection developed and discuss the mixed results of such a strategy.

Freedom of speech is a value that must be protected in a free and open democratic society. The protection of the expression of dissenting opinions is at the core of our society without which we would not have a free nor open debate about what is true or false, good or bad, beautiful or ugly, right or wrong (O'Neil 9). In Nicholas Wolfson's Hate Speech, Sex Speech, Free Speech he discusses the idea that the model for knowing truth in a liberal society is a post-modern, pragmatic, and plural one (12). In this model a society such as ours is not looking for an absolute or universal truth from which it can gauge the validity of speech. Instead we value the open exchange of ideas in with expectation that in the marketplace of ideas the best and truest ideas will win out. This relative validity of opinion leaves us with a problem when we try to draw a line and say that one person's speech is unacceptable while another person's speech is acceptable.

Rodney Smolla in Free Speech in an Open Society states that there are two obvious "easy answer" methods of determining policy on free speech and both of them come up short (43). The first is absolutism, the idea that all ideas can be judged based on a foundation of set ideas or ideals. This fails because we have no homogeneity in our culture for determining the basis of such an absolute stance. Since we as Christians would have to compromise to gain consensus in our heterogeneous culture we also could never decide on a basis without compromising the absolute nature of it. The second is history, the idea that original intent of the "freedom of thought, belief, opinion and expression" in the Canadian Charter of Rights and Freedoms in Canada could be the guide to understanding the complexity of free speech (Charter). Smolla asserts that this method also fails because the original intent is too difficult to determine. He states that "the human instinct to censor thrives, as it always will, living in irrepressible conflict with the human instinct to speak" (42).

The absolutist view expressed above is closely aligned with a traditional dogmatic Christian view. Wolfson also states that from a modern Christian perspective, the lack of any foundation in our modern society is nihilistic which makes public discourse an exercise in assertion instead of discussion (37). However he goes on to state that the goals of a free and open society promoting free speech are not at all contrary to those of a Christian worldview that sees God's revelation is continual and not dogmatic in nature. Since we do not have complete revelation we should approach our culture with humility. Thus we should engage in public discourse in a tolerant way that exchanges ideas and weighs them in common (38).

In view of the varied philosophical backing for the value of free speech in a democratic society there are certainly going to be different views on which speech should be protected and which should be deemed harmful. There are a few different criteria to base the distinction of acceptable and unacceptable speech on a society. The first is the truth of the statement. If the speech in question can be shown to be not true, then its value to society as an argument is negligible. However this argument is limited because similar to the idea of defamation, it is only applicable when it can be shown that the statement was one of fact not opinion (49). The line between the two is often slippery and most inflamed dialogue in society would not be considered attempts at making factual statements (50). Therefore the factual statement versus opinion method tends to limit valid expression and is not a good criterion for restricting speech.

The arguments for restricting hate speech are summarised according to Wolfson as follows:

> [F]irst [is] the scientific falsity of explicit or implicit racial or sexual [or other 'identifiable group'] stereotyping; and second, the harm such speech does to the victim…. The victim feels threatened, humiliated and diminished. It is asserted that he or she may suffer temporary or permanent psychological harm. Furthermore, such expression…tears the weave of the community in which the speech was made. (47)

In Canada hate speech and hate literature laws prohibiting violence or threat against a group have not always been a part of the Canadian legal system. According to the Report of the Special Committee on Hate Propaganda, in 1966 the commission stated that there was no law to protect a group from this kind of violence (36-37). The reason given was that individuals were already protected from many kinds of violence including threats as individuals not groups. Hence individuals are "protected from violence and threats of violence which are intended to compel them to abstain from doing anything they have lawful right to do or to do anything they have lawful right to abstain from doing... and also from threatening communications of all kinds..." (37).

Since individual rights were and are already protected it is unclear how overlapping group rights came into being. The Report goes on to give us a hint as to the cause and intent of the development of genocide law (37). Hate speech and hate propaganda against identifiable groups is closely related to genocide law. These three types of crime are grouped together in sections 318-320 of the Canadian Criminal Code. Apparently the influence of international bodies is a major factor in the development of Canada's genocide and implied within that is hate speech law.

[A]lthough Canada is a signatory of the United Nations Convention on Genocide and is bound thereby to implement anti-genocide measures in its domestic legislation; Canadian law so far has not been amended in accordance with the Convention. (37)

Furthermore the committee speaks on the supposed intent of the genocide law that it does not address laws geared at protecting individuals. "[T]he intent to destroy a racial, religious, ethnic or national group, which is an essential ingredient of the genocidal act, is not an element of any existing offence in Canadian law" (37).

The intent of group protection, as contrasted with laws protecting individuals, is primarily to protect a group from being "destroyed," as defined by the committee. The application of this law is obvious when it comes to genocide law protecting groups from physical violence; however, when hate law is extended to cover hate speech against a group, I believe it goes beyond the intent of preventing that group from being "destroyed." If a person threatens someone on the basis of ethnicity, that is a basis for hate speech. However, if a person threatens someone for an unknown reason he or she is instead guilty of some other personal offence such as assault. This in its essence strays from the original concept for protecting a group from being destroyed. I would suggest that the hate crime concept is similar to the idea of affirmative action except in the context of social interaction. These types of group protections have the potential to limit free speech just as affirmative action has the potential to stifle actual competition. Ultimately, of course, I agree with the goal of affirmative action and of that of the hate crime and hate speech law, I simply question the method by which we get to those goals. The expansion of hate crime and hate speech law must be met with very careful consideration because they have the possibility of reducing or chilling constructive speech as well as negative speech.

FREEDOM OF SPEECH/RELIGION

In view of the varied philosophical and historical backgrounds it is no wonder that the concept of freedom of speech is a hotly-contested area of law. There is a constant struggle between wanting to allow freedom to the widest range of speech possible while protecting the rights of individuals from the harm potential in speech. In this section I will argue that the Charter does not give adequate weight to freedom of expression including religious expression in the public sphere. I will give a reasonable basis for the expansion of the interpretation of these rights and finally a possible strategy for expansion of the interpretation of those rights.

The Charter guarantees that everyone in Canada has some basic fundamental freedoms and rights which are "subject only to such reasonable limits prescribed by law as can be demonstrably justified" (section 1). The Charter states in section two:

Everyone has the following fundamental freedoms:
a) freedom of conscience and religion;
b) freedom of thought, belief, opinion and expression, including freedom of the press and other media of communication;
c) freedom of peaceful assembly; and
d) freedom of association.

What are the reasons that can be demonstrably justified to limit freedom of opinion and expression? Often in the public sphere, speech that is religious is invalidated because its primary domain is seen to be private. We have allowed the idea that someone can sell us a vacuum in public space but we do not want to allow people to "sell" or attempt to persuade people to our religious opinions merely on the basis that the opinions are religious in nature.

Freedom of religion is primarily thought along the lines of personal belief and practices. Kim Vance, president of EGALE, Equality for Gays and Lesbians Everywhere, stated in a newspaper interview that she believes that religious speech must be limited. "There is a huge difference between someone being allowed to practice their religion and taking out ads in the newspaper saying that gay and lesbian people are sick and immoral. There is a line there, and it has been crossed" (qtd. in Moore 4). "Sick and immoral" may be condemning in nature, but it is not violent. Vance seems to be insisting that religious activity then is solely a personal activity, and does not enter the public sphere.

I would contend that this is an invalid presumption. Religious speech, except violent speech, whether controversial or not should be accepted on its own merit in the public sphere including newspapers and public speaking such as church gatherings. The idea that religious reasoning has no bearing on public life is a false assumption based on an idea that reason and its "religion" of atheism hold the default place in our culture. Ismail Royer, a writer about religion in the public sphere from an Islamic perspective, agrees:

> At the root of the notion that state neutrality between belief and disbelief is somehow fairer than neutrality between beliefs is the assumption that disbelief is man[kind]'s default nature... Thus, it is thought, it is less oppressive for a religious person that God's name be stripped from official expression than [visa versa]. Considering the presence of religion in nearly every human society throughout history, this assumption is false on its face. (7-8)

Religious speech is of course generally protected in section two of the Charter as a part of "freedom of thought, belief, opinion and expression." However, due to the "religion sterile" nature of the state, when religious expression comes in conflict with other interests in the public sphere it tends to be valued less than them.

A strategy to increase the association of religious speech under the protection of free speech laws has been under way in the United States for years. In the U.S. this imbalance of religious expression in the public sphere is being addressed under their broader freedom of speech laws. Stephen Brown writes the following in his book Trumping Religion:

> In general the New Christian Right has contributed little to the process-oriented strategies pioneered by the ACLU, American Jewish Congress, NAACP, and other litigating interest groups. But its forging of a new jurisprudence relationship between the free speech clause and religion is a legal contribution that has left a distinct impression on contemporary church-state litigation. (47)

I suggest that the court based strategy may be a route in Canada for Christian and possibly multi-religion alliances to expand the power of freedom of religious expression in the public sphere. A litigation strategy is a means by which the true meanings of "freedom of religion" according to the Charter can be interpreted and expanded.

HATE SPEECH AND EXPLORATION OF BILL C-250

While the current legal environment is not ideal from a religious freedom standpoint there is a balancing act that must be performed when we are trying to create and recreate a country that upholds the rights and values of all its citizens as morals and values change over time. Hate speech is of concern to many religious people because it could be construed that public negative commentary against certain lifestyles based on religious reasons could be criminalized. In this section I will first discuss the current laws pertaining to hate crime and secondly the amendment posed by Bill C-250. Thirdly, I will use a case to explore the potential implications and pitfalls of this bill.

The Criminal Code sections 318 through 320 entitled "Hate Propaganda" describe Canada's hate crime, hate speech, and hate propaganda laws. Section 318 of the code states that anyone who commits, advocates, or promotes genocide is guilty of a criminal offence. Genocide is defined as the intent to destroy in whole or in part any identifiable group. Section 319 makes a criminal offence the act of inciting hatred in a public place against any identifiable group.

Hate has been defined in several Supreme Court rulings (Dutton par. 3). Supreme Court Justice, Cory, stated that "To promote hatred is to instil detestation, enmity, ill will and malevolence in another ... clearly an expression must go a long way before it qualifies within that definition" (qtd. 3). In section 318 part four the term "identifiable group" is defined for that and the other two sections. Section 318 reads: "In this section, 'identifiable group' means any section of the public distinguished by colour, race, religion or ethnic origin." These three laws are intended to prevent hatred against people defined by these identifiable groups by the negative consequences procured by the offence part in each section of the law.

National Democratic Party member Svend Robinson introduced Bill C-250 that proposed to add the term "sexual orientation" in this list of identifiable groups contained in part four of section 318. This definition affects the two following laws that both make reference to it in order to determine which groups are eligible for protection under hate speech (section 319) and hate propaganda (section 320). Robinson who is openly homosexual says the bill is necessary to defend homosexual people from being 'targeted for violent hate crime' (qtd. in Dunfield par. 5). He states:

> What my bill would do is to recognise that just as we say it's
> wrong to promote hatred or violence against racial or religious
> or ethnic minorities, so too, should we say it's just as wrong
> to promote that hatred or violence directed at gay or lesbian
> people. (qtd. par. 6)

Robinson's first statement is that the law is intended to prevent what he is hearing from the police as a targeting of homosexuals for violent crime, but the law he has proposed to change has far more vast impact than violent crime, it also includes hate speech and hate propaganda. One thing that is easy to overlook in a statement such as this is that people are already protected from violent crime under the law. There are stiff penalties for committing acts of violence, and for making threats against someone's life. Therefore adding protection outside of this is a question that deserves careful attention. Dan McTeague a Liberal MP refused to vote for the bill because he believes that there is adequate protection for homosexuals within current laws.

Bill C-250's inclusion of the words "sexual orientation" in the list of identifiable groups is in of itself an interesting quandary. Ron Gray head of the Christian Heritage Party brought up the point that the Bill would amend the law to "protect all 'sexual orientations' - but it does not define the term" (Gray par. 5). If the Bill passed and was not struck down that leaves it open for interpretation as it is applied in court. Gray continues on to make an exaggerated point about how this term sexual orientation could be construed to give protection to pedophiles (par. 21). While that scenario is unlikely it does bring to the forefront a worthwhile discussion and casts a shadow over the merit of Bill C-250.

From a Christian perspective this is a critical issue because it highlights the distinction of criticism of homosexual behaviour versus the sexual orientation of homosexuality. Columbia University professor Randall L. Sell writes on how we define sexual orientation. Sell states:

> Today's preferred terms [homosexual, heterosexual, bisexual] and the term 'sexual orientation' itself have a wide variety of definitions in the literature [of researchers] but these generally comprise one or both of two components: a "psychological" component and a "behavioural" component. (par. 4)

These two correspond to a traditionally-held Christian perspective that there is a distinction between the behaviour and the orientation. The concern is summed up by Bruce Clemenger, head of the Evangelical Fellowship of Canada's Centre for Faith and Public Life, when he says that "the courts have not distinguished between the identity of the person and the activity. So sexual orientation refers to both the sexual disposition as well as the activity" (qtd. in Moore par. 4). This distinction is rejected by a homosexual spokesperson for EGALE (par. 6). This means that if a Christian wants to criticise the activity but not the orientation they have no means of doing it because the two are so closely tied.

In the case of Owens v. Saskatchewan the Saskatchewan Human Rights Commission decided against Hugh Owens who placed an ad in the Star-Phoenix paper that was offensive to three gay men who filed a complaint (Gunter par. 6-8). The ad contained references to Bible verses condemning homosexuality but did not quote them (par. 6). The court case under review by the Court of Queen's Bench upheld the commission's ruling:

> The use of the circle and the slash combined with the passages
> of the Bible herein make the meaning of the advertisement
> unmistakable. It is clear that the advertisement is intended to
> make the group depicted appear to be inferior or not wanted at
> best. When combined with the Biblical quotations, the adver-
> tisement may result in a much stronger meaning. It is obvious
> that certain [usage] of the Biblical quotations suggest more dire
> consequences and there can be no question that the advertise-
> ment can objectively be seen as exposing homosexuals to hatred
> or ridicule. (Owens v. Sas. section 9)

It appears that in this case it is hard to tell whether Owens' intent was to criticise homosexuals' behaviour which is a message with some social value to Christians or merely hatred which is of little societal value. The courts sided against the side of religious expression which aligns itself with the "state is anti-religion instead of religion neutral" conclusions I drew in the section on free speech and religious speech. Ruth Ross, director of the Christian Legal Fellowship in London, Ont., said in reaction to the outcome of this case that "[t]he religious opinion defence has been applied very narrowly ... based on the way court cases have been handed down recently, we have real concern as people of faith" (qtd. in Ward 2 emphasis added).

The outcome of the Owens case was the payment of fines to the offended parties. If Bill C-250 was in effect, it would be interesting to see what the results would be; possibly instead of fines, it would be a criminal offence. I am only able to speculate but the language used to describe hate offences in the Criminal Code and that used by the Court of Queen's Bench seems very similar.

Conclusion

In conclusion, I believe the fears that Bill C-250 could stifle religious expression are valid. It would also serve to protect homosexuals from oppressive actions. However, this is too high a price to pay to quiet some social discourse given that homosexuals are already protected by the rest of the law against harm and threat of harm. The concept of having double coverage for people, once as individuals and again as a group under the law, is also suspect for cooling free speech. I am disturbed by the lack of care given to define sexual orientation according to the law and the refusal of the courts to recognise the distinction between commentary on sexual behaviour and commentary on sexual identity.

The idea that I would like to close with is an anecdotal story of Benjamin Franklin who helped frame the founding documents of the United States. The story is that during the Constitutional Convention an anxious woman was waiting outside and inquired of Franklin, "Well, Doctor, what have we got, a [democratic] republic or a monarchy?" Franklin replied, "A republic, if you can keep it." (qtd. in Whitehead 123 emphasis added). This story in the context of this paper denotes the importance of our being vigilant to protect the market place of ideas in Canadian culture. Religious ideas as well as secular ones are valid even when controversial and in so doing we can bring about change that we, too, hope will end hatred.

WORKS CITED

"Bill C-250." Online Posting. 15 Oct. 2003
   <http://www.parl.gc.ca/37/2/parlbus/chambus/house/bills/private/C-250/C-250_1/372097bE.html>.

Bowman, John., et al. "MP's Vote to Protect Gays Under Hate Law." CBC News
   Online. 18 Sept. 2003. 25 Sept. 2003
   <http://www.cbc.ca/storyview/CBC/2003/09/17/hate030917>.

Brown, Steven P. Trumping Religion: The New Christian Right, the Free Speech
   Clause, and the Courts. Tuscaloosa: Alabama UP, 2002.

Canada. Minister of Justice. Report to the Minister of Justice of the Special Committee on Hate Propaganda in Canada. Ottawa: Queens Printer for Canada, 1966.

Canadian Charter of Rights and Freedoms. Online Posting. Department of Justice.
   20 Nov 2003 <http://laws.justice.gc.ca/en/charter/index.html>.

Dunfield, Allison. "MP's Vote to Extend Hate Crime Protection." The Globe and
   Mail. 17 Sept. 22 Oct. 2003
   <http://www.globeandmail.com/servlet/story/RTGAM.20030917. whate0917/
   BNStory/National/>.

Dutton, Alan. "Summary of Hate Crime Law in Canada." 1998. 19 Nov. 2003
   <http://mpd.selkirk.bc.ca/webdev/arcom/viewcontent.asp?ID=42>.

Gray, Ron. "CHP response to Bill C-250 being narrowly approved." Christian Heritage Party Online. 18 Sept. 2003. 22 Oct. 2003
   <http://www.chp.ca/homepage/response_to_C250.htm >.

Gunter, Lorne. "Koran hate literature? Won't Happen: But When a Christian
   Quotes Bible in an Ad, He and the Paper Get Fined." Edmonton Journal. 12
   Feb. 2003. 22 Oct. 2003
   <http://www.citizenimpact.ca/faith_hate_literature.html>.

"Hate Propaganda." Online Posting. Department of Justice. 25 Sept. 2003. 25 Sept.
   2003 <http://laws.justice.gc.ca/en/c-46/41491.html>.

Moore, Art. "The Bible as 'Hate Literature?'" World Net Daily. 21 Oct. 2002. 25
    Sept. 2003
    <http://www.worldnetdaily.com/news/article.asp?ARTICLE_ID=2932 8>.

O'Niel, Robert M. Free Speech: Responsible Communication in an Open Society.
    2nd ed. New York: Bobbs-Merrill, 1972.

"Owens vs. Saskatchewan." Online Posting. Canadian Legal Information Institute. 1
    Dec. 2002. 20 Nov. 2003
    <http://www.canlii.org/sk/cas/skqb/2002/2002skqb506.html>.

Royer, Ismail. "Religion in the American Public Square." Journal of Religion and
    Society. 5 (2003): 22 pars. 22 Oct. 2003
    <http://moses.creighton.edu/JRS/2003/2003-9.html>.

Sell, Randall L. "How Do You Define 'Sexual Orientation'?" Archives of Sexual
    Behaviour. 25.6 (1997): 12 pars. 18 Nov. 2003.

Smolla, Rodney A. Free Speech in an Open Society. New York: Knopf, 1992.

Ward, Marianne, Meed. "Is the Bible hate literature? 'Far-fetched,' say some, But
    Others Worry Bill C-250 Would Infringe on the Free Expression of Religious
    Beliefs." Presbyterian Record. 127.4 (2003): 21 pars. 18 Nov. 2003
    <http://infotrac.galegroup.com/itw/infomark/789/78/4343624 7w2/purl=rc1_
    CPI_0_A100734364&dyn=4!xrn_5_0_A100734364?sw_aep=trinitywu>.

Whitehead, John W. The Right to Picket and the Freedom of Public Discourse. Vol.
    3. Werchester: Crossway, 1984.

Wolfson, Nicolas. Hate Speech, Sex Speech, Free Speech. Westport: Praeger, 1997.

Religious Doctrine vs. Self-Preservation:
The Hutterite Dilemma

Jeremy Friesen

V

The Hutterite worldview embraces separation from society in order to preserve their ideals and beliefs. Canada is an excellent choice for Hutterite communities since Canada not only has many rural areas ideal for agriculture, but also laws that often favour freedom of religion. However, the cultural and religious beliefs Hutterites hold do not always fit with Canadian law. Exploring the relationship between Hutterites and the law reveals that Hutterites' need to survive is overriding their religious doctrine which prohibits the use of any kind of force, especially in court. The purpose of this essay is to show that the increase in Hutterite-initiated litigation is compromising the integrity of Hutterian internal law, and in doing so, may cause far reaching consequences to Hutterian society as a whole.

This topic will be developed as follows. A brief overview will be given of the four main Anabaptist sects and the differences between them, as well as their similarities. This section will impart a basic understanding of Hutterite culture, and will be necessary in understanding the importance of the following sections. The second section involves Government litigation against Hutterites. This will give an overview of the varying issues that Hutterites have had with the broader Canadian culture and its laws. The next section will deal with the Hutterite initiation of litigation, both against other Hutterites as well as against other Canadian citizens. The fifth section will discuss why the increase in Hutterite-initiated litigation is such a surprising and disturbing development, and what this might imply for the future of Hutterite communities. Also to be explored is the question, can the rejection of religious doctrine be a viable solution to prolonging the survival of Hutterite communities. Finally, the sixth section will give a Christian perspective on the Hutterite dilemma.

The various streams of Anabaptism all have the same roots. In 1517 Catholicism gave rise to the Protestant Reformation, and eight years later, in 1525, the even more radical Anabaptist movement further separated from Protestantism. As with any radical movement, the Anabaptists were heavily persecuted: many were killed for practising adult baptism. This practice interfered with both the civil and religious authorities of the time: "The Anabaptists placed the authority of the Scriptures above civil edicts . . . The young upstarts chose to follow their own interpretation of Scripture and the literal words of Jesus recorded in the New Testament" (Kraybill 2). As a result of this persecution, most Anabaptists relocated to remote areas of Eastern Europe and became farmers. This became the pattern for current Anabaptist groups who segregate themselves from their surrounding societies. At this time most Anabaptist groups migrated to North America with the promise of religious freedom.

There are four main streams of Anabaptism: Mennonites, Hutterites, Amish, and Brethren. The most well known are the Mennonites. This is primarily because many Mennonites merged with American culture to become less a separate religious entity and more an American sub-culture. However, many Old Order Mennonite communities continue to exist, remembering the teachings of their leader from the mid-fifties, Menno Simons. A large number of Old Order Mennonites have homes with electricity and telephones, though horse and carriage are still used for transportation, and meeting places for church services have no plumbing, electricity, or carpet. They farm and live among non-Mennonite neighbours, and while they are set apart by their plain clothing, the men do not usually have beards, as do many other Anabaptists groups.

The Amish are also relatively well known. This group originally separated from the Mennonites in 1693 under the leadership of Jakob Ammann. This new, more conservative sect had to find their own path in Europe, though many Amish groups reintegrated with Mennonites in the eighteen hundreds after coming to America. The Amish groups who remained separate from the Mennonites evolved

Perspectives On Christianity, Society & The Law

their own practices, continuing on their own path: Amish worship in their homes every other Sunday. They do not have electricity or electrical appliances. They use horse and buggy transportation, but have been known to rent vans for longer trips. The Amish most strictly prohibit the use of technology, and along with the Hutterites, are known for having relatively frequent conflicts with the governments of North America.

The Brethren division stems from Anabaptist roots as well, but was also heavily influenced by radical Pietism. The Brethren were formed in 1708 under the leadership of Alexander Mack Sr. Brethren views on immersion baptism yielded the nickname "Dunkers." They were very similar to Mennonites in their doctrines of "adult baptism, the separation of church and state, pacifism, and church discipline" (Kraybill 7). A key difference from other Anabaptist groups is the Brethren level of interaction with the larger society: they have cars, telephones, electricity, and very seldom, television and video for educational purposes. Many Brethren children attend public schools. It is not unusual for Brethren to own a business or to work in a non-Brethren occupation. As with all Old Order groups, the Brethren have traditional plain clothes. The Brethren are characterised by their near complete lack of German-speaking members, technological lenience, and varied occupations outside of farming, unlike the other three main Anabaptist groups.

The focus of our discussion is the Hutterites. Only three years after Anabaptism was created, the Hutterites emerged, under the leadership of Jacob Hutter. Their main distinction from the other Anabaptist groups is the practice of having only communal property. As of 2001, there are said to be "425 agricultural colonies, each averaging about ninety members" (Kraybill 21). While the Hutterite religious and home lives are very traditional, the same cannot be said of their work environment: "the colonists readily use the latest computerised equipment to operate large farms on thousands of acres" (Kraybill 4). Meals and religious services are held each day in communal buildings, and while families may live in private dwellings, no one has private property. The Hutterites are characterised by moral and residential, but not economic separatism, and selectively embracing technology in business applications.

What ties these four groups, as well as a number of minor Anabaptists off-shoots, are their similar ideals, most of which are still radically different from today's society:

Old Order pilgrims contend that:
The individual is not the primary reality.
Communal goals transcend personal ones.
The past is as important as the future.
Tradition is valued over change.
Preservation overshadows progress.
Newer, bigger, and faster are not necessarily better.
Personal sacrifice is esteemed over pleasure.
Local involvement outweighs national acclaim.
Work is more satisfying then consumption.
Obedience to authority brings order and unity.
Spiritual salvation comes via the grace of community.
Friends are more important than status, fame, or wealth.
Yielding to community brings meaning, identity, and belonging.
Maintaining the unity of community is the supreme value.
(Kraybill 19)

These principles are the foundation for Hutterite communities, along with the principles of "Gelassenheit," the surrendering of the self to God's will, and "Ordnung," the adherence to rules and discipline.

Clearly, for Hutterites, as well as other Anabaptist groups, community is valued above all else, especially over personal goals. As with all humans, Hutterites do not always succeed in maintaining these lofty ideals: "Pride, envy, jealousy, and greed sometimes fracture community harmony" (Kraybill 19). When these problems occur, litigation is sometimes used as a weapon. Hutterites who become dissatisfied with their communities often use the law of the country in which they live to take revenge—often this is an attempt to gain personal property after leaving the community. This is a very disturbing event for a Hutterite community because it is expressly forbidden for a Hutterite to be involved in any litigation. The use of force is inconceivable in the minds of most Hutterites: "Their commitment to peace prevents them from filing lawsuits, which are viewed as tools of coercion. [They] are also reluctant to defend themselves in court . . . Serving as a police officer is unthinkable and would be cause for excommunication" (Kraybill 184). One may wonder how far this situation can go. Can Hutterites afford to be so mindful of these anti-force principles when the fate of their religious freedom is at stake? Is it worse for a Hutterite leader to defend his colony's welfare in court or to let the community suffer at the hands of outsiders? These questions will be the main focus of the following section, in which we will discover the extent of litigation against Hutterites.

Both in the United States and Canada, Hutterites have been the target of aggressive government litigation, usually with the intention of eliminating the Hutterite way of life. While the main focus of this essay is the Hutterite relationship with Canadian law, it is notable to consider their treatment by US law in order to gain an understanding of how North American culture in general has felt about Hutterites in the past.

In South Dakota in 1922 the case of State ex rel. Chamberlain v. Hutteriche Bruder Gemeinde was presented. The claim of Chamberlain was that the Hutterite community could not be allowed to continue existing as a corporation. Hutterite communities enjoyed corporate status as it relieved many of the legal issues resulting from their communal ownership of property. The government was very aggressive in its attempt to essentially exterminate Hutterites in South Dakota through legal action.

The seriousness of this case spurred a massive Hutterite exodus to Canada, especially after a very negative judgement was found. Professor Alvin Esau, who has researched the topic of Hutterite litigation extensively, makes note of the outcome of this case: the corporation was ordered to dispose of all of its real estate over the amount of fifty thousand dollars, amend its by-laws to exclude all secular pursuits, and failing compliance, appointed a receiver to take over and liquidate the property. Esau also aptly characterises this result as a significant blow against Hutterites: "So much for freedom of religion in 1922 in South Dakota" (Litigation). After most South Dakota colonies moved to Canada, an appeal was heard, which successfully overturned this judgement. As opposed to the trial judge, the Court of Appeal stated that the Hutterite community did not break US law in any way, except by refusing military service (the First Amendment clearly allowed them exemption as engaging in military service would directly encroach upon their religious beliefs). On the same basis the court found that religious freedom did not include the right to incorporate as a religious organisation. This ruling forced the Hutterite community to disband as a corporation; however, they were still able to exist in an non-incorporated form by designating trustees to hold all the land and possessions in their name.

In Canada, many of the same issues had to be faced in regards to income tax, debtor's rights, municipal zoning, and especially communal property. During the Second World War, Canadian law discriminated against Hutterite communities by preventing them from spreading and prospering: The Alberta Land Sales Prohibition Act of 1942 prohibited any sale of land to Hutterites. After World War I, this Act was replaced by another which instead limited Hutterites from buying land. "For example, no colony could purchase land within forty miles of an existing colony or increase its holdings beyond a certain number of acres" (Esau, Litigation). In 1960 a board was created solely for the purpose of approving Hutterite land purchases. In 1973 the Act was eliminated.

The reasons for such discrimination were primarily due to fear of the continued growth of Hutterite communities. Once established, most Hutterite communities were very prosperous, even in the face of depression and war, partly due to certain tax exemptions and the communal work ethic of such communities.

In regards to income tax, some Hutterite communities believed they should be exempt from any income taxes, both personally and corporately. They characterised their communities as religious organisations or charities. The Tax Review Board rejected this claim, finding that the farming operations were a secular activity and members of the community directly benefited from profits of said activities, and should be liable to pay personal income taxes based on the profit of the community divided by the number of members. On appeal to a trial judge, the decision was upheld, but in the Federal Court of Appeal and subsequently the Supreme Court of Canada, the Hutterites were successful. The Court decided that they only needed to pay income tax on what the colony gave them to survive (such as food and clothing), rather than paying an amount based on the profit of the colony evenly

Perspectives On Christianity, Society & The Law

divided between members of the colony. Of course, while this exempted Hutterites from the majority of personal income taxes, being taxed as a corporation was still perfectly legal.

The crux of these issues is for the courts to decide the balance of religious freedom of Hutterite communities with their level of corporate status. While religious freedom is a very important edict in Canadian law, the courts cannot allow Hutterite communities to be wholly tax exempt, as this gives them an unfair advantage over other farmers trying to sell goods in the same markets. The concern of whether defending themselves in court can be theologically viable might partially be answered here by agreeing with Donald Kraybill's assertion that they "see this more as a matter of following God than of resisting government. Scripture instructs them to 'obey God rather than men'" (Acts 5:29) .

While defending themselves in court can be theologically rationalised, it is much more difficult to do so with litigation initiated by Hutterites or Hutterite communities. Some examples of this would include instances in which an excommunicated member continually invades the property of his/her former community, and the community obtains restraining orders to prevent them from doing so, or instances in which the formation of a "daughter colony" was promised but then not created (a "daughter colony" is a new colony formed with the money of a 'parent colony' that had grown too large for its facilities). Despite the aversion felt by Hutterites in initiating litigation, Hutterites who leave the community tend to be less troubled over filing suits to gain personal property proportional to their perceived share of property while part of the community. These cases usually involve whether privatisation of Hutterite communal property should be allowed, or if some division between multiple communal pots should be allowed.

In one example, ex-Hutterites sued for a portion of communal property. In the 1970 case of Hofer v. Hofer, the Supreme Court of Canada dealt with a situation in which some members of a Hutterite colony joined a different church and after being expelled from membership in the Hutterite colony. They sued the colony for a share of the assets. The Court held that they were not entitled to any of the colony property. The Federal Court of Appeal and Supreme Court of Canada stated that Hutterites through their articles of association or trust deeds essentially renounced any claim for shares in the corporation or trust community, other than the right to be sustained on the colony.

This, of course, can be rationalised as strictly non-Hutterite-initiated litigation, even if the plaintiffs still held themselves to be Hutterite. However, even earlier in Canada, more issues came up. In 1962 an Alberta colony successfully sued a real estate agent in Saskatchewan who refused to return money that was left in trust with him. Then in 1982 a Saskatchewan colony sued for specific performance of a land transaction. The colony claimed that it had bought the land for $672,000 and wanted the title to it, but the defendant claimed that the sale was subject to a prior option to buy from another party, which option was exercised. The court found that the colony did have notice of the prior option to purchase, so the Hutterites lost the lawsuit.

No rationalisation for ignoring the anti-litigation norms of Hutterite beliefs immediately comes to mind in these cases. We will discuss this in further detail in a later section. Another example of Hutterite-initiated litigation involves the sale of land to Hutterites in which an intermediary was used to purchase the land. A colony in Alberta bought land in Montana in 1947 by using an agent who did not disclose to the vendor that he was acting for a Hutterite colony. The contract for the sale of the land was assigned to the colony and the colony moved onto the land and commenced operations, but the vendor did not convey the land to the Hutterite colony, presumably due to prejudice against Hutterites. The vendor eventually sued in state court to have the contract cancelled. The colony then sued in Federal court for specific performance of the contract. "It is unclear on the record available to me which side sued first" (Esau, Litigation).

Despite who sued first, this is significant because the Hutterites directly initiated a lawsuit, seemingly in direct contradiction of the normal anti-force behaviour of Hutterite communities. Another case, this time in the US, involved a lawyer who convinced a Hutterite community to sue for defamation. According to author Vance Joseph Youmans, in 1962 a newspaper ran an article claiming that Hutterites were:

[T]he world's oldest Communists . . . claim religion as their basis . . . They have registered in the state as a church but have no affiliations or missions with any churches or sects other than their own . . . Our main objection is that they operate a farm under the guise of religion . . . They want and get many concessions tax-wise that permit them to make more money. They turn around and try to pressure us into selling them our farms . . .

This may not seem like enough evidence to support a lawsuit for defamation, but the article continued:

Mrs. Peterson, pointing to the Russian background of the ancient religious sect, calls attention to the fact that the Hutterite land virtually surrounds two Air Force missile sites which are vital components of the Spokane Air Defense Sector. You wonder if they bought their land close to missile sites by accident or by design.' The colony, on the urging of a lawyer, sued and won a modest settlement for defamation, as well as a public apology in the newspaper. (qtd. by Esau, Litigation)

These cases draw attention to why the communities abandoned their usual "turn the other cheek" approach in favour of litigation. The next section will further illustrate why the use of courts by a member of a Hutterite community is so objectionable, and will present the arguments for and against the question of whether these cases constitute a fracture between edict and practice.

All of the cases discussed so far beg the question of whether they constitute a break from the Hutterite norm of not using force, especially through courts, and if so, what it might mean for Hutterite communities. To do so, one must understand why using courts is considered morally unacceptable to the Hutterite community.

The list of principles at the end of page four can be thought of as an extension of one of the key theological standards of Hutterite life, "Gelassenheit." According to Kraybill, this term essentially means fully surrendering oneself to the will of God. By this principle, Hutterites maintain that using force against others is wrong. If someone has wronged one, it is only God who may pass judgement; hence one must simply bear the wrong, "turn the other cheek," or submit to evil. Kraybill defines it as: "the opposite of assertive individualism . . . The expression of "Gelassenheit" includes plainness, simplicity, obedience, humility, lowliness and meekness . . . 'Yeildedness' is the supreme virtue of an obedient life" (Kraybill 182-183).

The Hutterites believe that defending oneself in court, which is still considered forbidden, is not nearly as bad as the use of "offensive" litigation, as Esau points out:

> It is my contention that defending lawsuits brought against
> you is less problematic in terms of violating Anabaptist norms
> as compared to bringing a lawsuit against someone . . . in the
> latter category you are asking for a court order backed by the
> violence of the state to coerce someone . . . This invocation of
> state violence is problematic. (Litigation)

Such Hutterite-initiated cases are problematic because a Hutterite community suing for defamation appears to be not only directly ignoring the taboo against litigation, but also indirectly ignoring "Gelassenheit" through the use of force. There are approximately ten cases of Hutterite-initiated litigation: "Even though we have five cases in the United States and about the same number in Canada, the existence of any cases at all raises the question of whether the norm against litigation was still stable..." (Esau, Litigation). It is reasonable to assert that the norm is definitely breaking down, especially in Manitoba where numerous Hutterites have engaged in manufacturing and selling products. When goods are delivered to a customer but payment is never received, how long would it take for a Hutterite business to fail if it became public knowledge that they did not sue over such a breach of contract? Practically, it is clear that Hutterites in such businesses cannot easily submit to such circumstances, but morally, it still seems to be in opposition to "Gelassenheit". The defence of this assertion might be that Hutterites, until recently, did simply suffer the wrong if a solution could not be reached short of going to court. The wrong that would have been suffered in the cases where litigation was initiated by a Hutterite may have been circumstances where the wrong that would have been suffered was simply too grave to allow. An example of this would be a situation where the entire way of life for Hutterites would have been in jeopardy, such as the South Dakota case discussed above. However, as more Hutterites move into non-agricultural businesses, we will likely see more litigation involving Hutterites.

The above section was meant to discuss the issue of breaking away from the "Gelassenheit" norm and give possible interpretation of the situation. This purpose of this section is to end the discussion and come to a conclusion from a Christian perspective. Hutterites clearly believe that using litigation is wrong, and until very recently there were hardly any reported cases of Hutterites using the "force of the state" to coerce anyone. The recent increase in such cases can be seen in two ways: 1) as an indication of the breakdown of Hutterite society or 2) as an indication of the strength of the Hutterite community to conform in the face of mounting extra-societal pressure. The Christian belief in God and following the example Jesus set certainly lends itself to admiring the Hutterite way, and while they might seem morally superior in many ways, they too are susceptible to human failings. Should the principles of "Gelassenheit" be allowed have a line drawn through it at any point? The ideals of submission to evil and allowing God to be the judge are admirable, but it is inconsistent if they are not applied once a Hutterite community is in danger. The principles of "Gelassenheit" must be universally applicable to be a truly solid foundation for Hutterites. This would entail allowing people to take advantage of Hutterite businesses, using law to disband entire Hutterite communities, and submitting to such punishment in faith that God's will shall prevail.

If "Gelassenheit" should truly be universal, then the recent increase in Hutterite litigation does indicate a possible chink in the armour of the tight Hutterite societal structure. However, if "Gelassenheit" is applied universally, Hutterite communities might face extinction via exploitation. The question left to the reader is whether either path might result in the eventual vanishing of Hutterite communities in Canada.

There is evidence of Hutterite initiation of litigation that cannot be easily rationalised by another internal religious edict. There is also reason to believe that this is this indicative of a problem in Hutterian society. Despite this, I must conclude that this problem will not have far reaching consequences, such as the eventual extinction of Hutterites in Canada or North America.

Through the torture and murder of the fifteen hundreds to the discrimination of the nineteen hundreds, the Hutterites have not only survived, but also prospered and multiplied. Their strict social control and submissive obedience to the principles of "Gelassenheit" not only make them radically different from the outside society, but also binds them together so strongly that they may survive as long as the outside societal policy, and thereby laws, hold religious freedom in such high standing. Hutterite groups constantly have to maintain their Old Order identities while adapting to pressures for social change. Each independent community does this on a daily basis, and has been doing so for over 450 years, simply to survive. The strength of the Hutterite community will no doubt leave them unscathed, even in the face increased need for litigation. While this essay has asserted that Hutterite-instigated litigation disrupts the Hutterite norm, the final conclusion must be that their approach is one means by which Hutterite communities can and will adapt to the modern world.

WORKS CITED

Aksamit, Nichole. Heavy with History. Nov 1999. 12 Feb. 2004
    <http://www.in-forum.com/specials/awa/1114b.html>.

Eichler, Evan. A Brief History of the Hutterian Brethren (1755-1879). 2 April 1997.
    17 Feb. 2004 <http://feefhs.org/hut/frg-hut.html>.

Esau, Alvin J. Hutterite Litigation. 1997. 9 Feb. 2004
    <http://www.umanitoba.ca/faculties/law/Courses/esau/litigation/huttlitigation-
    web.htm>.

____. Law and Property: The Establishment and Preservation of Mennonite Semi-
    Communalism and Hutterite Communalism in North America: 1870-1925.
    2001. 12 Feb. 2004
    <http://www.colonialpropertycolloq.law.uvic.ca/papers/Esau.htm>.

____. The Judicial Resolution of Church Property Disputes: Canadian and American
    Models. April 2003. 16 Feb. 2004
    <http://www.albertalawreview.com/abstracts/abs40.asp>.

"Federation of East European Family History Societies." Hutterite Genealogy
    HomePage. 1 March 1997. 16 Feb. 2004
    <http://feefhs.org/hut/frg-hut.html>.

Gingerich, Orland. The Amish of Canada. Waterloo, Ontario: Conrad Press, 1972.

Greaves, Thomas C. Endangered Peoples of North America: Struggles to Survive
    and Thrive. Westport, CT: Greenwood Press, 2002.

Hartman, Joel. Summary of School Court Cases. 7 Oct. 2003. 9 Feb. 2004
    <http://www.missouri.edu/~rsocjoel/rs150/courtcases.html>.

Hofer, John. The History of the Hutterites. Altona: D.W Friesen & Sons Ltd. 1998.

Kafka, Joe. Hutterites Deny Patent Infringement. 4 Nov. 2003. 14 Feb. 2004
    <http://www.aberdeennews.com/mld/aberdeennews/news/7179768.htm>.

Keim, Albert N. Compulsory Education and the Amish: The Right not to be Mod-
    ern. Boston: Beacon Press, 1975.

Kraybill, Donald B. On the Backroad to Heaven: Old Order Hutterites, Mennonites, Amish, and Brethren. Baltimore: Johns Hopkins University Press, 2001.

Nolt, Steven M. A History of the Amish. Intercourse, PA: Good Books, 1992.

Oyer, John S. They Harry the Good People Out of the Land: Essays on the Persecution, Survival and Flourishing of Anabaptists and Mennonites. Goshen, IN: Mennonite Historical Society, 2000.

Peter, Karl A. Dynamics of Hutterite Society: An Analytical Approach. University of Alberta Press: Edmonton, Alberta. 1987.

South Dakota Supreme Court. Decker v. Tschetter Hutterian Brethren, Inc., 1999 SD. 26 May 1999. 12 Feb. 2004
<http://www.sdbar.org/opinions/1999/May/1999 _062.htm>.

Unknown Author. "Gaithersburg Man Crosses the Bruderhof." The Daily Record. 31 Aug. 2000. 14 Feb. 2004
<http://www.apologeticsindex.org/news/an200831.html>.

Waldner, Jacob. Hutterian Brethren Pamphlet. Decker Colony. 1999.

Waldner, Mark. The Hutterian Brethren: Hutterites Living in Community in North America. 2 Jan. 2004. 15 Feb. 2004 <http://www.hutterites.org/>.

Youmans, Vance J. Spokane's Hutterite Community: A Place Where History Lives. Fall 2000. 9 Feb. 2004
<http://www.washingtonhistory.org/wshs/columbia/articles/0300-a2.htm>.

Zellner, W. W. Sects, Cults, and Spiritual Communities: A Sociological Analysis. Westport, CT: Praeger, 1998.

Publicly Funded Discrimination:
An Examination of Homosexuals in the Government Funded Catholic School System of Ontario

Danielle Hildebrand

VI

When a homosexual Ontario Catholic school student brought the Durham Catholic District School Board to court, following a refusal to allow his boyfriend to escort him to prom, publicity surrounding government-funded Catholic schools truly escalated. Ontario's seventy-two District school boards consist of thirty-one English-language public boards, twenty-nine English-language Catholic boards, four French-language public boards and eight French-language Catholic boards. The funding formula for all the school boards was nearly identical; the public school boards received the same percentage of funding from the Government of Ontario as the Catholic school boards. This caused concern because Catholic school boards have the right to run their schools in accordance with Catholic teachings, which often discriminate against certain individuals, namely homosexuals.

My thesis is that Catholic school boards, that receive government funding, do not have the right to discriminate against homosexuals even though homosexuality may be in conflict with Catholic teachings and curriculum.

INTRODUCTION

In order to provide context for my thesis, this paper will discuss how the controversy surrounding government-funded Catholic schools discrimination against homosexuals exposed the inevitable conflict between freedom of religion and the dictates of the state. For the purposes of this paper, when referring to Catholic schools, I will be referring to Catholic schools in Ontario only. I will begin by looking at the case study of Marc Hall vs. the Durham Catholic District School Board ("Marc Hall vs. Durham"). This case deals with a homosexual Catholic student who was discriminated against because of his sexual orientation. Secondly, I will look at the Ontario Catholic school system and discuss the requirements and exclusions they are subject to, as well as the funding formula used by the Ministry of Education to distribute money to the school districts. I will also examine who is responsible for the education of students in Ontario. Lastly, I will review upon the place of homosexuals within the Catholic school system by examining their rights and freedoms. I will also be discussing the Catholic viewpoint as well as the Bible's perspective of homosexuality and the interpretation employed today.

MARC HALL CASE

In April 2002, Marc Hall, a student at Oshawa's Monsignor John Pereyma Catholic High School attempted to buy a ticket for his boyfriend, to escort him to his senior prom. He was denied the ticket by the principal of the school and later, when it was brought before the Durham Catholic District School Board ("Durham Catholic"), was rejected again. His reaction was to sue the School Board for the right to bring his boyfriend to the prom. When the case was brought before the court, the courtroom was filled with supporters of Marc; they actually outnumbered anti-gay religious forces by five to one. David Corbett, Hall's lawyer argued his case around several important points: first, The Charter of Rights and Freedoms ((Charter) principle of "substantive equality" and Hall's freedom of expression and freedom of association; second, the Education Act ("Act") which sets the standard that are applied to the different classes of schooling; third, that the boards decision breaches the common law fiduciary duty of educators; and fourth, that Section ninety-three of the Constitution of 1867 (Constitution) which recognises and provides special protection for denominational schools.

In their defence, the Durham Catholic's counsel argued that Hall had no valid question to be tried, because the Constitution provided absolute protection for religious decisions by denominational schools, and placed the Board's decision beyond Charter scrutiny. They also claimed that it was Hall's decision to attend a

Catholic school, and if he did not agree the values of the Church, he does not have to attend school there.

After two days of hearings Justice McKinnon made his decision. In his ruling he brought up a few previous cases of significance. In his judgement Justice McKinnon quoted the following:

> The Supreme Court of Canada in Trinity Western University, which stated that 'the freedom to hold beliefs is broader than the freedom to act on them' and that 'neither freedom of religion nor guarantee against discrimination based on sexual orientation is absolute.' At the heart of the Trinity Western University decision lies a distinction between holding a discriminatory view and actively discriminating against someone.

As it relate to the Hall case, it meant it was tolerable for him to be gay; he just could not act gay. Another case that was cited was a case involving the United States Supreme Court v. Bob Jones University, which recognised that public funds would not be used to subsidise discriminatory practices even where it is asserted that those discriminatory practices are founded on religious beliefs. This is relevant because Catholic Schools funded by the government should not discriminate against anyone or engage in discriminatory practices. In response to the argument of the Constitution, Justice McKinnon stated, "In 1867 homosexual activity was viewed both as a crime and as a sickness. Today it is viewed as neither. Canadians' understanding of human behaviour and of its people has changed over the last 135 years." In the end, Justice McKinnon sided with Hall, signalling that when an institution accepts public funds, they accept public regulations.

ONTARIO SCHOOL BOARDS

According to Wayne Burtnyk, the Ontario's Ministry of Education's Director of Transfer Payments and Financial Reporting, The Ministry of Education in Ontario sets a curriculum policy and defines what teachers are required to teach and what students are expected to learn in each grade and subject area. A consistent, province-wide curriculum is thereby ensured. However, teaching and assessment strategies are left to the professional judgement of teachers, enabling them to address individual students needs and to deliver the curriculum in a context that is logically meaningful. In Ontario, education is managed mainly by the Act and its regulations which set out the duties and responsibilities of the Ministry of Education and the duties and responsibilities of school boards, school board supervisory officers, principals, teachers, parents and students. The Act sets out standards that are applied to different classes of schooling in Ontario, which include public, private, Catholic and home schooling. These standards comply with the Human Rights Code of Ontario, which require that everyone is to be treated fairly, regardless of race, religion or sexual orientation. Most Catholic school boards have accepted this code of conduct, but many make decisions that violate the code, thus making the code irrelevant. Under section fifty-two of the Act, "A Roman Catholic board may establish and maintain programs and courses of study in religious education for pupils in all schools under its jurisdiction." This allows Catholic schools to include Catholic teachings, largely the Catechism of the Catholic Church, in their curriculum.

The Ministry of Education in Ontario is responsible for the education of all Ontario students. Along with developing curriculum they set policies and guidelines for school trustees, directors of education, principals and other school board officials; set requirements for student diplomas and certificates; and prepare lists of approved textbooks and other learning materials. Below the Ministry are all the school boards in Ontario. These school boards are responsible for providing education programs that meet the needs of the school community, including special education; carefully managing the funds allocated by the province to support all board activities, including education programs for elementary and secondary school students and ensuring schools abide by the Education Act and its regulations. Principals within each school are accountable for the quality of instruction at their school and for student discipline. Teachers prepare lesson plans and exemplify good citizenship and respect for all groups of people. Educators have a duty owed towards their students. Using the curriculum provided by the Ministry of Education, it is the educators' duty to determine how to teach that curriculum as it applies to their students. They owe a fiduciary duty to their students; teacher-student relationships are based on trust. Noticeably, if anyone within the Ministry of Education demonstrated discriminatory views towards homosexuals, the entire Ministry would be affected.

The Constitution Act of 1867, formerly titled the British North America Act, is a statute that was passed by the Imperial Parliament in Great Britain in 1867. The Constitution guarantees two systems of publicly funded education in Ontario— a Roman Catholic "separate" system and the public system. Section ninety-three of the Constitution says that Catholic schools are exempt from any law that may prejudicially affect any rights Catholics might have had concerning education at the time of Confederation. An article by Ailsa M. Watkinson, entitled "Public Funding for Public Education: A Humans Right Issue" argues for an end to public funding for all religious based schools and school divisions in Saskatchewan, Ontario and Alberta. Watkinson refers to the Constitution:

> The section protects only Protestant and Catholic denomination rights and no others. Originally Quebec and Newfoundland, along with Saskatchewan, Alberta and Ontario, had separate or denominational schools. The provincial governments in Quebec and Newfoundland reorganised their education systems in 1997 and 1998 respectively to bring an end to the religious component of public education.

One important feature of the Constitution is that the authors of the Constitution were taking education into consideration at the time of Confederation, some one hundred and forty years ago. As Justice McKinnon acknowledged, there are many aspects of the Constitution that are no longer applicable today because times have drastically changed since the Constitution was established, and although some sections of the Constitution are still relevant, others should be carefully explored to determine their relevance today.

The amount of funding an Ontario school district is to receive is based upon numerous factors, including the number of students attending school in that district, and the distance the district is from the city center. After speaking with Ryan

Putnam, the Comptroller of Finance for the Durham Catholic, I learned that the funding formula that they utilise is as follows:

- 67.5% funding from the Government of Ontario
- 22% funding from the Municipality
- 10% funding from other school boards and local developers
- Less then 1% funding from the Government of Canada

This formula is very consistent with most of the Catholic School Boards in Ontario. When investigating the funding formula for public schools in Ontario, I contacted Terry Henderson, the Comptroller of Finance for the Durham District Public school board. He informed me that the funding they receive is:

- 67% funding from the Government of Ontario
- 27% from the Municipality
- Balance from fees, rentals of school, facilities, interest income

Clearly, the funding formulas are similar, varying within a few percentages of each other. Therefore the Government of Ontario allocates the same percentage of money to both the Catholic District School Board and the Public School Board. From the previous information, it seems that Catholic Schools are exempt from certain laws and provisions that Public Schools have to comply with, yet it would seem that their money all comes from the same areas.

What is interesting is that in addition to all the public and Catholic schools in Ontario school boards, there are also private schools. These private schools receive absolutely no funding from the government. This seems hypocritical because there are quite a few Christian private schools such as Baptist and Anglican, but because they were not recognised in the Constitution, they do not get the same funding benefits Catholic schools receive. However, the Ministry of Education may inspect a private secondary school that has requested authorisation to grant credits in subjects leading to the Ontario Secondary School Diploma. Judging from the combination of financial and education information, I believe that Catholic Schools

Perspectives On Christianity, Society & The Law

should abide by the same rules and regulations that the Ontario public schools have to abide with.

HOMOSEXUALITY IN THE CATHOLIC CHURCH

In Canada, before 1969 sodomy same-sex practices between consenting adults were considered crimes punishable by imprisonment. In 1969 the Canadian government passed a bill decriminalising private sexual acts between two people over the age of twenty-one. This was the first time equality was granted to same-sex couples. Legislation has come a long way in granting rights, freedoms and equality to homosexual individuals. A source that addresses how homosexuals ought to be treated is the Ontario Human Rights Code ("Code"). The purpose of the Code is to provide equal rights and opportunities and recognise the dignity and worth of every person in Ontario. The Code states that "Every person has a right to equal treatment with respect to services, goods and facilities, without discrimination because of race, ancestry, place of origin, colour, ethnic origin, citizenship, creed, sex, sexual orienta-tion, age, marital status, same-sex partnership status, family status or disability." I believe this should eliminate the discrimination of homosexuals in Catholic schools because they are entitled to the same treatment as heterosexual in Catholic schools. The Canadian Human Right Act ("CHRA") is a means of preventing the unequal treatment of gay men, lesbians and bisexuals. It was not until 1996 when sexual orientation was included among the groups of people against whom discrimination was prohibited against. Section two of the CHRA expressed that homosexual persons should have an:

> Opportunity equal with other individuals to make for them-
> selves the lives that they are able and wish to have and to have
> their needs accommodated, consistent with their duties and
> obligations as members of society, without being hindered in or
> prevented from doing so by discriminatory practices based on
> race, national or ethnic origin, colour, religion, age, sex, sexual
> orientation, marital status, family status, disability or conviction
> for an offence for which a pardon has been granted.

Considering the Catholic schools in Ontario and see them as public institutions, one would have to agree that any discrimination based on homosexuality should be abolished.

The Charter is an instrument used in Canada to set out those rights and freedoms that Canadians believe are necessary in a free and democratic society. According to the Charter everyone has the following fundamental freedoms: freedom of conscience and religion; freedom of thought, belief, opinion and expression, including freedom of the press and other media of communication; freedom of peaceful assembly; and freedom of association. Therefore homosexuals have the right to express their sexual orientation. They should be able to be open about their sexuality as well as the fact that they are Catholic. Section fifteen of the Charter speaks to the substantive equality, meaning that every individual has the right to the equal protection and equal benefit of the law without discrimination and, in particular, without discrimination based on race, national or ethnic origin, colour, religion, sex, age or mental or physical disability. Although sexual orientation is not included in the list of groups, the courts have held that section fifteen also protects equality on the basis of other characteristics that are not specifically set out in it.

Homosexuality has become a highly prominent topic in the last twenty years, but homosexuality itself has been around for thousands of years as demonstrated by the references made to it in the Bible. In the original Hebrew, Aramaic and Greek texts, the words "homosexual" and "homosexuality" are not found, these words date from the late nineteenth century. The authors of the Bible rarely referred to sexual orientation and in fact their language did not have words for the concepts. These authors used a variety of words and phrases to refer to homosexuality, including "without natural affection ,""defile themselves with mankind" and "going after strange flesh." Their perspective was that everyone was heterosexual, but that some heterosexuals engaged in sex with persons of the same gender. The first reference to homosexuality occurs in Genesis 19, but in Leviticus 20:13 a more important passage can be found: "If a man lies with a man as one lies with a woman, both of them have done what is detestable. They must be put to death; their blood will be on their own heads." This is a good example of how the Bible interprets homosexuality, obviously

Perspectives On Christianity, Society & The Law

as a sin. Actually, all references made to homosexuality according to the Bible, are negative. In the Bible, it is clear that homosexuality is a sin, but the sin can be overcome and forgiven. In 1 Corinthians 6:9-10:

> Know ye not that the unrighteous shall not inherit the kingdom of God? Be not deceived: neither fornicators, nor idolaters, nor adulterers, nor effeminate, nor abusers of themselves with mankind, Nor thieves, nor covetous, nor drunkards, nor revilers, nor extortioners, shall inherit the kingdom of God. And such were some of you: but ye are washed, but ye are sanctified, but ye are justified in the name of the Lord Jesus, and by the Spirit of our God.

Although God loves all people, including homosexuals, He does not like sinning because sinning hurts people.

Looking at homosexuality from a Catholic viewpoint, you will get different explanations. The Catechism of the Catholic Church ("Catechism") is a collection of Catholic beliefs. In the two thousand year history of the Catholic Church, we have read the Scriptures and interpreted them in the light of the Apostles. Homosexuality appears approximately four times in the Catechism. It defines homosexuality: "Homosexuality refers to relations between men or between women who experience an exclusive or predominant sexual attraction toward persons of the same sex." It explains that its psychological genesis remains largely unexplained. The Catechism describes homosexuality as contrary to natural law, and disordered, and under no circumstances should it be approved but proceeds to say:

> The number of men and women who have deep-seated homosexual tendencies is not negligible. This inclination, which is objectively disordered, constitutes for most of them a trial. They must be accepted with respect, compassion, and sensitivity. Every sign of unjust discrimination in their regard should be avoided. These persons are called to fulfil God's will in their lives and, if they are Christians, to unite to the sacrifice of the Lord's Cross the difficulties they may encounter from their condition.

So the Catechism believes that homosexuals are not natural, but that they are human beings, and they should not be treated any differently then heterosexuals.

Not all Catholics are in agreement with how homosexuality should be dealt with. The discrepancy of the Catechism causes many Catholics to have conflicting opinions of homosexuals. A few Catholics believe that homosexuality is natural, and is not something someone chooses to be, they cannot change as, it is genetic. Others accept homosexuals, but purely based on the idea that God created them, and that God loves everyone. In 1986 the Roman Catholic Church issued a letter approved by His Holiness, Pope John Paul II, to the bishops of the Catholic Church on the Pastoral Care of Homosexual persons. The letter reads that if you "choose someone of the same sex for one's sexual activity, you annul the rich symbolism and meaning, not to mention the goals, of the Creator's sexual design." The letter forbade any support for groups that did not clearly oppose homosexual acts. In 1992 the Vatican wrote to American bishops and urged Catholics to oppose legislation that would protect the civil rights of gays and lesbians. The letter said that homosexuals were "intrinsically disordered" and `"in no case to be approved of," but continued to say that they were human persons and had the same rights as all persons including that of not being treated in a manner which offended their personal dignity.

Obviously the Ontario Catholic School boards comply with the Catechism and the papal encyclicals from the Vatican. In a statement made by the Chair of the Board, Mary Ann Martin for Durham Catholic she is quoted "The Catechism accepts homosexuals as a person who should be treated like any other person... with respect, compassion and sensitivity. At the same time, however, the Catechism notes that homosexual behaviour is unacceptable and cannot be approved." Martin also notes that Catholic high schools accept all people, and makes no distinction based on race, colour, language or sexual orientation. Where the Catholic school boards will draw the line, however, is not approving of homosexual behaviour, as in the Hall case. Bishop Tony Meager points out that a system that allows a seventeen year-old boy to take another male as his "date" for the prom will be a clear and positive approval, not just of the boy's orientation, but of his adopting a homosexual lifestyle.

The victory in the Hall case was not only a triumph for himself, but also triumph for all homosexuals in Catholic schools. Justice MacKinnon's judgement showed that there may be a place in a Catholic school system for them. The effect of the Hall case was felt throughout the Catholic community. Catholic students have to learn to accept and respect fellow students, regardless of their sexual orientation. Educators within the Catholic schools have to welcome homosexual students and include them in all school activities.

Conclusion

Almost half of the school boards in Ontario are Catholic school boards and get over one-third their funding from the Government of Ontario. This is unfair, as the Constitution is discriminating against other Christian denominations by not allowing them to educate their students with the assistance of the government. Outside of Ontario, most Catholic schools receive no funding from the government, making them solely private institutions. Private institutions have the right to make decisions and regulations based on the principles they wish to follow. The private schools in Ontario are given that same privilege. Catholic school boards should not receive the same amount of funding as the public school boards if they do not wish to comply with the Government of Canada's, and the Government of Ontario's laws and regulations. I understand that forcing Ontario Catholic schools to accept and approve of homosexual behaviour threatens their freedom of religion, but Ontario Catholic school boards have to realise that by accepting public funds, they are just as much a public institution as any other schools within the public school boards. Homosexuality is considered a sin, and is unnatural, based on Catholic principles, but if Catholic schools wish to continue to live by these practices, they must gather funds from sources other than the government.

Ananova. Teenager Wins Gay Prom Sate Court Battle. May 2002. 18 Sept. 2003
    <http://www.ananova.com/news/story/sm_585545.html>.

Burtnyk, Wayne. Letter to Danielle Hildebrand.

Carmichael, Amy. Fate of Gay Prom Date in Court. Canadian Press. May 2002.
    <http://www.canoe.ca/CNEWSLaw0205/06_gayteen-cp.html>.

Catechism of the Catholic Church. Revisions Sept. 1997. 19 Nov. 2003
    <http://ccc.scborromeo.org.master.com/texis/master/search/
    ?sufs=0&q=homosexual&s=SS>.

Canada. Department of Justice. Canada Canadian Charter Of Rights and Freedoms.
    Ontario, 1982. 20 Nov. 2003
    <http://laws.justice.gc.ca/en/charter/index.html>.

Canada. Minister of Supply and Services. Canadian Human Rights Code. Ontario,
    1989.

Durham Catholic District School Board. Financial Statements: For the Year Ended
    August 31, 2002. 19 Nov. 2003 <http://www.durhamrc.edu.on.ca/assets/other_
    images/PDF/ budget2002/DCDSB2002F1.pdf>.

Egale Canada. Court Opens Way For Gay Teen To Attend Prom. Press Re-
    lease. May 2002. 23 Sept. 2003 <http://www.egale.ca/index.asp?lang=&me
    nu=72&item=275>.

Egale Canada. Excerpts From The Judgement of MacKinnon J. In The Marc Hall
    Case. May 2002. 23 Sept. 2003 <http://www.egale.ca/index.asp?lang=&menu=7
    2&item=290>.

Egale Canada. Marc Hall Hearing. May 2002. Henderson, Terry. Re: Funding
    Formula, 12 Nov. 2003. 23 Sept. 2003 <http://www.egale.ca/ index.asp?lang=&
    menu=72&item=291>.

Holy Bible. New International Version. Zondervan. Michigan, 1989.

Lex View. The Court Claims to Extend its Jurisdiction to Church Matters. Mar.
    2003. 20 Nov. 2003 <http://www.culturalrenewal.ca/lex/lex-52.htm>.

Perspectives On Christianity, Society & The Law

Martin, Mary Ann. Statement by the Chair of the Board. April, 2002. 18 Sept. 2003 <http://www.durhamrc.edu.on.ca/html/pr-chair-04-08-02.html>.

Meagher, Anthony G. Letter to Dalton McGuinty. April, 2002. 18 Sept. 2003 <http://www.durhamrc.edu.on.ca/assets/other_images/PDF/bishop-letter.pdf>.

Ontario. Human Rights Commission. Sexual Orientation: Your Rights & Responsibilities. Ottawa, 2001. 20 Nov. 2003 <http://www.ohrc.on.ca/english/guides/sexual-orientation.html>.

Ontario. Ministry of Education. Code of Conduct. Ottawa, 2001. 20 Nov. 2003 <http://www.edu.gov.on.ca/eng/document/brochure/conduct/conduct. html>.

Ontario. Ministry of Education. Student Focused Funding. Ottawa, 2002. <http://www.edu.gov.on.ca/eng/funding/t0102.pdf>.

Ontario. Ministry of Education. Education Act. Ottawa, 1990. 20 Nov. 2003 <http://www.e-laws.gov.on.ca:81/ISYSquery/IRL7606.tmp/9/doc>.

Ratinger, Joseph. Letter to the Bishops of the Catholic Church on The Pastoral Care of   Homosexuals Persons. Oct.1986. 20 Nov. 2003 <http://www.catholicinsight.com/political/homo/pastoralc_799.html>.

Watkinson, Ailsa M. Public Funding for Public Education: A Human Rights Issue. 2003.

To Spank or Not to Spank:
A Response to the Controversial Issue of Corporal Punishment of Children in Canada

Heather Jahnke

VII

To spank or not to spank? This has become a very controversial issue in Canada over the last three years. Is spanking a child considered abuse or discipline? Should spanking be a criminal offence? Some people argue that spanking in any form, with any instrument, such as a spoon, should not be allowed, while others argue that there should be no restrictions on spanking. Still others argue that parents should only spank children with their hand and nothing else, such as a paddle or belt. I will argue that spanking is an effective means of discipline for some parents to use on some children. Parenting requires freedom to choose the best form of discipline. My thesis is that government regulations on the corporal punishment of children infringe upon a parent's responsibility to nurture their children in such a way that the children grow into responsible members of society.

Many questions are raised regarding the physical discipline of children. What are children's rights? Are children's rights different from that of adults when it comes to assault and battery? What is reasonable force with a child? Is spanking the root of other rampant problems in society such as violence in schools and sado-masochism? Does spanking have long-term psychological effects? Does the Bible condone or condemn spanking? All of these questions are valid and important to consider as the answers may have significant implications for Christian parents today.

I would like to introduce the Hildebrandt family of Alymer, Ontario. Henry Hildebrandt is a pastor, husband, and father of seven children. On July 4, 2001 a child-welfare worker called for the removal of all seven children on the grounds of child abuse. Hildebrandt routinely spanked his children as a form of discipline. The children have since been returned to their home on the condition that they are not to be spanked until a verdict has been determined. While judges are making a decision, social workers are "vigorously" monitoring the house (Byfield). Seven children were torn from a loving home by a social worker on the basis of spanking and nothing else. The children did not feel abused by the parents and had not complained of abuse to anyone. The social worker simply took matters into her own hands upon her brief observation of the children. In this type of situation, who are children supposed to listen to, their parents or the state? (Byfield) Who knows what is best for children? Their parents or the government?

The Repeal 43 Committee, made up of activists against the corporal punishment of children, argues that Section Forty-three of the Canadian Criminal Code is contradictory to the laws against assault and violates children's rights as human beings; thus Section Forty-three should be eliminated. Section Forty-three states: "Every schoolteacher, parent, or person standing in the place of a parent is justified in using force by way of correction toward a pupil or child, as the case may be, who is under his care, if the force does not exceed what is reasonable under the circumstances" (qtd. in Turner 18). The term "reasonable" is extremely vague, but it is the basis for arguments that allow for the physical punishment of children.

It is argued that the elimination of Section Forty-three will: a) reduce child abuse in general; b) reduce the risk of children becoming abuse victims when older; and c) reduce violence in schools and society. I will take an in-depth look at these three claims in the following section.

The first claim is that the elimination of Section Forty-three will reduce child abuse. This argument stems from the belief that all physical punishment of children is abusive, be it spanking, slapping, flicking or any form of restraint. Thus, if all physical forms of punishment are considered abuse, the surface of this argument is true. Webster's dictionary defines abuse as follows: "1) to use wrongly; 2) to mistreat; 3) to insult; revile" (Webster's 3). There is nothing in the definition that defines specific actions as abuse; rather the misuse, or wrong use of something is defined as abuse. I argue that spanking in itself is not an abusive action, however, it can be misused. The freedoms to eat sugar, drink alcohol, and drive a car are often abused. As a society, we do not eliminate alcohol, sugar, and the ability to drive simply because there is a possibility of abuse; rather, we have regulations and guidelines that define what abuse of these privileges may include. In the same way, spanking can be, but is not always, abusive. Making spanking illegal will not significantly reduce child abuse.

Criminal intentions must be taken into consideration as well. One must ask the question, do individuals that break the law have any regard for the law? What I am implying by this question is that parents who intend to abuse their children are going to abuse them whether or not there is a law prohibiting it. Instead of saving children from abuse, responsible parents are stripped of an effective means of discipline.

To discern what is and is not abuse can be very difficult, and I believe that it depends on the child, the parent, and the situation. An appropriate act of punishment cannot be determined apart from the situation and circumstances of the misbehaviour. In a similar manner, cases involving death require an examination of the circumstances and evidence in order to determine the precise charge and terms of punishment.

The second claim is that eliminating Section Forty-three will result in reduced violence in schools and society. Some have said that spanking teaches children violence, and children who are spanked are more prone to violence as adults than those who are not spanked. However, current indicators show otherwise. One leading expert writes, "Our society is now experiencing youthful behaviour of practically unprecedented violence...the first generation raised with little or no spanking is proving to be the most violent we have yet spawned—precisely the opposite of what was promised" (Byfield, Ted). Thus, according to this statement, the elimination, by private sectors, of corporal punishment, as encouraged by theorists, has proven the exact opposite of what was hypothesised. Elimination of corporal punishment does not reduce violence in children or society. In my research, I found no evidence directly linking spanking as a child to violence in an adolescent or adult.

The third claim is that the elimination of Section Forty-three will reduce the risk of adults either being abusive or being abused themselves. There is no denying that events and circumstances of childhood have an affect on adulthood. Children who are abused have a greater likelihood of being abusive or abused as adults, but in reality it all comes down to the choices one makes. One theory that regards spanking as a specifically destructive form of abuse that is later displayed in adulthood is that of Irwin A. Hyman, Director of the National Centre for the Study of Corporal Punishment and Alternatives and Professor at the School Psychology at Temple University. The theory is that spanking arouses sexual desires in children, within the context of pain and confusion, and is a direct root of sadomasochism. Hyman writes, "the nerves of the behind, the place on children's bodies that get spanked the most, are also hooked with the nerves that go to the sexual organs" (qtd. in Turner 195). This implies that when children are spanked and accompanied with the words "I'm doing this because I love you" or "this is for your own good," children learn to associate pain with pleasure. In relation to the apparent flourishing of sadomasochism, Susan M. Turner writes, "many adults . . . require pain before they can feel any sexual pleasure . . . spanking with the hand as well as other instruments is, judging from the Internet, one of the most popular means of satisfying [these desires]" (195). I think this claim is very loosely tied to general spanking or abuse, i.e. spanking by parents or spanking with the loving motive of correction. For there to be a link sexually, I believe there must have been sexual abuse involved simultaneously with spanking. To conclude that spanking alone will create sexual desires in a child that will lead to the need to be spanked as an adult in order to experience sexual pleasure is an extreme inference. There is no credible link between the act of spanking and children's sex drives and development.

Another argument against spanking is that it encourages children to lie. Activists for this argument claim that children only learn the discomfort of spanking and therefore lie in order to avoid future spankings. Abraham A. Andero writes, "another emotional reaction of the child to corporal punishment is a desire to avoid punishment . . . thus the child escapes this potential situation" (Andero). While a child may seek to avoid punishment, they need to learn that there are consequences to their actions. I question whether or not avoidance is a negative reaction. When parents discipline children, is not the main objective for the children to stop whatever "bad" action they were doing and to avoid doing it again in the future? If parents cease to discipline a child because they may react negatively, then what is the point of any form of discipline? This concept in itself is abusive as it will not direct a child away from self-destructive behaviour, or behaviour that is harmful to others.

One expert writes, "punishment implies aggressive behaviour on the part of an adult, the very behaviour we oppose in children" ("Should"). In this argument, it is implied that spanking is contradictory to its purpose. Hyman calls this the "Modelling Theory" because "almost all behaviour is learned by watching others . . . children learn to imitate the behaviour of their parents" (49). While this may be true, parents are responsible for teaching their children discernment. Even if children only modelled everything their parents did they would still do wrong. People perform actions everyday that are not ideal. The world is not perfect. People are not perfect. Thus the modelling argument is not very strong due to its reliance on an idealistic world.

There is no denying that the behaviour of many of today's youth is out of control. Perhaps you have experienced the screaming child in the grocery store or the child throwing a tantrum in your favourite restaurant. When I observe scenes like these, where a child is defying an adult, I immediately think that this child's parent does not know how to discipline his or her child. In my mind, the child could use a good spanking; however, others argue that there are better and more effective means of discipline. The subsequent section will look at some of these alternative forms of discipline.

In response to aggressive behaviour, Dr. Spock, author of baby and child care books, suggests that "if your child is hurting another or looks as if he were planning murder, pull him away and get him interested in something else" (Azerrad). Many other doctors suggest similar tactics in pulling a child away or other forms of distraction, as well as soothingly and reassuringly talking to them about the situation. In an article entitled "Why Our Kids Are Out of Control," Jacob Azerrad and Paul Chance suggest that children's misbehaviour is due to misguided adult attention. Azerrad and Chance suggest that parents are too focused on discipline. Rather than focusing on all the bad things children do, parents and caregivers should focus on the positive things children do. Just as "gardeners . . . nurture the flowers not the weeds," Azerrad and Chance suggest that spanking, distracting, or reasoning with children is misplaced attention, because these forms of dealing with the problem focus on the negative things children are doing, not the positive. Children only get attention for the negative actions they perform and in turn grow up to be unruly, negatively-oriented people. Hyman, in his book The Case Against Spanking, also addressed this idea. He states, "if you treat children as if they are bad, they will come to believe that they are bad and therefore act as bad kids" (78). Hyman argues that one should never ever have to hit a child and prevention is the key to good behaviour in children, like the old adage "an ounce of prevention is worth a pound of cure." Hyman suggests many methods of prevention as alternative forms of discipline. Some guidelines Hyman suggests are: make sure the child understands who the parent is; praise and encourage children for good behaviour; use soft reprimands rather than harsh threats; and teach children to express emotions verbally (82-85). Parents should set a behavioural example for their children. Hyman also suggests physical affirmation, such as hugging, kissing, and cuddling, should happen at least once a day (83). Parents need to be patient with their children and teach them empathy, cooperation, and rational problem solving from the earliest possible age (83-84). Consistency in child rearing tactics with one's spouse is crucial to effective discipline (84). Parents need to set limits and provide structure for children (85). Hyman also gives some warnings of parental behaviour to avoid, such as: threatening punishment one is not willing to carry out; comparing children to siblings or other children; loosing control while punishing a child; and avoid scolding and screaming at or psychologically putting down a child; (85). Other methods of discipline are time-out and counting before taking action. Thomas W. Phelan, Ph.D., a renowned expert on child discipline, suggests that counting to a maximum of three and then sending a child to "time out" is the best method of discipline for children age two to age twelve (Phelan). "Time-out" as a disciplinary tool is simply removing a child from a situation and having them think about their actions; some common methods are: sitting a child on a chair in a corner or sending him or her to their room. These are all alternative forms of discipline that can be used in place of spanking. However, most of the alternatives could be used abusively and are therefore no better or worse than spanking.

Many activists argue that Section Forty-three is contradictory to the Canadian Charter of Rights and Freedoms (Charter) sections Seven, Twelve, and Fifteen that state:

> 7. Every one has the right to life, liberty and security of the person and the right not to be deprived thereof except in accordance with the principles of fundamental justice.
> 12. Everyone has the right not to be subjected to any cruel and unusual treatment and punishment.
> 15. (1) Every individual is equal before and under the law and has the right to equal protection and equal benefit of the law without discrimination and, in particular, without discrimination based on race, national or ethnic origin, colour, religion, sex, age or mental or physical disability. (Canadian)

Those against the corporal punishment of children argue that spanking violates the child's rights to security, to not be subjected to cruel treatment, and to equal protection under the law. Section Forty-three creates "tension" with the Charter, and as Turner argues, "we appear to have a conflict of legal rights: the legal right of parents to discipline their children as they see fit versus the legal rights of children to security of the person" (160). In response, I argue that just as an adult gives up his rights when he commits a crime, so does a child when they disobey and or misbehave. There are many exceptions to the law due to the flaws of humanity and society. Section Forty-three is one of these needed exceptions, which protect people, but also to allow for physically corrective measures to be used by parents on their children.

Corporal punishment of children in Canada should remain legal. Spanking and some other forms of physical punishment are effective means of discipline. Spanking used properly is not abuse. I propose that there are some practical guidelines that ought to be used to determine the abusiveness of an action. The age of the child, their particular learning style and comprehension abilities should be taken into consideration. One should not be spanking infants, or children who have reached puberty. The type and severity of misbehaviour committed are two other important factors to take into consideration. Many times parents are too quick to spank their children. The punishment must fit the act. The location on the body that a child is spanked is important as well. Hitting a child in the face, on the head, or upper body is unacceptable. Spanking should be reserved for the buttocks or upper thighs of a child. The number of times a child is spanked is important as well. Beating a child excessively would be an abuse of spanking.

The use of various instruments other than the hand to administer spankings is acceptable, but dependant upon a) the age of the child and b) the capacity of the adult. The instruments used should be subject to appropriateness and guidelines developed by the courts. I do not believe that parents should be beating children with random objects, or whips. However, I think the use of spoons, spatulas, hands, and belts are all acceptable depending upon the situation.

Parents themselves must take careful consideration of who they are individually and what discipline means are appropriate for them to use. Just as someone who had alcoholic parents must take careful measures not to become an alcoholic themself; so too, parents who were abused as children or have short tempers, etc. must be careful what means of discipline they choose to use. It is important that parents not spank their children in anger, but for corrective purposes only.

Discipline tactics are not as important as how they are implemented. I mentioned earlier, several alternative forms of discipline such as counting and "time out." I argue that even some of those mentioned could be abusive to a child. If a parent put a child in "time-out" locked away in a closet for an extreme amount of time, their practice would be considered abusive and negligent. All forms of discipline mentioned in this paper can be both effective and ineffective. The distinction between discipline and punishment is important to recognise. Discipline is more than punishment. Webster's dictionary defines discipline as "1) training that develops self-control, efficiency, etc. 2) strict control to enforce obedience 3) orderly conduct 4) a system of rules, as for a monastic order 5) treatment that corrects or punishes" (Webster's 171). Whereas, punishment is simply defined as "1) a punishing or being punished 2) the penalty imposed 3) harsh treatment" (477). These definitions are important to understand when determining whether or not spanking is an effective means of discipline or not. If spanking is only punishment, then the arguments of only teaching children what not to do would be valid and it would not be an effective means of discipline at all. I argue that spanking used properly, coincides with numbers two, "strict control to enforce obedience," and five, "treatment that corrects or punishes," of Webster's definition of discipline (171). Add some training and reasoning, in relation to the age of the child, along with spanking and achieve effective discipline.

Spanking is not battery. At their most basic definition, battery and spanking appear to be the same. The Section 265 of the Canadian Criminal Code (Code) states:

> A person commits assault when (a) without the consent of another person, he applies force intentionally to that other person, directly or indirectly; (b) he attempts or threatens, by an act or a gesture, to apply force to another person, if he has, or causes that other person to believe on reasonable grounds that he has, present ability to effect his purpose; or (c) while openly wearing or carrying a weapon or an imitation thereof, he accosts or impedes another person or begs. (Canadian)

Section 268 of the Code states "everyone commits an aggravated assault who wounds, maims, disfigures or endangers the life of the complainant" (Canadian). However, I argue that motivation must be taken into account. There are many times in society that assaults and batteries are carried out and it is both legal and necessary. Take for example the police force. A police officer may "threaten" an individual, who is holding up a convenience store at gun point, that if he/she does not put the gun down and come out with his/her hands up he/she may be shot, or taken down by force. This is acceptable for the safety of those in the store and surrounding area. Spanking can be used similarly. If a child is misbehaving, a parent may threaten him/her with a spanking, and if the child does not obey, then he/she must be spanked, to take corrective action. This teaches children the value of one's word and how it is important to follow-up words with action, as well as the principle that certain actions have certain consequences. Acceptable and unacceptable behaviour can be taught to children through the process of warning and spanking.

Spanking is a recommended form of discipline by family physicians and pediatricians. A study was conducted to determine whether or not family doctors and pediatricians are in support of corporal punishment of children. The study concluded, "Most physicians and pediatricians support the use of corporal punishment . . . "(McCormick). The study also found that pediatricians offer discipline guidance for families more often than physicians. From this study, it can be concluded that spanking is an effective means of discipline and not as detrimental to children's health, physically, emotionally, or psychologically, as many people believe. Grant Hill, Reform MP, a medical doctor writes:

> Using force is a reasonable way to discipline children, but it must not go beyond reasonable force . . . Spanking and discipline in this manner has been a part of parenting for centuries. I do not believe that the social engineers and interfering lawmakers of today know better than the generations of parents who reared their children using spanking. (Moore)

Hill makes an important statement and raises the question of tradition and history. Should centuries of tradition and success be eliminated in a matter of a few years and court rulings? If the system was so messed up, how did it last so long? I agree with Hill, that the lawmakers and social policy activists of today do not know any better than parents of previous generations. I have not witnessed nor discovered anything in my research that indicates people today have more wisdom and discernment than people of the past.

On January 30, 2004 in a six to three judgement, the Supreme Court of Canada (Court) rejected the Canadian Foundation for Children, Youth, and the Law's (CFCYL) request to have Section Forty-three repealed. The Court found that Section Forty-three is not in contradiction with Sections Seven, Twelve, and Fifteen of the Charter (Canadian F.). However, the Court did establish some guidelines for the spanking of children. Parents are only permitted to spank children between the ages of two and twelve years old, and with their hand only.

This verdict has significant implications for Christians today and it is important to understand the severity of the decision. Spanking one's child with anything other than a hand is now a criminal offence, punishable by imprisonment or fines, not to mention the potential removal of children from the home, as was experienced by the Hildebrandt family. If a parent spanks their toddler one day short of his or her second birthday it is a criminal offence. In my opinion, this criminalization of spanking is in conflict with the teachings of the Bible, in regard to corporal punishment, and infringes on the rights of Christian parents to raise their children in accordance with the Bible. Proverbs 23:13-14 states "Do not withhold discipline from a child; if you punish him with the rod, he will not die. Punish him with the rod and save his soul from death" (New 978). Christians are called to discipline their children and it is implied that spanking with a rod is okay, as it will not kill a child. The word rod in this verse can be taken both literally and figuratively for punishment of various kinds. The Hebrew word for rod used in theses verses is also used in reference to a staff, or a stick used to assist in walking, discipline or guidance (Zondervan 1496). Proverbs 13:24 states, "He who spares the rod hates his son, but he who loves him is careful to discipline him" (New 964). Hate is a very strong word and indicates the severity and importance of disciplining children. The Bible Knowledge Commentary gives the following comments on this verse:

> A loving parent inflicts temporary discomfort on his children
> (by spanking with a rod) to spare them the long-range disaster
> of an undisciplined life. Refusal to discipline one's child when
> he needs it shows that a parent's love and concern are questionable. (934)

In Proverbs 29:15 it is written, "The rod of correction imparts wisdom, but a child left to himself disgraces his mother" (New 986). The Bible Knowledge Commentary comments on this passage:

In Hebrew, the rod of correction literally reads 'the rod and correction.' Either the rod is the instrument of correction (in which case a figure of speech called hendiadys is used), or both the rod (physical punishment) . . . and verbal correction (lit., 'rebuke') are to be used. A child who is not disciplined and is left to himself (allowed to do as he pleases and have whatever he wants) will become an unruly person. (968)

The implications from these verses are very strong. Christian parents are called to discipline their children, both physically and verbally. These verses do not say to abuse children, but rather the discipline of children gives them wisdom. In fact the Bible goes so far as to say not only does a parent not love his child if he does not discipline him, but he hates him. As Christians, we need the right to discipline our children in the manner prescribed by God.

Some may argue that these verses are no longer applicable because they are from the Old Testament. However, the New Testament does not abolish the Old Testament. The New Covenant described in the New Testament is in reference to the law. The Book of Proverbs is a book of wisdom and is still very applicable today. One can also study the life and teachings of Jesus for further insight into this matter. Jesus frequently quoted Old Testament scriptures to people, validating the applicability of the Old Testament for believers under the New Covenant. There are no direct references to spanking in the New Testament because the previous verses of the Old Testament are still valid. The New Testament does however, comment on the importance and significance of discipline. Hebrews 12:9-11 states:

We have all had human fathers who disciplined us and we respected them for it . . . our fathers disciplined us for a little while as they thought best; but God disciplines us for our good that we may share in his holiness. No discipline seems pleasant at the time, but painful. Later on, however, it produces a harvest of righteousness and peace for those who have been trained by it. (New 1874)

Perspectives On Christianity, Society & The Law

In this passage, a parallel is drawn between God the Father disciplining His children and the discipline of earthly children by their fathers. If discipline was corrupt and not to be practised then God would not apply it to His children. As Christians, God is the ultimate authority and example; God is good, not evil. Thus, discipline is good and should be carried out in direct response to the example and commands God has set.

Parents are largely responsible for developing the character of their children and the Bible supports this. Proverbs 22:6 states, "Train a child in the way he should go, and when he is old, he will not turn from it" (New 976). Here it is implied that parents are to train or nurture their children in the way that he or she is manifesting their own personality, and this will require discipline, in order to instruct them so that they do not turn from it when they are older. Ephesians 6:1,4 indicates the importance of obedience, training and instruction of children; "Children obey your parents in the Lord, for this is right . . . Fathers, do not exasperate your children; instead, bring them up in the training and instruction of the Lord" (New 1799). Parents are responsible for the upbringing of their children. The statement "Fathers, do not exasperate your children," indicates that parents must surrender feelings they may have, in order to act reasonably towards their children. The verse specifies that parents do not have the freedom to do whatever they feel like, but rather what is useful for training and teaching of the Lord. In Colossians 3:20-21 it is written, "Children obey your parents in everything, for this pleases the Lord . . . Fathers, do not embitter your children, or they will become discouraged" (New 1817). Children are to obey parents. Parents are to place boundaries on children and then enforce them.

The guidelines handed down with the verdict by the Court gives parents limited freedom to discipline their children. As Christians, we should fight for the repeal of these guidelines and ask for a legal test to be developed as has been done for many other areas of law. I feel that the guidelines developed by the Court are not reasonable and do not address the real problem. Child abuse is a very real problem today, but spanking is not child abuse. Spanking is an effective disciplinary tool used to instruct, train, and nurture children. Specific age requirements, in regard to the issue of spanking, are not reasonable because children develop at different stages. The age guideline basically places the difference between criminal and non-criminal action of a parent on one-minute. I do not think parents should be allowed to spank children with anything they desire, however, they also should not be limited to using their hand only. Discipline is a very important part of the development of children. In his book entitled Seven Things Children Need, John M. Drescher gives a good definition of discipline and its importance. Drescher writes,

> Discipline is usually defined as punishment to bring about obedience. This is far too narrow . . . Discipline involves the total molding of the child's character through encouraging good behaviour. Punishment is the part of discipline which provides a short-term, temporary deterrent . . . Discipline includes also the responsibility of the parent to draw out, encourage, and build good behaviour to take the place of the bad. Discipline includes both discipline and restriction . . . Discipline includes everything a parent does or says to help the child learn and develop to maturity. (Drescher 103)

Discipline is critical to child development, and punishment is a part of this. Spanking is an effective tool of punishment. Drescher also states, "At times discipline may hurt, physically and emotionally, but parents do their children an injustice to hold off discipline because it may hurt momentarily" (Drescher 105). Pain is a part of life, part of the growing process and cannot be a defence to not spank.

Section Forty-three of the Criminal Code of Canada allows for the corporal punishment of children by parents and caregivers and should remain in effect. Three claims for the elimination of Section Forty-three are: There will be less child abuse in general; the risk of becoming an abuse victim as an adult will be reduced; and there will be less violence in schools and society. There are many other factors that contribute to the problems that are supposed to be reduced by the repeal of Section Forty-three. No direct link can be found between spanking and adult abuse or violence in schools and society. Spanking a child does not create perverse sexual desires in children nor a need to be spanked to experience sexual pleasure as an adult. A child's right to security, as a person, is not violated by spanking, nor is spanking assault or battery. Spanking is an early childhood disciplinary tool, and subject to various criteria for use, such as: age, personality, and mental capabilities of the child; the offence committed; as well as the personality and given tendencies of the parent. Spanking is not effective for every parent to use on every child, however it is effective for a majority, and must remain a disciplinary option. Most family physicians and pediatricians are supportive of spanking as a disciplinary method.

In conclusion, spanking is a disciplinary tool that can sometimes be misused. Spanking is an effective disciplinary action for many parents to use on their children. In response to the question, "to spank or not to spank?" parents should have the individual right to decide. The government should continue to uphold Section Forty-three, which gives parents the right to decide whether or not to spank their children, but revise their newly mandated guidelines by developing a legal test to determine whether or not the spanking in questionable cases was abusive. There are multiple tools and methods to use in disciplining children. Most of them can be misused and result in child abuse. The Bible supports the use of physical discipline for the correction of children, within the framework of discipline and careful instruction and the development of their character, in order to be a contributing member of a peaceful, law-abiding society.

WORKS CITED

Andero, Abraham A. "Issue of Corporal Punishment: Re-examined." Journal of Instructional Psychology. June 2002 <http://findarticles.com>.

Azerrad, Jacob and Paul Chance. "Why Our Kids Are Out of Control." Psychology Today. Sept./Oct 2001, Vol. 34 Issue 5. <http://search.epnet.com/direct.asp?an=4976248&db=bsh>.

Bible Knowledge Commentary, The. Old Testament, New International Version. John F. Walvord and Roy B. Zuck, ed. Colorado Springs, CO: Chariot Victor Publishing, 1985.

Byfield, Link. "Conservatives Actually Lost the Anti-spanking Court Challenge, But as Usual Won't Admit it." Report / Newsmagazine. (Alberta Edition): 4 Feb. 2002, Vol. 29 Issue 3. <http://search.epnet.com/direct.asp?an=5979292&db=bsh>.

Byfield, Ted. "Surely the People who Should be on Trial are Those Ontario Children's Social Workers." Report / Newsmagazine. (Alberta Edition) 20 Aug. 2001 Vol. 28 Issue 16. <http://search.epnet.com/direct.asp?an=5088764&db=bsh>.

Canadian Charter of Rights and Freedoms. <http://laws.justice.gc.ca/en/charter>.

Canadian Foundation for Children, Youth, and the Law v. Canada. (Attorney General) <http://www.lexum.umontreal.ca/cscscc/en/rec/html/2004scc00 4.wpd. html>.

Drescher, John M. Seven Things Children Need. 2nd ed. Scottdale, PA: Herald Press, 1988.

Hyman, Irwin A. The Case Against Spanking: How to Discipline Your Child Without Hitting. San Francisco: Jossey-Bass, 1997.

McCormick, K.F. "Attitudes of Primary Care Physicians Toward Corporal Punishment." JAMA. 267: 3161-3165. 1992. <http://jama.ama-assn.org>.

Moore, Charles W. "The Spanking Wars Go To Court." <http://www.geocities.com/Athens/Agean/9318/spanking.html>.

Perspectives On Christianity, Society & The Law

New International Version Study Bible, The. Kenneth Barker, Ed. Red Letter ed. Grand Rapids, MI: Zondervan, 1985.

Phelan, Thomas W. Ph.D. 1-2-3 Magic: Effective Discipline for Children 2-12. Glen Ellyn, Il: Child Management INC, 1995. 2nd ed.

"Should you Punish Your Child?" Psychology Today. Sept./Oct 2001, Vol. 34 Issue 5. <http://search.epnet.com/direct.asp?an=4976223&db=bsh>.

Turner, Susan M. Something to Cry About: An Argument Against Corporal Punishment of Children in Canada. Waterloo, ON: Wilfrid Laurier University, 2002.

Webster's New World Dictionary. Pocket Books Paperback ed. New York: Prentice Hall, 1995.

Zondervan NIV Exhaustive Concordance. Edward W. Goodrick, et al. Ed. Grand Rapids, MI: Zondervan, 1999.

WHO IS GUARDING THE FLOCK?
Affinity Fraud, Liability and the Church's Response

Tim Kreiter

Fraud touches every aspect of our lives, from telemarketing schemes to credit card theft and misuse, identity theft and Internet scams. On the corporate scene, large-scale fraudulent behaviour has been epitomised by companies such as Enron, WorldCom and the accounting giant Arthur Anderson. Too many people have, unfortunately, accepted fraudulent practices, as just another aspect of doing business in today's marketplace.

Fraud is not limited to dealings at the higher levels of the business world, but is most often perpetrated by a person with an investment proposal presented to an individual with little or no business or financial experience. In fact, frauds are often directed towards people who "share the same religion, race, ethnicity, career or other social characteristic and then deceives them in some kind of financial transaction (Henderson par. 1)." Churches are extremely vulnerable to fraud, especially that form generally referred to as affinity fraud, because "members of religious groups . . . typically expect someone of the same religion to follow its moral principles" par.4). Too often church members make their financial decisions based on personal relationships and trust in authority figures (Chattaway par. 18) which can lead to a situation where a congregation could be led, like sheep, to their financial slaughter. And what of the shepherd of that flock, what is his duty or responsibility in the event of an affinity fraud?

My thesis is that pastors, their churches and supporting denominational conferences would be liable under a potential negligence action where an affinity fraud has been allowed to occur within a church setting or religious network. This liability should not be minimised, even though the church has done little or nothing to alert or educate pastors to the ever-increasing problem of affinity fraud.

To better understand affinity fraud and the issues surrounding pastoral liability I will start with an overview of fraud, including some historical background and definitions. I will then review an actual affinity fraud that arose in a church setting and apply the three-part test of a negligence action to assess the scope of pastoral liability. To assist in describing liability I have included several classic case law examples that have provided the basis that the courts have relied on when deciding liability. The paper will conclude with a consideration of the impact that affinity fraud has on the churches witness in the world.

To start, fraud is a term that is not always clearly understood. In fact the simple recognition of fraud as a distinct criminal act is a fairly recent development in the history of law; for most of human history crime was generally held to be violent assaults, thefts, robbery and murder (Surette 25-35). It has only been since the nineteenth century that fraud has been actively codified, and only in the last hundred years has fraud even come close to receiving serious consideration from the courts (Working Paper 37-50). Black's Law Dictionary describes fraud as "an intentional perversion of the truth for the purpose of inducing another in reliance upon it to part with some valuable thing belonging to him or to surrender a legal right" (625). The Quebec Court of appeal in R v. Littler said that fraud also includes:

> All these calculated and wilful false statements, half truths,
> omissions, even mere secrecy, all these direct or indirect lies
> and falsehoods, disloyal or fraudulent means deliberately used
> by its [sic] author to his benefit or the benefit of third parties,
> which may not be characterised fully as a false pretence, but
> which create a state of mind inducing a person to follow a
> course of action to its [sic] detriment and injury.(Nightingale 2)
> In Working Paper 19, Criminal Law, Theft and Fraud, chaired
> by the late Honourable Antonio Lamar, it was noted that the
> "underlying notion is simple: 'don't be dishonest'"(3). Justice
> Lamar also noted that fraud must be intentional; knowledge of

a falsehood or a complete disregard for the truth in a statement would constitute fraud, but a statement given with a mistaken belief as to its accuracy, honestly given, even with a failure to confirm the content of the statement itself, was not a fraud (32).

The simplest way to define fraud is in contrast with the associated offence of theft; theft is when someone takes something from you without your consent, whereas fraud is when someone tricks you into turning over an item of your own free will. Fraud, which has a better financial return then robbery and a correspondingly low level of detection or apprehension, can be characterised as robbery at the point of a pen rather than at the end of a gun (Lindskoog 256). While criminal law has slowly evolved to regard fraud as a serious problem, the entertainment industry, and in particular television, has continued to present crime in a limited context, namely as violent acts against the person (Surette 25-35). Movies, such as Paper Moon, The Sting and Ocean's Eleven have perpetuated the myth that fraud is just good, clean fun with no serious legal or moral implications for the perpetrators.

More recently, the movie version of Catch Me If You Can, Frank Abagnale's autobiography, continues to romanticise the fraud artist, portraying him as a "Robin Hood" prototype (Stansfield 65), the con man with a heart of gold (Faron 29). Abagnale was the consummate affinity "fraudster", able to complete so many of his schemes by pretending to be a Pan Am pilot. His apparent affiliation with the highly respected airline convinced bank tellers, hotel clerks and many other people world-wide to cash his counterfeit cheques. Those cheques, totalling over $2.5 million dollars calculated in sixties dollars, were cashed over a very short period of time, covering only the last few years in his adolescence (Abagnale 4 -5).

Why did those honest, and basically decent, people unwittingly assist Abagnale? There were a number of reasons, not the least of which was that awareness and prevention of fraud was seriously lacking in the sixties. Beyond that, Abagnale's success depended on his convincing people through his many assumed guises, including his pilot persona, that this pleasant, charming and affable young man was exactly who he claimed to be, not the impostor that he really was. Abagnale convinced people that they could trust him because he supposedly belonged to an organisation they knew and trusted. This tactic is still used by affinity "fraudsters" today; they join the local service clubs, business organisations and, all too often, churches, pursuing this affiliation with the group in an effort to further their schemes and swindle as many people as possible (Faron 30). Once inside a targeted organisation the "fraudster" befriends the prominent people, the people in leadership positions, with the hopes that these leaders will influence the other members of the group to trust him.

Affinity is described in Black's Law Dictionary as "a close agreement; relation; spiritual relation or attraction held to exist between certain persons . . . in a larger sense . . . kindred," (59) virtually a familial relationship. The Concise Oxford Dictionary defines affinity as a "similarity of character suggesting relationship" (22). Advertisers exploit the public's identification and sense of kinship with sports stars and other celebrities and use this "similarity of character" to influence consumer attitudes and decisions. This is a practical application of the human tendency to stereotype others as a shortcut to identifying whom we should trust (McShane 161-65, Sumner interview). Affiliation is also used by sports teams, the military and many corporations to develop "esprit de corps" in their members, resulting in a positive form of stereotyping that benefits both the group and all its members.

This need to belong has not gone unnoticed by the criminal element of society. Street gangs, outlaw motorcycle groups and the Mafia all use symbols, passwords, gang colours and jargon in a perversion of affiliation. Fraud artists, like Frank Abagnale, also exploit affinity for their nefarious purposes. Henderson in Crimes of Persuasion, noted that in religion-based scams, the affinity "fraudsters" want to get close to the church leaders to "lull members into a misplaced trust by selling first to a few prominent members, then pitching the scam to the rest by using the names of those previously sold" (par. 6). This defeats "the natural scepticism of the individual member . . . " (par.7). As Brad Sumner, a minister at North Langley Community Church noted, parishioners want to be on good terms with their pastor; they look to him for spiritual guidance, counselling and dispute resolution, they accept the pastor's authority on moral and religious issues. That acceptance is then readily transferred to other matters, such as finances, even when the pastor has no specific knowledge in that area. Once the "fraudster" has gained the pastors' friendship, he can translate that to a tacit endorsement of his character and, by extension, his schemes, and prepare his snares for other victims.

Pastors, of all people, should be intimately knowledgeable of the many aspects of sin, including fraud, since the Bible abounds with tales of deceit and trickery. The Old Testament tells of the serpent tricking Eve in the Garden of Eden (NIV Gen. 3:1-7), and of Jacob receiving the elder sons blessing by impersonating his brother Esau (NIV Gen. 27:1-40). The New Testament church was not immune to fraud either, as noted in Acts 5:1-11, where Ananias and his wife Sapphira sold their home and donated the proceeds to the fledgling church. Rather then turn over all the money, they decided to keep some for themselves, claiming to have given it all to the church.

When confronted by the Apostle Paul, Ananias and Sapphira denied the fraud and were struck dead. Following this:

> No one else dared join them, [in trying to deceive the church]
> even though they [the Christians] were highly regarded by the
> people. Nevertheless, more and more men and women believed
> in the Lord and were added to their number.
> (NIV Acts 5:13 & 14)

Churches have fared poorly in the centuries following the Apostolic Age. From the relics and indulgences sold by the Roman Catholic Church in the Middle Ages to the many charlatans of the Age of Enlightenment, the church has been a ripe target for fraud. In more recent centuries, the Church has seen Joseph Smith and his "divine" revelations that led to the founding of the Mormon Church (Martin 169-83), the plagiarism of Mary Eddy, the founder of Christian Science (128-33) and "Pastor" Russell, the founder of the Jehovah's Witnesses and his miracle wheat seed (38-43). All in all, religious history has been a sorry litany of frauds and impostors. Notwithstanding all the examples of the Bible and the historical record, fraud continues to be a problem for the contemporary church. An example that received wide press coverage in the late nineties was the Greater Ministries International, also known as GMI, scandal. Greater Ministries, of Tampa, Florida, perpetrated one of the largest affinity frauds ever, separating some eighteen thousand churchgoers from an estimated $448 million dollars (Bergal par.10, Greater Ministries 1). The founder of GMI, Gerald Payne, offered a "Double Your Money Gift Exchange" program that promised to double parishioner's money over a short period of time, all thanks to GMI's alleged investments in precious metals and mines in Africa. People were encouraged to empty their bank accounts and sell off all their assets to invest with GMI.

In the beginning, because GMI was paying off the initial investors with funds from subsequent investors, many people did make money and readily endorsed the programs. Ironically, in the end, GMI collapsed after it lost most of the money after having deposited it in a crooked bank (Greater Ministries 4). Payne was convicted and sentenced to twenty-one years for running a "Ponzi scheme" (Bergal par.10).

"Ponzi schemes," and the related "pyramid" schemes, are the most common scams perpetrated against churches. Ponzi schemes are named after Charles Ponzi, an Italian immigrant who conned thousands of Americans in the early nineteen hundreds. Ponzi sold international postage return coupons, claiming he could make huge profits for investors on the difference in the exchange rates between the United States dollar and the foreign currencies used to buy and sell the international mail coupons (Faron 145). Ponzi did provide returns of up to fifty percent to the initial participants in the scheme. So many people wanted to invest with him that he could not be bothered to count the money; he simply stuffed it by the handfuls into desk drawers, boxes and suitcases. Most of Ponzi's victims continued to reinvest their money with him; consequently all he had to pay out was the interest. Since the investors were not asking for their principal, Ponzi simply stopped buying the mail coupons and used the money from the new investors to pay out the old investors (146). As always happens, Ponzi's scheme finally collapsed when there were no more new investors to provide the money he needed to pay out the earlier investors.

Ponzi schemes are typically run by one "fraudster" and ultimately he is the only one who realises any real gain from the investment scam, as all the profits that the victims have been promised are usually only on paper and are never actually paid out. Any money that victims do receive will usually be "interest payments" on their investment, amounting to only a small sum of the money that they have invested with the con man. "Pyramid" schemes, a variation of Ponzi schemes, operate on the same general principals, needing an ever-increasing number of new investors to provide the funds necessary to pay out the initial "investors." The main difference between the two schemes is the number of perpetrators running it. In a pyramid there is often a core group of people who begin the scheme and recruit new victims to invest. These investors are encouraged to recruit ever-increasing numbers of new people to participate in the scheme and provide the money that will run the scam. They are promised, like GMI's victims, that there are huge profits to be made as a result of receiving a share of every new participant's investment. The bulk of the money always goes to the group that is running the pyramid and only the people at the top will make any money. In "pyramids," as in Ponzi schemes, the same problem always arises; there are never enough new investors available to allow anyone other than the top few people to actually make any money, a return on the losses suffered by everyone else.

These classic scams, with some technological improvements, are still being used by the current generation of "fraudsters" with great success. Theses schemes will not be called "pyramids" or Ponzi schemes, rather they will be disguised with a variety of aliases such as "investments," "gifting programs," "blessing plans," or with a combination of religious sounding names such as "Jubilee Trust Fund, Oracle Trust Fund and Elkosh Trust Fund" (Henderson 35). The Ponzi scheme is especially effective when the initial investors, and subsequent beneficiaries, of one of these fraudulent investment schemes is a pastor or an elder. When a church leader receives a substantial sum of money, it legitimises the scheme and can provide the opportunity for a con artist to set up and fleece an entire congregation (Henderson par.7 - 8; Sumner interview, Atchison interview).

Having looked at the definition of fraud and how it can be perpetrated against a congregation, we will now move on to an examination of a classic example of a Ponzi scheme. Laurie Davis used the tactics of affinity fraud to promote her schemes to the congregation of the Faith Works Church in Charlottetown, Prince

Edward Island. Davis was invited, at the request of the pastor, to present her program called "Personal Empowerment Program" (PEP). PEP was touted as a lifestyle program for people to "make positive changes in their lives" and as a "great business opportunity" (R v. Davis 4). At these meetings Laurie Davis promised "revenues forecast in the millions" (5). Laurie Davis was enthusiastic, impressive and above all, convincing, selling a dream of success with the "potential to help people with their lives and to reward financially the people who became involved" (5). People who had come to the initial sessions got caught up in the hype and came back with friends and family to listen to "testimonials [that] were given by people who had been helped by the program or by people who were excited about the program, the word spread" (5). People signed up for personal training programs and were sold "membership packages that included workbooks, videos, training manuals and other miscellaneous support tools that allegedly enable them to sell PEP" (BC Security Commission Bulletin 195) to others, all the while helping to spread the PEP message.

While holding seminars and meetings the Davis' were also recruiting investors for one of their many companies. Enthusiasm for the program continued to grow, spurred on by the Davis' promises that an "investment of five thousand dollars would return $9,465.63 in only three years" (5). Many of the people who came to these meetings and subsequently invested had no idea what they were getting into; they joined because friends and family urged them to. The Davis' said, "they were looking for smaller investors so the common person could be involved" (8).

After an investigation by securities regulators in Atlantic Canada, the Davis' were charged with trading in an unlicensed investment product. At their trial, the judge noted that there was a "lack of sophistication in investing in the case of many of the witnesses we heard from" (9). The witnesses said that they had invested because of the high rate of return and because the projects were promoted as being risk free. In the end most of the people who invested with Laurie Davis did so because friends and family members brought them into the program. R v. Davis, et al is a classic example of affinity fraud; Davis had convinced her victims that she was just like them, an ordinary person with a desire to help other people. People wanted to be part of the dream, but in the end the only person that she helped was herself.

While R v Davis, et al illustrates a classic Ponzi scheme; the trial record made only passing reference to the minister who provided the initial venue for the Davis'. Under other circumstances could an affinity fraud lead to pastoral liability? Would the pastor be liable for the losses suffered by his congregation, leading to a tort for negligence? To better understand that question we need to go back to the three-part test for negligence; the duty owed, the duty breached and the harm caused by that breach of duty. Pastors clearly have a duty of care to the congregation regarding spiritual matters and are understood to be the guardians of their parishioner's spiritual lives, the shepherd of the flock (Sumner interview, Spencer interview). Should that duty of care extend to financial losses suffered in a fraud?

When the pastor has failed to detect a fraud, or worse invited the "fraudster" into the church, has he breached a duty to the congregation? If he was directly involved in the fraud, like Gerald Payne and Greater Ministries, then there could be no argument that he had breached his duty and also committed the criminal offence of fraud (Smyth 221). If he simply failed to prevent the fraud due to a lack of care, or complete incompetence, failing to conduct himself to the standard expected by a "reasonable person," he would still be expected to have foreseen the results of his actions. As previously noted, this question would be answered by the use of the standard three part test of a negligence tort would be used; first, was there a duty owed, secondly, was it breached and third, did that breach of duty actually cause harm to the plaintiff. The popular assumption is, if there is a loss it must be as a result of the breach of duty, but that is not always true. Rather, the process has to be followed from the beginning to the end; from the duty owed, to the duty breached, to the harm caused. Where there is no duty owed then there can by no breach or liability for the harm suffered.

The classic textbook case that defines a negligence tort is Donoghue v. Stevenson, in which a manufacturer sold a defective product that caused a third party to fall ill (Smyth 57 - 58). This was the first case to impose a duty on a defendant to those persons further removed from any direct dealings with the defendant by including the principle of reasonable foreseeability. Lord Atkin said,

The rule that you are to love your neighbour becomes in law, you must not injure your neighbour: and the lawyers question, Who is my neighbour? receives a restricted reply. You must take reasonable care to avoid acts or omissions which you can reasonably foresee would be likely to injure your neighbour. Who then is my neighbour? The answer seems to be—persons who are so directly affected by my act that I ought reasonably to have them in contemplation as being affected when I am directing my mind to the acts or omissions which are called in question. (Jepson par.6)

"Who is my neighbour?" refers to the well-known biblical parable of the Good Samaritan. When the lawyer asked, "Who is my neighbour?" Jesus turned the question back on him and the lawyer then answered that the neighbour was the man "who had [shown] mercy to [the man who had been robbed]". Jesus replied, "Go and do likewise" (Luke 10:25-37). Matthew Henry in his Commentary in One Volume says, "It is the duty of every one of us to succour, help, and relieve all that are in distress and necessity, and of lawyers particularly" (1449). This concept, as set out by Lord Atkin, leads us to examine our actions; we must always be alive to the possibility that our actions, or inaction's, may harm another and deal with the risks accordingly.

Anns and Others v Merton London Borough Council took the principles laid out in Donoghue v Stevenson further, confirming that where there was foreseeability and proximity, the connection of the defendants actions to the plaintiffs injuries, then there was a duty of care (Swarb par. 16). These decisions expanded the principal of the duty owed to cover a wider group of plaintiffs. This has been upheld in subsequent court decisions, particularly Crocker v. Sundance Northwest Resorts Ltd. which imposed a greater burden of duty when there was a commercial, or a special relationship. In that case, Sundance Resort had held a competition where people slid down a ski hill in tire inner tubes. Crocker signed the entry and waiver form without reading it, paid the entry fee and entered the competition. He had been drinking and had received a cut over his eye in the first run down the hill. At the start of the second run, Crocker was quite noticeably drunk and the owner of Sundance

Perspectives On Christianity, Society & The Law

suggested that Crocker should not compete. The resort manager also questioned Crocker's participation, but neither did anything more to prevent Crocker from sliding down the hill a second time. During the second run there was an accident and Crocker hurt his neck, leaving him a quadriplegic (Crocker par.1).

The matter went to trial, eventually ending in an appeal before the Supreme Court of Canada. The issue before the court was whether the ski resort had a "positive duty at law to take steps to prevent a visibly intoxicated person" from competing in its competition. The decision by the appellate court was that Sundance, in promoting a dangerous sport and in also supplying alcohol to Crocker, owed a definite duty of care to Crocker to take all reasonable steps to prevent his further participation when it was obvious that he was drunk, especially when the resort owner and an employee had directly asked Crocker about his ability to continue (Crocker par.23). In considering the duty of care the judges wrote that,

> the common law has generally distinguished between negli-
> gent conduct (misfeasance) and failure to take positive steps to
> protect others from harm (nonfeasance). The early common
> law was reluctant to recognise affirmative duties to act. Limited
> exceptions were carved out where the parties were in a special
> relationship (e.g. parent and child) or where the defendant had
> a statutory or contractual obligation to intervene. (par. 17)

The justices noted that the law to that point had not required people to actively look out for the well being of another person except where there was a "special relationship." They further noted that the Canadian courts had become "increasingly willing to expand the number and kind of special relationship to which a positive duty to act attaches" (par.18). Thus, it could be seen that where there was foreseeable and unreasonable risk created by an action, or a failure to act, on the part of the defendant; and there was a connection between the two persons, in this instance a commercial relationship, the reasonable conclusion was that there was a duty owed to the plaintiff. Where there was an increased risk of serious injury, even greater care would be expected. Further, wherever a person is unable, "either through youth, intoxication or other incapacity" (par.21) to deal with a situation then the duty is even greater. Given that the courts are willing to expand the duty of care in a commercial relationship, how much further would they take it in light of that special relationship that exists between a pastor and the members of his congregation?

The concept of the duty of care was expanded in Dube v Labar, where Justice Estey, writing for the majority, noted that Dube, who was drunk, choose to ride in a car driven by Labar, who was also drunk. As they were driving, Labar swerved towards the edge of the road. Dube grabbed the wheel to try and correct the situation. This lead to the car going off the road completely and Dube was injured in the crash. Labar raised that defence of "volenti non fit injuria" which means, "to one who is willing no harm is done". Justice Estey noted,

> The question is whether the plaintiff gave an express or implied consent to accept or assume the risk without compensation. In other words, did the plaintiff really consent to absolve the defendant from his common-law duty of care, saying or implying, in effect, I am prepared to take the risk of your negligence and if I am injured you will not be legally responsible for my damages. The question is not simply whether the plaintiff knew of the risk, but whether the circumstances were such as necessarily to lead to the conclusion that the whole risk was intentionally incurred by the plaintiff. (par.22)

Justice Taggart, in his contribution to the decision, stated that, even considering the contributory negligence ascribed to Dube due to his self-induced intoxication, the jury had clearly not accepted that Dube had given away all his rights by getting back into the car and the defence raised by Labar could only be used where,

> [I]t is clear that the plaintiff, knowing of the virtually certain risk of harm, in essence bargained away his right to sue for injuries incurred as a result of any negligence on the defendant's part . . . only where there can truly be said to be an understanding on the part of both parties that the defendant assumed no responsibility to take due care for the safety of the plaintiff, and that the plaintiff did not expect him to. (par. 6)

A pastor, who had been negligent, or even grossly incompetent, could not raise a defence that the congregation had abdicated all responsibility for their own actions, or waived all their rights in regards to any actions that their pastor might take, unless there was a very clear understanding between both parties that those rights had been surrendered. However, as noted in Crocker v. Sundance the courts still held that "people should remain free to agree to waive their legal rights, at least under conditions of free and informed choice" (Crocker par.32). The courts have clearly held that there is a duty of care in special relationships and in other circumstances, such as in "Dube," and further that the duty cannot be summarily bargained away. The question remains, what is the standard of care owed by a pastor?

Obviously there are certain expectations of religious leaders relating to moral standards and ethical conduct, but does that same high standard apply to financial advice or participation in questionable investment strategies? The determination of the standard of care has long been by way of the "reasonable person" test; what a hypothetical "reasonable person" could or should have done in the same circumstances as the defendant. The standard, as noted in the Justice Institute of BC Police Training Bulletin, is "a minimum standard" and quoted Justice Laidlaw in his decision in Arland v. Taylor where he defined the reasonable person as:

> [N]ot superhuman; he is not required to display the highest skill of which anyone is capable; he is not a genius who can perform uncommon feats, nor is he possessed of unusual powers of foresight. He is a person of normal intelligence who makes prudence a guide to his conduct. He does nothing that a prudent man would not do and does not omit to do anything a prudent man would do. He acts in accord with general and approved practice. His conduct is guided by considerations which ordinarily regulate the conduct of human affairs. His conduct is the standard "adopted in the community by persons of ordinary intelligence and prudence. (Novakowski)

Consider then, the pastor at Faith Works Church, who not only failed to prevent an affinity fraud in his congregation, but also actually invited the "fraudster" into the church. There is no doubt that he has a duty to guide his flock spiritually and that there is clearly a "special relationship" (Black's 626) with his congregates which places him in a position in which he owes a duty of care to the congregation. Further to that, he is also required to conduct himself with at least a minimum standard, as set out in "Arland." This standard should not be beyond his grasp, given the special knowledge that a pastor has regarding the sinful nature of man. It would not be unreasonable to expect that a pastor should be less trusting than the average person and more aware to the pitfalls possible in business transactions, but this seldom seems to be the case. Christians, especially pastors, who make a living dealing with sin, continue to conduct their business affairs as if there was no such thing as sin (Chattaway par.23), treating everyone as if they held to the same principles, even where there is nothing to substantiate that faith.

A pastor has a further duty to his congregation, beyond the special relationship arising from his spiritual duties, a clear fiduciary duty, defined as "a duty to act for someone else's benefit, while subordinating one's personal interests to that of the other person . . . "(Blacks 625). Sumner suggested that he felt it was his duty to ensure that the congregation's donations were spent properly and accounted for fully; beyond that he did not want to be involved in the finances of the church, or in the financial arrangements of the parishioners.

Examining fiduciary duty further, considerations should be given to a quote in an article written for a labour law seminar. In the article, James Maxwell quoted Justice Gautreau's Canadian Bar Review article, "Demystifying the Fiduciary Mystique" where Justice Gautreau said,

> A fiduciary relationship will occur where a person undertakes . . . to act in . . . the interests of another . . . the other person relies on . . . this undertaking, and, as a result, is in a position of vulnerability . . . and the first person knows, or should know, of such reliance and vulnerability. The nature and circumstances giving rise to the undertaking are such that loyalty and good faith are intrinsic elements of the consequent duty. (10)

Notwithstanding the mere fact of the clear fiduciary duty owed by a pastor to his congregation, the courts have begun to apply the standard of fiduciary duty in a narrower manner. In a recent English Court of Appeals decision on the duty of lawyers to their clients, the justices cited a previous decision in Girardet v. Crease & Co., observing that "the term 'fiduciary' is flung around now as if it applied to all breaches of duty by solicitors, directors of companies and so forth . . . but to say that simple carelessness in giving advice in such a breach is perversion of words" (Law-PRO "Fiduciary"). The Court of Appeal went further, saying that even if there were a fiduciary relationship, it did not mean that every duty that was owed to a client was a fiduciary duty. In other words, a person who gave their best effort and still failed to competently complete the task would not necessarily have committed a breach of fiduciary duty. There has to be an active part to the breach of fiduciary duty, namely the commission of a disloyal or unfaithful act ("Fiduciary"), echoing Mr. Justice Lamar's words of thirty years ago (Working Paper 32). A number of jurisdictions, in particular Colorado and California, have taken the concept of fiduciary duty into account and have passed laws providing some protection for churches against lawsuits for breaches of fiduciary duty, realising that such lawsuits could destroy a church and it's governing body or conference. The laws protect the church but do not necessarily prevent suits against individual pastors for their criminal actions, only in the area of fiduciary duty (Lloyd 1).

While the careless action, made in good faith by the pastor, may not be a breach of fiduciary duty there is still the question of vicarious liability on the part of the denomination, since the pastor was acting directly as an agent of the larger church body, the same church body that in many instances has taken no steps to provide any training to the graduates of it's seminaries (Spencer interview). Turning again to Black's Law Dictionary, liability is defined as:

> [A]broad legal term . . . of the most comprehensive significance, including almost every character of hazard or responsibility, absolute, contingent, or likely . . . an obligation one is bound in law or justice to perform . . . condition of being responsible for a possible or actual loss, penalty, evil expense, or burden (914).

Based on that definition, a church body should certainly be concerned about vicarious liability arising from the carelessness or incompetence of one of its pastors.

There have been a number of decisions that speak to the question of vicarious liability, the classic being U.S. v Carroll Towing Co. During World War II a barge loaded with flour belonging to the United States government was inadvertently set adrift by employees of a tug working for Carroll Towing when they shifted some mooring lines. While the barge was adrift, she was holed by another ship and sank, losing the cargo of flour. The barge owners had signed a contract requiring that a person be on board at all times, however at the time of the accident the barge was unsupervised as the barge attendant had taken a day off. The court found that the cargo could have been saved if someone had been on board the vessel (Beirs, "Carroll"). The owners had a duty to prevent the barge from breaking away and the court applied "Hands Theorem," an equation that measures the damages sustained if an accident occurs; the probability of that accident occurring; and the burden, or cost, of taking precautions to prevent the accident from occurring (Queens "Introduction" pt. IX 2 a).

The courts acknowledged that there are times where the costs of taking adequate precautions are high and that it is impossible to make every situation completely safe under all circumstances. Further, where the harm to society is greater, if the task is avoided because it is unsafe, then the cost of continuing with the activity, then the defendant, if he had taken all reasonable and prudent precautions, would not be liable for negligence. In the case of the barge, the cost of the precaution, which was having a person on board the barge, was minimal, and the loss of a shipload of flour, vital to the war effort, was substantial, the courts held that the barge company was held liable for the loss (Biers)

This "cost/benefit" analysis of the duty owed to another has been reviewed in depth in Law Estate v. Simice. This was a negligence action that arose from the death of Jason Law, which occurred due to a misdiagnosed cerebral aneurysm. In the course of Law's medical treatment there had been symptoms that indicated a possible intra-cranial lesion, but this was not followed up, due in part to the cost of the tests needed. Justice Spencer, in writing for the court noted:

Doctors testified that they feel constrained . . . to restrict their requests for CT scans as . . . such sophisticated equipment is limited and costly to use . . . in my opinion, those constraints worked against the patient's interest by inhibiting the doctors in their judgement of what should be done for him . . . The severity of the harm that may occur to the patient who is permitted to go undiagnosed is far greater than the financial harm that will occur to the Medicare system if one more CT scan procedure only shows the patient is not suffering from a serious medical condition. (par. 28)

Clearly Justice Spencer held to the rule as set out in U.S. v Carroll, that the cost of prevention must be considered against the very real likelihood of harm and the costs associated to that harm. When compared to the millions lost to affinity fraud and the cost of educating pastors to those dangers, a seminary or church governing body would be hard pressed to support their decision not to educate their seminary graduates to this problem since most seminaries provide only rudimentary sessions on ethics, let alone any specific education regarding finances or fraud.

In an interview, Dr. Archie Spencer of the Associated Canadian Theological Seminary (ACTS), Langley, BC, said that in the pastoral programs, the teaching on ethics issues consists of one 3-credit course over a four-year program. In that course, financial issues account for a total of one 3-hour class. This hardly allows for more than a brief overview of the varied financial issue that a pastor could face, let alone providing any time to deal with fraud, which, according to Spencer, is seldom mentioned. Spencer was quick to point out that in setting up their course of study, ACTS consulted over twenty of the degree awarding seminaries and universities in Canada and that the ACTS program closely mirrors those other programs, which was confirmed by a review of a number of seminary websites. In the area of ethical training, the secular universities may actually be ahead of the seminaries as a number of universities offer a variety of ethics courses, but this is a fairly recent situation. In interviews with several established accountants and a financial adviser, they all said that their training regarding fraud had been acquired on the job, not at school (Hotte, Simpson, Atchison, interviews).

In light of the recent trends, as noted in "Dube" and "Simice," and given the many lawsuits that have arising from the residential schools scandals, it is apparent that the Canadian courts have moved a long way towards holding institutions, including churches, and the individuals acting on their behalf, liable for almost any harm that befalls a person participating in a program offered by that institution. With the traditionally slow response by churches and other institutions to any form of change, it is inevitable that a religion based affinity fraud will soon lead to a negligence suit.

Beyond the courts stance is an issue of greater concern; the damage that affinity fraud is doing to the witness of the church. When the secular world sees that another affinity fraud has been perpetrated against God's people, they must think, as did Bono, lead singer of the band U2, that, "I can't tell the difference between the ABC News, Hill Street Blues and a preacher on the Old Time Gospel Hour stealing money from the sick and the old. But the God I believe in isn't short of cash, Mister" (Bullet the Blue Sky).

God does not want our last dollar, but he does require stewardship. This was God's commandment when He gave Adam dominion of the earth (NIV Gen. 1:28). Stewardship is the ultimate fiduciary duty since we are in a "kinship" relationship with our Father, a Father who has given us many blessings and placed a higher standard on us, His children, when we use His gifts. Every time another church-based affinity fraud occurs, it undermines the credibility of Christians with respect to our ability to exercise good stewardship (Graves 81-92). The money that has been squandered in the pursuit of the impossible profits promised by affinity frauds is no longer available to be used to the benefit of the poor, the desperate and the lost. It is a condemnation of the worst part of our Western culture and the never-ending quest to "store up . . . treasures" (NIV Matt. 6:19-21). This poor stewardship, coupled with the apparent greed of the people who participate in these fraudulent schemes, destroys our credibility in the eyes of the world. Those who profess to be Christians are scrutinised daily and any breach of the standard set for Christ's followers is pounced upon and presented as yet another reason to reject the "Word." In our post modern world, faith of any sort is seen as unsubstantiated foolishness and affinity fraud goes a

Perspectives On Christianity, Society & The Law

long way to support that view. We have sometimes been called fools for Christ (NIV 1 Cor. 1:17-19) but that does not mean that we are to be less diligent or thoughtful in our approach to money and investing.

During Jesus' ministry on earth he spoke more often of money, wealth and riches in their many forms then he did of prayer, and these teachings did not condemn money, only "the love of money" (NIV 1 Tim. 6:10). Christians who would not sit down to a meal with out asking God's blessing on the food, will throw away their life's savings without asking a question, all because it is done in "God's name." Christians often proclaim that we "are in the world, not of the world," misquoting Jesus' prayer for his followers, "not that you take them out of the world but that you protect them from the evil one. They are not of the world, even as I am not of it . . . as you sent me into the world, I have sent them into the world" (NIV John 17:15-18). Christians have been removed form the world and spared the condemnation of sin, but that does not absolve us from our responsibilities, rather it binds us to a higher standard and places us in the highest position of duty as a "a guardian, or trustee."

We have been blessed with material wealth beyond much of the world's grasp, and we have come to believe that we deserve it and more. That expectation is what allows affinity frauds to flourish time and again in our midst. Considering the billions of dollars lost world-wide and the damage to our witness, Christians can no longer ignore the issue of affinity fraud. Pastors and churches may, in the end, be found negligent in the courts, but when we, as the body of Christ, fail to be diligent in the prevention of fraud, we will all stand condemned in the court of public opinion.

WORKS CITED

Abagnale & Associates. 19 Sept. 2003 <http://www.abagnale.com/index2.asp>.

Abagnale, Frank W., and Stan Redding. Catch Me if You Can. 1980. New York, New York: Broadway Books, 2002.

Atchison, John. Personal interview. Langley, British Columbia. 29 Oct. 2003.

Barnhart, Clarence, ed. Thorndike-Barnhart Comprehensive Desk Dictionary. Garden City, New York: Doubleday and Co. 1967.

Beirs, Sam. "U.S. v. Carroll Towing Co." 4Lawschool.com. 11 Nov. 2003 <http://www.4lawschool.com/torts/carroll.htm>.

Bergal, Jenni. "Religion-based scams take Lord's name in vain." South Florida Sun-Sentinel. 26 Jan. 2003. 20 Sept. 2003 <http://www.rickross.com/reference/general/general527.html>.

Black, Henry Campbell. Black's Law Dictionary, with pronunciations. 6th ed. St. Paul, Minnesota: West Publishing Co., 1990.

British Columbia Securities Commission. 2002 BCSECCOM 195. 18 Oct. 2003 <http://www.bcsc.bc.ca:8080/comdoc.nsf/0/ 2087a2ca0478000788256b7900614f7c/ $FILE/2002%20BCSECCOM%20195.pdf>.

Canada. Law Reform Commission of Canada. Working Paper 19, Criminal Law, Theft and Fraud Offences. Ottawa: Ministry of Supply and Services, 1977.

Canadian Legal Information Institute. 6 Oct. 2003 <http://www.canlii.org>"Law Estate v Simice" (1994-05-03) BCSC A914631- /bc/cas/bcsc/1994/ 1994bcsc10687.html>.

Chattaway, Peter T. "Con men Fleece the Sheep." BC Christian News. July 2000. 18 Sept. 2003 <http://www.canadianchristianity.com/cgi-bin/bc.cgi?/bc/bccn/0700/conmen>.

Faron, Fay. Rip-off: A Writers Guide to Crimes of Deception. Cincinnati, Ohio: Writers Digest Books, 1998.

Graves, Stephen R., Thomas G. Addington. Behind the Bottom Line; Powering Business Life with Spiritual Wisdom. San Francisco, CA: Jossy-Bass, 2003.

Henderson, Les. "Affinity Fraud Investment Scams." Crimes of Persuasion. 20 Sept. 2003 <http://www.crimes-of-persuasion.com/Crimes/InPerson/MajorPerson/affinity.htm>.

Hotte, Roger. Personal interview. Langley, British Columbia. 12 Oct. 2003.

Huntley, Helen. "'Affinity Fraud' A Common Investment Scam." St. Petersburg Times. 27 July 2003 < http://www.sptimes.com/2003/07/27/columns/_Affinity_fraud_a_co.htm>.

Jepson, Peter. "Tort Cases." <http://www.peterjepson.com/law/tort_cases.htm>.

Lawindexpro. "Anns and Others v. Merton London Borough Council." Case Law. <http://www.swarb.co.uk/c/HL/1977Anns_Merton.html>.

LexUm. University of Montreal Faculty of Law. 7 Oct. 2003 <http://www.lexum.umontreal.ca>.

____. "Crocker v. Sundance Northwest Resorts Ltd." [1988] 1 S.C.R. 1186 - /csc/1988/1988csc62.html.

____. "Dube v. Labar " [1986] 1 S.C.R. 649 - /csc-scc/en/pub/1986/vol1/html/1986scr1_0649.html.

Lindskoog, Kathryn. Fakes, Frauds & Other Malarkey: 301 Amazing Stories and How Not to Be Fooled. Grand Rapids, MI: Zondervan Publishing House.

Llyod, Jillian. "Churches Seeking Shield From Lawsuits." The Christian Science Monitor. 28 Oct. 1999 <http://search.csmonitor.com/durable/1999/10/28/pls4.htm>.

Martin, Walter. The Kingdom of the Cults. Minneapolis, MN: Bethany House Publishers,1985.

McShane, Steven L. Canadian Organizational Behaviour. Toronto, Ontario: Mc-Graw-Hill Ryerson Limited, 2001.

Nightingale, Brenda L. The Law of Fraud and Related Offences. Scarborough, Ontario: Carswell Thompson Professional Publishing.

Novakowski, Mike. "Reasonable Grounds: Through Your Eyes Only." Justice Institute of BC Training Bulletin Number 4. <http://www.jibc.bc.ca/police/police-TrainingBulletins/bulletin4/trainingbulleting4.htm>.

PracticePRO. Case Study: Fiduciary Duty. 11 Nov.2003 <http://www.practicepro.ca/information/duty.asp>.

Prince Edward Island. The Official Website of the Government of Prince Edward Island, Canada. "Laurie J. Davis". <http://www.gov.pe.ca/photos/original/oag_davis_ judge.pdf>.

Quicksilver. Queens University An Introduction to the Law of Torts. Nov.2003 <http://qsilver.queensu.ca/~lss/outlines/1y/tort--01.doc.>.

Simpson, Perry. Personal interview. Langley, British Columbia. 16 Sept. 2003.

Smyth, J.E., D.A. Soderman, A.J. Easson. The Law and Business Administration in Canada. 10th ed. Toronto, Ontario: Pearson Prentice Hall, 2004.

Spencer, Archie. Personal interview. Associated Canadian Theological Seminaries. Langley, British Columbia. 14 Oct. 2003.

Surrette, Ray. Media, Crime and Criminal Justice: Images and Realities. Belmont, California: Wadsworth, Inc., 1992.

The NIV Study Bible, 10th Anniversary ed. Grand Rapids, MI: Zondervan Publishing House, 1995.

U2. Rattle and Hum. Island Records, 1988.

A Christian Response Against Marijuana Decriminalisation

Sara Lanting

IX

The most frequently used illicit drug1 in Canada is marijuana. According to the Senate Special Committee on Illegal Drugs, roughly 325,000 Canadians use marijuana on a daily basis. Close to thirty percent of the population admit to using marijuana in their lifetime (15). In response to the continuing increase in the use of marijuana among Canadians, the Cannabis Reform Bill, also known as Bill C-38, was introduced in the House of Commons on May 27, 2003. Bill C-38 is an Act to amend the Contraventions Act and the Controlled Drugs and Substances Act. Under Bill C-38 possession and production of marijuana would remain illegal but the possession of small amounts of marijuana would be decriminalised.

In the Christian faith, the law, whether established by God or the government, is to be upheld. Therefore, Christians need to be aware of the suggested changes to the law, such as those proposed in Bill C-38, and need to provide a response. My thesis is that Christians should not support the decriminalisation of marijuana in Canada, as outlined in Bill C-38, because marijuana decriminalisation will adversely affect Canada's young people as well as lead to an increase in marijuana use among a vast number of Canadians, thus damaging society's overall health.

To substantiate my thesis I will separate my paper into four main sections. First, I will provide an overview of the history of marijuana legislation in Canada. Second, I will review what the Bill proposes. Third, I will give five main arguments in support of the Bill. Fourth, I will provide a Christian response, which will include the arguments against the Bill.

At the outset, it is important to give a brief summary of the use and effects of marijuana. Marijuana, also known as cannabis, is the dried leaves of the cannabis sativa plant. Hashish or "hash" also comes from the sativa plant and is the dried resin from the leaves and flowers. Marijuana is commonly smoked as a hand-rolled cigarette, known as a "joint," or in a pipe. Marijuana can also be ingested when baked in certain foods such as brownies. The primary active ingredient in marijuana is tetrahydrocannabinol (THC). Once inhaled or ingested THC is quickly absorbed and distributed to areas of the body that have significant fat content such as the brain. Because the body's natural process for eliminating fat-soluble substances is very gradual, THC exits the body very slowly. Half of the THC from one "joint" will often stay in the body for a week, and THC can take four to six weeks until it is completely eliminated.

The effects of marijuana can vary, but normally marijuana intoxication causes the feeling of ecstasy, intensifies the body's senses, impairs information processing and the ability to perform simple tasks, and slows reaction time. It also raises a person's blood pressure and causes dryness in the throat and mouth. Sometimes people experience dizziness and nausea when smoking marijuana.

Marijuana first came to Canada in the sixteenth century. At that time, cannabis was used primarily to make rope, paper, and sails for ships. The strong, stringy fibres from the plant's stalks were harvested, cut, dried, and woven into a variety of materials. In the early nineteenth century, these uses began to decline as other resources evolved and replaced cannabis. It was at this time that the use of marijuana as a narcotic2 began to increase and regulations were established.

Marijuana became illegal in Canada in 1923 when cannabis was added to the list of illicit drugs in the Opium and Narcotic Drug Act (ONDA) of 1911. The import, manufacture, and sale of marijuana became prohibited under the ONDA. The ONDA continued to be the basis for marijuana legislation in Canada for many years.

In 1961 Canada joined the United Nation's Single Convention on Narcotic Drugs. This led to an amendment to the law, increasing the minimum sentence for cultivation of marijuana to seven years and exportation and importation of marijuana to fourteen years.

In 1997 the Controlled Drugs and Substances Act (CDSA) came into effect, combining marijuana laws previously found in the Narcotic Control Act and Parts III and IV of the Food and Drug Act. The CDSA made significant changes to the law regarding the regulation of marijuana by setting it apart from all other illegal drugs. Cannabis was no longer classified as a "narcotic" but as a Schedule II drug, while other drugs like cocaine and heroin were included in Schedule I. Because of this separation, the maximum sentence one could receive for possessing or trafficking marijuana became based on the quantity of marijuana in possession. Today the CDSA continues to be the current law regulating marijuana in Canada.

Under the CDSA, the maximum penalty for possession of thirty or less grams of marijuana is six months in jail and a one thousand dollar fine while the maximum penalty for possession of thirty grams or more is five years less one day in jail. For trafficking less than three kilograms of marijuana, the maximum penalty is five years less one day in jail, while for trafficking more than three kilograms, the maximum sentence is life imprisonment. In the CDSA, the maximum prison sentence for production of marijuana is seven years and the maximum sentence for importing and exporting marijuana is life imprisonment.

After the CDSA came into effect in 1997 another important event in the history of Canada's marijuana legislation took place. It began when Terrance Parker, an epileptic who used marijuana to alleviate his seizures, was accused of possession, cultivation, and trafficking of marijuana. This was not the first time Parker had been charged, but this time he argued that the charges violated his rights listed under the Canadian Charter of Rights and Freedoms (Charter).

On December 10, 1997 Ontario Judge Patrick Sheppard ruled in Parker's favour on the charges of marijuana cultivation and possession, but convicted Parker of marijuana trafficking since. Parker had admitted to giving some of his marijuana to friends for their ailments. The judge gave Parker one year probation and ordered that three marijuana plants be returned to Mr. Parker. Judge Sheppard wrote,

Mr. Parker stands a daily risk of being deprived of his right to life, liberty, and security . . . Health is fundamental to the life and security of each person . . . It does not accord with fundamental justice to criminalise a person suffering a serious chronic medical disability for possessing a vitally helpful substance not legally available to him. (qtd. in Young)

The Crown appealed Judge Sheppard's ruling, but on July 31, 2000 the ruling was upheld by the Ontario Court of Appeal. The Ontario Court of Appeal ruled that the prohibition of the possession of marijuana was unconstitutional and that the wide ban of possession of marijuana was contrary to the Charter. The court suspended their ruling for one year in order to give Parliament "time to amend the federal legislation to comply with the Charter" (qtd. in "Ontario court"). If Parliament did not act in one year, possession and cultivation of marijuana in Ontario would become legal.

On July 30, 2001 "Canada became the first country [in the world] to adopt a system regulating the medical use of marijuana" (Wood and Ali). Under the Marijuana Medical Access Regulations, (MMAR) those suffering from a terminal illness or severe chronic disease, and who could prove that marijuana was their only option to treat their illness, qualified to use the drug for medical purposes. In addition, to qualify, a recommendation for the drug's use had to come from a certified doctor. On July 9, 2003 MMAR was amended to include an interim policy on how to acquire the drug lawfully. Today MMAR continues to be the current law on the production and sale of cannabis for therapeutic purposes.

In 2002 the Senate and House began reviewing Canada's anti-drug policies and legislation. In September 2002 the Senate Special Committee on Illegal Drugs released its final report on the issue. In the report, the Senate recommended an amendment to the Controlled Drugs and Substances Act. The amendment called for the legalisation of possession and production of marijuana for personal use and declared that any Canadian citizen should have the right to obtain a license to commercially produce and distribute marijuana to licensed users. Although the committee recognised that cannabis had physical and mental health risks, they also found marijuana to be less harmful than alcohol and therefore called for the legalisation of marijuana (52-53).

Two months after Senate published its report, the House of Commons released its own findings on marijuana in the Report of the Special Committee on the Non-Medical Use of Drugs. The House found that "[c]annabis products are potentially harmful and should continue to be prohibited under the law." However, the House concluded that "[t]he consequences of conviction for possession of a small amount of cannabis for personal use are disproportionate to the potential harm associated with that behaviour," but "[a]ny movement toward legalising cannabis carries the potential for causing even greater harm than the present law" (208-09). Therefore, based on their findings, the House recommended that the Canadian Minister of Justice and Health propose a decriminalisation Bill for possession of small amounts of marijuana. The House also concluded that any trafficking of marijuana should remain a criminal offence (223).

As the Senate and House have called for reforms of Canada's marijuana laws, many recent judicial rulings are also pressuring the legislature to make reforms and, unfortunately, adding confusion to the current law. In January 2003, Ontario Justice Douglas Phillips dismissed two drug charges against a sixteen year-old Windsor boy, suggesting marijuana possession laws are no longer valid.

In another ruling over marijuana possession charges in British Columbia (BC), Justice Mary Southin "wrote [that] she has sat on 'over 40 cases which had something to do with this substance'" and, according to her, marijuana "'appears to be of no greater danger to society than alcohol'" (qtd. in Yearwood-Lee).

Another BC judge, Patrick Chen, ruled on September 16, 2003 that the marijuana possession laws no longer stand. He concluded that because the Ontario Court of Appeal ruled that the Controlled Drugs and Substances Act was invalid in the Parker case, the law became void. He wrote, "As a result, there was no longer any prohibition or penalty . . . for simple possession of marijuana. It follows, therefore, there is no offence known to law at this time for simple possession of marijuana" (qtd. in Hall).

On May 27, 2003 partially in response to the Senate and House's findings and the recent judicial rulings, Justice Minister Martin Cauchon introduced and tabled the Cannabis Reform Bill, Bill C-38, in the House of Commons. Bill C-38 is an Act to amend the Contraventions Act and the Controlled Drugs and Substances Act (CDSA). Under the Bill, possession and production of marijuana would remain illegal, but penalties for possession of small amounts of marijuana would decrease and penalties for large-scale growers of marijuana would increase. On October 9 and 10, 2003 a motion to refer the Bill to the Special Committee on the Non-Medical Use of Drugs was debated and the motion was carried on October 21st, 2003. The Bill is currently being reviewed and is awaiting a second reading in the House of Commons.

Bill C-38 is most commonly known as the "decriminalisation bill." The term decriminalisation is important to understand when evaluating the Bill. Decriminalisation is the "removal of a behaviour or activity from the scope of the criminal justice system" (Senate Special Committee on Illegal Drugs, 3). Decriminalisation is not legalisation. "Decriminalisation concerns only criminal legislation, and does not mean that the legal system has no further jurisdiction of any kind in this regard" (3). Under the Bill, possession of small amounts of marijuana would be decriminalised and would no longer be a criminal offence, but would continue to be illegal and regulated.

To understand decriminalisation in more detail it is important to recognise that in the Bill under clause five, which is an amendment to the CDSA, the possession of small amounts of marijuana would be considered a "contravention" under the Contraventions Act.

> [The Contraventions Act] adopted in 1992, created new, simpli-
> fied procedures for dealing with selected federal offences, as
> an alternative to the summary conviction procedure set out in
> the Criminal Code. Under this Act, offences can be designated
> as "contraventions" by regulations. One of the original goals
> of the Act was to distinguish between more serious criminal
> offences and other less serious federal offences. (Lafreniere)

Therefore, under the Bill, possession of a small amount of marijuana would no longer be charged as a summary conviction, as it currently exists under the CDSA, but rather the offence would be prosecuted as a contravention by means of a ticket. This ticket would be very similar to a ticket issued for a traffic violation. The amount of the fine would vary based on the quantity of marijuana in possession and the age of the guilty party. By prosecuting the offence as a contravention by means of a ticket, the accused would no longer have to appear in court and would not receive a criminal record, thus decriminalising the offence.

The Bill divides the penalties for possession into four main categories. First, those guilty of possession of one gram or less of cannabis resin (hashish) are liable for fines up to three hundred dollars for an adult and two hundred dollars for a young person. In the Bill, a young person is someone under the age of eighteen. Second, those guilty of possession of fifteen grams or less of marijuana (about fifteen to thirty joints) are liable for fines up to $150 for an adult and one hundred dollars for a young person. Third, those guilty of possession of one gram or less of cannabis resin or fifteen grams or less of marijuana where certain circumstances exist are liable for fines up to four hundred dollars for an adult and $250 for a young person. The certain circumstances include possession while operating a motor vehicle, while committing an indictable offence, and while in or near a school. Fourth, in cases of those guilty of possession of fifteen to thirty grams of marijuana the police have free judgement to either charge the guilty party with a contravention and issue a ticket, or charge a criminal offence and issue a criminal court order. The ticket would be up to three hundred dollars for an adult and two hundred dollars for a young person. The summary conviction would be for a fine up to one thousand dollars and/or up to six months in prison.

In addition to possession, the Bill's amendments to the CDSA also alter the penalties for growing marijuana. Currently under the CDSA, the maximum sentence one can receive for production of marijuana is seven years imprisonment. The Bill separates the penalties for production of marijuana into four categories based on the number of plants grown. First, for growing no more than three plants the penalty would be a fine of up to five thousand dollars or a one-year jail sentence. Second, for growing four to twenty-five plants the penalty would be a fine of up to twenty-five thousand dollars and/or eighteen months in jail, or five years less a day imprisonment if pursued by indictment. Third, for growing twenty-six to fifty plants the penalty would be a ten-year jail sentence. Fourth, for growing more than fifty plants the penalty would be a sentence of up to fourteen years imprisonment. The Bill also states that a person convicted of growing more than three plants when aggravating factors are present will likely receive a prison sentence. Aggravating factors include growing plants on the land of a third party, growing plants that create a safety hazard in a residential neighbourhood, growing plants near children, and setting traps to purposely injure another person where the plants are grown.

The Bill does not amend the CDSA for the trafficking, importing, or exporting of marijuana. The Bill also does not annul the criminal records of those who have received criminal records for marijuana possession in the past.

There are five main arguments in support of the Bill. First, many feel that the Bill should pass because the majority of Canadians support it. "A May 2000 survey . . . found that sixty-five percent of people said the concept of decriminalising marijuana is an excellent, very good, or good idea. Twenty-two percent responded negatively" (Khoo). Directly attached to this argument, many argue that the Bill's amendments are necessary because cannabis use is becoming the norm in Canada. As mentioned previously, according to the Senate Special Committee on Illegal Drugs, roughly 325,000 Canadians use marijuana on a daily basis (15). These numbers have dramatically increased as cannabis is now the most widely-used drug in Canada. Close to thirty percent of the population admit to using marijuana in their lifetime (15).

A second argument in support of the Bill is that marijuana is less harmful than alcohol and therefore marijuana should be viewed as a public health issue not a criminal issue. Many who support the Bill admit that marijuana is in fact harmful to the body, but since some studies have shown that only five to ten percent of marijuana users become addicted (27), they argue that the effects of smoking marijuana are less harmful than the effects of drinking alcohol. As a result, they conclude that these two substances should be regulated in the same manner.

Third, many argue that prosecuting people for possession of small amounts of marijuana is a waste of the government's scarce resources and ties up the court system. "The cost of prosecuting drug offences in 2000/01 was fifty-seven million dollars with approximately five million dollars or roughly ten percent of the total budget relating to prosecuting cannabis possession offences" (25). Those who support the Bill believe this money could be better spent on public education programs that present the negative health aspects of marijuana. They also argue that since the Bill would decrease the amount of court orders given to people charged with marijuana possession, the courts would have more time to focus on cases of greater importance.

A fourth argument in support of the Bill is that the current level of punishment for marijuana possession is too harsh. Under the current law, any adult convicted of possession of marijuana can be sentenced to jail. However, the majority of those convicted of marijuana possession do not go to jail but do receive a criminal record. Those supporting the Bill argue that this penalty is too harsh because a criminal record has drastic effects on anyone's life, limiting opportunities in employment, international travel, and even in education, such as getting into medical school. "An estimated 600,000 Canadians have criminal records for marijuana possession" (Wood).

Finally, many support the Bill because they believe the Bill will be evenly enforced across Canada. They argue that current laws are unfairly enforced. For example, "in large urban centres, police are much less likely to lay a charge for possession of small amounts of cannabis than in other parts of the country, and where a charge is laid, the accused is more likely to receive a discharge" (Health Canada). Those in support of the Bill also argue that the current legislation is being unevenly enforced in many courtrooms across Canada.

Now that the groundwork for marijuana legislation in Canada, Bill C-38, and the arguments in favour of the Bill have been established, it is important to respond to the Bill from a Christian perspective. In the Christian faith, the law, whether established by God or the government, is to be upheld. Romans 13:1 states, "Everyone must submit himself to the governing authorities, for there is no authority except that which God has established" (The NIV Study Bible). Therefore, Christians need to be aware of the suggested changes to the law and need to provide a response.

Christians should not support the decriminalisation of marijuana, as contained in Bill C-38, for two main reasons.3 First, it presents a harmful message that will particularly have an adverse effect on Canada's young people. Like many members of society, Christians believe young people need to be protected from harmful substances. The youth of Canada should not be exposed to and affected by mind-altering drugs, but sadly, they are. The Senate Special Committee on Illegal Drugs, in its September report, found that one in every three Canadian kids ages fifteen and sixteen have smoked marijuana at least once in the past month and that "the average age of introduction to cannabis is fifteen" (15). They also observed that marijuana use is the highest among people between the ages of sixteen and twenty-four and that Canada has the highest rate of young people who use marijuana, with one million smoking marijuana in the last year and 225,000 smoking it daily (15). These statistics demand that any new legislation on the issue must be aimed at decreasing the use of the marijuana among young people. Unfortunately, Bill C-38 does not focus on this task. Instead the Bill promotes the "soft-on-youth" approach. Those who support the Bill argue that the "soft-on-youth" approach will benefit children because children found guilty of possession will no longer receive criminal records. Although on the surface this argument may sound just, it is pointless. Under the current marijuana legislation, young offenders, those under eighteen years old, already cannot receive a criminal record (The Addictive Drug Information Council).

If the Bill does not remove the stigma of criminal records from children, what does it do? The Bill increases the social acceptance of marijuana among young people by presenting the message that marijuana is not a harmful substance. In the Bill, penalties for marijuana possession for young people, those under the age of eighteen, are lower than the penalties for adults. This separation makes a child's offence seem less severe. While speaking on marijuana decriminalisation, prominent government figures have made flippant remarks that the Bill's "soft-on-youth" approach is necessary because in today's world we expect kids to experiment with marijuana. Liberal MP John Bryden stated, "Police forces and courts . . . [should] not [be] wasting their time on young people who are experimenting with small amounts of pot" (qtd. in Foster).

Through this type of speech and through the introduction of Bill C-38, the government has led many young people to believe that marijuana is not harmful and that its effects on the body do not need to be taken seriously. In reality, the harmful effects of marijuana on the body and especially on children who are still growing and developing are great. However, by ignoring the dangers of marijuana the Bill creates greater social acceptance of marijuana among young people and, in turn, will likely lead to an increase of its use. A prime example of this happened in the Netherlands, when after decriminalising marijuana there was a "two hundred percent rise in adolescent [use of] marijuana" (Sabet). Although some argue this increase was due to the fact that decriminalisation allowed young people to admit they used the drug, this is quite unlikely considering the enormity of the rise.

To combat the message that marijuana is no longer a dangerous drug the federal government has attached a five-year $245 million anti-drug program to the Bill. However, this is "half the amount the Liberals had promised to counter Canada's multi-billion-dollar drug problem" (Tibbetts, A1), and when analysing the government's previous anti-drug programs it is clear that the government rarely spends the amounts they promise. In 1992 funding for a five-year program of $270 million was approved, but during that time only about one hundred million dollars was actually spent. In addition, the government claims that its anti-drug strategy is "based on four pillars: education and prevention; enforcement and control measures; treatment; and research and information." However, "in a 2001 report, the Auditor General indicated that of the approximately five hundred million spent annually by the 11 federal departments to address illicit drug use in Canada, roughly ninety-five percent was spent on supply reduction" (Lafreniere). It is therefore safe to conclude that the federal government's anti-drug program attached to this Bill will do very little in the way of teaching children about the harms associated with marijuana use.

Titus 2:6 says, "Similarly, encourage the young men to be self-controlled. In everything, set them an example by doing what is good. In your teaching show integrity, seriousness, and soundness of speech that cannot be condemned" (The NIV Study Bible). In many Christian homes, parents try to follow the instruction of Titus 2:6 when teaching their children about the harmful effects of marijuana. It is therefore discouraging when the government introduces a Bill that confuses and misinforms young people on this issue.

The second reason that Christians should not support the decriminalisation of marijuana in Canada is that it will lead to an increase in marijuana use among a vast number of Canadians, thus damaging society's overall health. The Bill will cause the use of marijuana in Canada to increase in two main ways. First, decriminalisation will allow more dealers, those who traffic marijuana, to "escape" the fair punishment for their crime. Although the Bill does not lower the current penalties for trafficking marijuana, the Bill does make possession of fifteen grams or less (fifteen to thirty joints) no longer a criminal offence. Under this new law, many dealers caught carrying fifteen grams or less of marijuana will claim the drug is for their own personal use and will only receive a ticket. This will in turn allow more dealers to "stay on the street" and greatly reduce the risk of trafficking small amounts of marijuana, and therefore lead to an increase in the distribution and use of marijuana.

The increase in the social acceptance of the drug among the adult population is a second and more alarming reason marijuana decriminalisation will likely lead to an increase in the use of marijuana. Young people are not the only ones using the drug and being sent the message that smoking marijuana is no longer harmful. In 2000, University of Lethbridge sociologist Reg Bibby surveyed Canadians and found that "today just thirty-four percent of Canadians think drugs represent a 'very serious problem'" (qtd. in Harvey). The Senate Special Committee on Illegal Drugs observed that almost "two million Canadians over the age of eighteen have used cannabis during the previous twelve months" (15). The president, Grant Obst, of the Canadian Police Association found that every time the government "'speaks publicly about [its] intention to decriminalise marijuana, many people are inferring . . . possession would be legal or less serious . . . Ultimately, this sends the message that cannabis use is harmless'" (qtd. in Foster). If the Bill were to pass, this type of social acceptance and ignorance of marijuana's harmful effects would only increase.

An increase in the public's acceptance and use of marijuana should be a major concern for Christians since marijuana has many negative physical and psychological effects that are damaging to all of society's health. What many people do not realise is that marijuana is a much stronger substance today than it was ten years ago. New ways of cultivating marijuana and the development of hybrid plants have greatly increased marijuana's active ingredient THC. In recent years, potency of cannabis plants has increased from less than one percent THC to today's average THC level of four percent to eight percent. In the new hybrid plants, the THC level is commonly thirty percent (Pinger et. al. 309).

This increased potency has increased the harmful physical effects of the plant. "One marijuana cigarette is akin to four tobacco cigarettes in terms of the amount of tar, five tobacco cigarettes in terms of the amount of carbon monoxide intake and ten tobacco cigarettes with respect to the amount of damage to the airways" (Sabet). Marijuana contains over four hundred chemicals including carbon monoxide, nitrosamines, and benzopyrene all of which are known to be dangerous (Pinger et al. 321). Therefore, repeated marijuana use can lead to throat and lung cancer as well as injury to the trachea and major bronchi. In his study of the "Sub-clinical Pulmonary Effects of Marijuana Smoking," Dr. Donald P Tashkin "selected twenty-eight men who had smoked at least four joints a week for the past six months. They were all in splendid health and did not use other drugs" (Mann 114). He then tested them over a period of "forty-seven to forty-nine days" using "sophisticated lung-function tests . . . at frequent intervals." He found that "all the subjects had 'significant lung function impairment in several areas. These impairments were similar to those found by other researchers studying people who had smoked tobacco moderately too heavily for many years'" (115).

Marijuana can also lead to addiction. Because marijuana activates the pleasant-reward system of the brain and exits the body slowly, marijuana causes mild withdrawal symptoms. An original study conducted by Nadia Solowij found that sixty percent of ex-cannabis users claimed to feel dependent on cannabis and that the "idea of cutting down [use] was not feasible" (Solowij, 219-20). Canada's Health Minster Anne McLellan stated, "Marijuana can lead to addiction, it can lead to all sorts of situations within local communities, and you need to be ready with information, with education and with treatment" (qtd. in Smith).

Many who support the Bill argue marijuana is less harmful than alcohol. However, a large difference exists between the two substances. While a person can have a glass of wine and not become intoxicated, a person who smokes one "joint" will within seconds becomes intoxicated and partially impaired. This is alarming when considering the effect marijuana can have on driving. "Research studies show that marijuana effects can be just as driver-impairing as the effects of alcohol, and in some cases more so" (Mann, 267). Marijuana reduces drivers' concentration, slows their reaction time, and impairs their judgement (Pringer et. al. 320). While driving impaired under marijuana will remain a criminal offence under the Bill, there are currently no "screening devices capable of determining whether a driver is 'stoned'" and according to Alliance MP Vic Toews, the Opposition's senior justice critic, "'People will begin to favour marijuana [over alcohol] because it's not as detectable as alcohol'" (qtd. in Foster). This should be a great concern to all of society when considering a Bill that will likely increase the use of marijuana.

For many years, chronic marijuana use has also been linked with the amotivational syndrome. Long time users of cannabis are likely to lack motivation and become lethargic and passive. Users often find school and work more challenging and may lose even the ability to meet the everyday demands of normal living (Pringer et al. 315). Although some argue that the amotivational syndrome is not a direct effect of marijuana, it has been proven that marijuana has a significant impact on the brain. Because the brain is one-third fat and cannabis is highly fat-soluble marijuana mainly collects in the brain cells when smoked. A study on the human brain conducted by Dr. A.M.G. Campbell looked at "ten chronic pot smokers, aged eighteen to twenty-six, [who all] used the drug on a regular basis for three to eleven years . . . Campbell found that a loss of brain substance had resulted in atrophy of the brain, comparable to that which occurs in people seventy to ninety years old". This study explained why marijuana often leads to abnormal irritability and hostility, abrupt mood wings, and impaired short-term memory (Mann, 184-85).

The Christian faith teaches that a Christian's body is the temple of the Holy Spirit. In I Corinthians 6:14 it says, "Do you not know that your body is a temple of the Holy Spirit, who is in you, whom you have received from the Lord? You are therefore not your own; you were bought at a price, therefore honour God with your body" (The NIV Study Bible). Christians believe that smoking marijuana does not allow a person to honour God with their body. Rather smoking marijuana allows harmful substances to enter one's body, which can cause disease, addiction, and can even harm a person's ability to function in society. For this reason, Christians should not support legislation that will likely increase the use of marijuana and adversely affect society's health.

In conclusion, I have presented an overview of the history of marijuana legislation in Canada, spanning from the first time Canada banned the use of marijuana in the Opium and Narcotic Drug Act to the recent introduction of Bill C-38 in the House of Commons. I have also reviewed what Bill C-38 proposes and have given five main arguments in support of the Bill. Finally, I have provided a Christian response, stating that Christians should not support the decriminalisation of marijuana in Canada as outlined in Bill C-38 because it will have an adverse affect on young people as well as lead to an increase in marijuana use among a vast number of Canadians, causing more individuals to suffer from its harmful effects.

The issue of marijuana decriminalisation is a display of how secular society and the Christian community are at odds. With approximately 325,000 Canadians using marijuana on a daily basis, marijuana is already having a detrimental affect on many Canadians through disease and addiction. If marijuana is decriminalised these damaging effects on society will only increase. For this reason, the Christian community must make its voice heard and take a firm stance against marijuana decriminalisation in Canada.

Notes

1   Drug is defined as "any chemical agent that alters the biochemical or physi-
    ological processes of tissues or organisms . . . Also used to refer to illicit rather
    than licit (such as nicotine, alcohol or medicines) substances" (Senate Special
    Committee on Illegal Drugs, 3).

2   Narcotic is defined as a "substance which can induce stupor or artificial sleep"
    (Senate Special Committee on Illegal Drugs, 5).

3   Although these arguments are presented as a Christian response, it may be
    noted that many non-Christians also contend against the Bill on similar points.

WORKS CITED

Barker, Kenneth, ed. The NIV Study Bible. Grand Rapids: Zondervan, 1995.

Foster, Scott. "Marijuana Legislation One of Parliament's Top Issues." Ottawa Hill
Times. 4 Aug. 2003. 20 Sept. 2003
<http://www.mapinc.org/drugnews/v03/n1177/a02.html>.

Hall, Neal. "BC's Marijuana Law Doesn't Exist Judge Rules." Vancouver Sun. 16
Sept. 2003. 20 Sept. 2003
<http://www.mpp.org/states/site/quicknews.cgi?key= 4928>.

Harvey, Bob. "Support Grows for Legalising Marijuana: 5 Years ago, one-third of
Canadians Favoured Making Drug Legal; Today About Half Do." Canadian
Foundation for Drug Policy. 22 May 2001. 30 Sept. 2003
<http://www.cfdp.ca/general4.htm/#may17>.

Health Canada. "Cannabis Reform Bill." Health Canada Online. 28 May 2003. 30
Sept. 2003
<http://www.hc-sc.gc.ca/english/ media/releases/2003/2003_34bk2.htm>.

House of Commons Special Committee on Non-Medical Use of Drugs. "A Policy
for the New Millennium: Working Together to Redefine Canada's Drug Strategy." Report of the Special Committee on Non-Medical Use of Drugs. 15 Nov.
2002.

Khoo, Lisa. "Up in Smoke? Canada's Marijuana Law and the Debate Over Decriminalisation."
CBC News Online. May 2001. 30 Sept. 2003
<http://www.cbc.ca/ news/indepth/background/marijuana_legalize.html>.

Lafreniere, Gerald. "Bill C-38: An Act to Amend the Contraventions Act and the
Controlled Drugs and Substances Act." Parliamentary Research Branch. 11 July
2003. 9 Nov. 2003
<http://www.parl.gc.ca/common/Bills_ls.asp?lang=E&Parl=37 &Ses=2&ls=C38
&source=Bills_Individual#backgroundtx>.

Mann, Peggy. Marijuana Alert. United States: McGraw-Hill, 1985.

"Ontario Court Ruling Pushes for Medical Marijuana Law." Ontario Court Ruling
on Medical Marijuana. 6 Aug. 2000. 30 Sept. 2003
<http://canadaonline.about.com/ library/weekly/aa080600a.htm>.

Pinger, Robert R., et al. Issues for Today: Drugs. 2nd ed. St. Louis: Mosby, 1995.

Sabet, Kevin A. "Staff Position on Pot Ignores Growing Costs." Harvard Crimson. 17 April 2002. 9 Nov. 2003 <http://www.thecrimson.harvard.edu/>.

Senate Special Committee on Illegal Drugs. "Cannabis: Our Position for a Canadian Public Policy." Report of the Senate Special Committee on Illegal Drugs. Sept. 2002. PDF File. 30 Sept. 2003.

Smith, Phillip S., ed. "Canada Marijuana Decriminalisation Legislation Delayed." The Week Online with DRCNet. 6 May 2003. 30 Sept. 2003 <http://www.mapinc.org/drugnews/ v03/n718/a10.html>.

Solowij, Nadia. Cannabis and Cognitive Functioning. Cambridge: Cambridge University, 1998.

Tibbetts, Janice. "New Drug Bill Gets a Rough Ride from all Sides." The Vancouver Sun. 28 May 2003: A1-2.

The Addictive Drug Information Council. "Proposed Marijuana Legislation Misguided." Vancouver Board of Trade. 27 May 2003. 20 Sept. 2003 <http://www.boardoftrade.com/ vbot_page.asp?pageID=910>.

Wood, Owen and Amina Ali. "The Need for Weed: Medical Marijuana." CBC News Online. April 2001. 30 Sept. 2003 <http://www.cbc.ca/news/indepth/background/ medical_marijuana.html>.

Wood, Owen. "Statistics." CBC News Online. 26 May 2003. 30 Sept. 2003 <http://www.cbc.ca/news/indepth/ marijuana/statistics.html>.

Yearwood-Lee, Emily. "Canadian Alliance MP Lashes Out against Pot Ruling." CNews. 23 June 2003. 30 Sept. 2003 <http://cnews.canoe.ca/CNEWS/Law/Marijuana/20 03/ 06/23/118080-cp.html>.

Young, Alan. "Ontario Judge Rules in Favour of Medical Marijuana; Health Canada Says It Will Approve Marijuana Prescriptions." Jan. 1998. 30 Sept. 2003 <http://www.ndsn.org/jan98/medmj2.html>.

Pastoral Counselling:
Safeguards Against Potential Liability
Laura McVety

X

Lawsuits against churches have become increasingly common. One church tax and law expert states that negligence and irresponsible counselling is one of the greatest legal risks churches face (Slaybaugh). In this paper I will argue that in order to have a successful counselling ministry, pastors and churches need to recognise and safeguard against the legal risks connected to pastoral counselling. The term pastoral counselling refers to the act of a pastor performing counselling duties such as soliciting people's problems and offering to help the patient come to the best solutions. The legal risks associated with pastoral counselling that I will address include negligent counselling, sexual misconduct, breach of confidentiality, and confusing counselling with ministering.

Churches across North America have a great responsibility to their congregations. People look to the church not only for spiritual guidance, but also for direction in making major life-planning decisions. If a lawsuit is brought against a church, all of the church's assets would be available to satisfy a legal judgement. This financial vulnerability means that the actions of one leader bringing down an entire church! The ramifications of a successful legal action against a church counsellor would be enormous.

In the case of the Vancouver College and Christian Brothers that began in 1989 and lasted thirteen years (Rowland et al / Christian Brothers of Ireland In Canada v. Attorney General of British Columbia), an employee of the Christian Brothers in Newfoundland was found guilty of child molestation, and the victims were awarded sixty-seven million dollars in damages. Upon realising that the Christian Brothers had general corporate assets of no more than four million dollars, the liquidator was permitted to claim the assets of two schools in Vancouver that were held by the Christian Brothers as a special purpose charitable trust. In this instance, the actions of one man in Newfoundland had huge ramifications for the entire organisation. The representation of Vancouver College settled out of court rather than have their school sold to satisfy the judgement (Cart).

I will discuss three issues related to the thesis statement in this paper: first, what common areas of pastoral counselling churches need to safeguard against, second, how churches should protect themselves from legal actions, and third, why churches need to recognise these legal risks and how to safeguard against them.

First, I will address what main legal issues involved in pastoral counselling churches need to be aware of. As stated above, the four most common areas of liability in pastoral counselling are negligence, sexual misconduct, confidentiality and distinguishing counselling from ministering. If pastors and churches familiarise themselves with these four areas and take preventative actions, to avoid leaving themselves vulnerable to lawsuits, the counselling ministry's success will not be undermined.

Negligence is the careless causing of injury to the person or property of another (Smyth 49). Negligent pastoral counselling involves pastors giving poor advice, or advice on topics that the pastor has no expertise in. The aspects of negligence counselling that I will address next are: tort law, duty of care, liability, and duty of professionals. Negligence is a division of tort law. The law of torts by definition is a wrongful act done to the person or property of another, intended to compensate victims (Smyth 46). Most lawsuits brought against churches involve tort law (Moreland). The most common basis for legal action in tort is negligence. To determine whether a negligence action can be established, the courts must determine if there was a duty owed by the defendant to the plaintiff, whether that duty was breached and finally, if there was harm caused to the plaintiff due to the defendant's negligence (Smyth 49).

In pastoral counselling, the pastor has a duty to honestly portray his qualifications to the counselee, and to remain within the boundaries of his training while counselling. For example, the pastor should not be treating a patient with a serious mental illness, such as depression. If the pastor portrays himself as an expert in the field of counselling, and proceeds to give the patient advice that may be detrimental to the patient's health, the pastor is guilty of breaching his duty to this counselee, and is liable for any injuries that occur.

The foundational issue for establishing a negligence claim is determining whether there was a duty of care owed to the plaintiff. Duty of care is defined as the duty to take reasonable care to avoid injury to others (Smyth 49). The primary deciding factor of the existence of duty of care is that the alleged wrongdoer, in this case the church or pastor, should have foreseen that his or her actions might do harm.

The legal issue of liability has two subdivisions that are relevant to negligence: strict liability and vicarious liability. Strict liability is the liability that is imposed regardless of fault, in other words, anyone who caused direct injury to another had to pay compensation (Smyth 46). For example, if a troubled young woman came into a church, spoke with a pastor about her problems, then left and committed suicide, the pastor would be liable under strict liability. Regardless of whose fault her death was, or whether the pastor's conduct was justified, the pastor would be held liable.

Vicarious liability is the liability of an employer to compensate for harm caused by an employee (Smyth 49). Vicarious liability indicates that the church or denomination is liable for any harm the pastor causes while the pastor is in the course of employment. Continuing on with the same example as above, if the family of the deceased woman was to seek compensation for their loss, they could sue not only the pastor, but also the church and the church's conference. Even if the church specifically told the pastor not to counsel anyone on any issue other than the Bible, the church would still be liable for negligent acts of the pastor.

Pastors are considered professionals in the field of ministering. The specific duties of professionals are fiduciary duties, contractual duties and duties in tort.

The first professional duty – fiduciary duty – is the duty imposed on a person who stands in a special relation of trust to another (Smyth 71). Pastors hold a special relation of trust with any member of his congregation simply because he has a pastoral role. According to Wilson J. in the Supreme Court of Canada, the three general characteristics that must be established in order for the pastor to have a fiduciary role are:

1. The pastor must have scope for the exercise of some discretion or power.
2. The pastor can unilaterally exercise that power or discretion so as to affect the beneficiary's legal or practical interests.
3. The beneficiary is peculiarly vulnerable to or at the mercy of the pastor. (Smyth 71)

A pastoral relationship fulfils all of these characteristics. Pastors must be aware of this liability because it is a great source of vulnerability for lawsuits.

The second duty assumed by professionals is the contractual duty – an agreement to provide professional services to a client containing a promise to perform those services with due care (71). Most legal action against churches involves torts or breach of contract (Moreland). In pastoral counselling, if a contract has been drafted and signed by both parties, and the pastor breaches his promise, the client may then sue for damages.

The next issue involved in counselling is sexual misconduct. Pastoral counselling is profoundly affected by sexual misconduct, or false claims of sexual misconduct, and pastors need to take extra precautions to avoid leaving themselves vulnerable to these lawsuits. The two main aspects of sexual misconduct that I will address are pastors involved in affairs and child molestation.

One study has found that seventy-one percent of pastors involved in affairs began these affairs through pastoral counselling sessions (Gibbs). The reason that having an affair is a legal liability in pastoral counselling is because sexual relations between a counsellor and a patient is illegal to have. In the case Odenthal v. Minnesota Conference of Seventh-Day Adventists (Subject Matter), a pastor began giving marriage counselling to a troubled couple, and then initiated an affair with the wife. The church leaders learned of the relationship but did not take any action. The church president eventually confronted the pastor who subsequently resigned and married the woman. The husband sued the church for vicarious liability and negligent employment and the pastor for negligent counselling, intentional infliction of emotional distress, clergy malpractice and breach of fiduciary duty. The courts dismissed the husband's claims of intentional infliction of emotional distress, clergy malpractice, and breach of fiduciary duty against the pastor on summary judgement. The remaining claims against the church and the pastor for negligent counselling were valid (Subject Matter). This particular case is still in trial, so the outcome of the lawsuit is unknown; nevertheless the case is applicable because it shows the consequence of pastoral affairs in society today.

In the case Mary Doe v. F.P. (Brockmann) a priest, F.P., was assigned to Mary Doe's parish. The two worked closely together planning music for the services. They mutually discussed their personal problems with each other, including F.P.'s sexual relationships with other women and Doe's dissatisfaction with her marriage. They eventually began a sexual relationship.

Doe and her family sued F.P. and the diocese claiming that F.P. was practising psychotherapy during the time of the affair. The courts judged in favour of F.P. stating that the communications between Doe and F.P. did not constitute psychotherapy (Brockmann). The case above is another example of how common pastoral affairs are, and it proves that these affairs need to be guarded against.

Child molestation is a serious issue in church liability. According to Richard Hammar the biggest worry from pastors in regards to lawsuits is sexual misconduct, and the focus is on incidents of child molestation. This is such a concern because exorbitant awards have been given in previous child abuse cases against churches and pastors (Hammar).

Three common allegations that are brought against churches in regards to child abuse cases are that the churches were negligent in hiring the offender, supervising the children, and failing to take proper action when molestation is suspected or reported (Moreland). In one case, a pastor molested nine young boys at one church. Investigations showed that the church representatives were aware that this pastor was charged with this same offence at his previous church and transferred the pastor because of the transgression.

If the church has proven to take all necessary precautions in hiring the pastor, and he then proceeded to sexually abuse any children, the church may still be found to be vicariously liable. In the case Bazley v. Curry Supreme Court of Canada (Making Someone Pay), the appellant, The Children's Foundation (Foundation) operated a residential care centre for troubled children. The Foundation's employees were responsible for all parental duties such as bathing and putting the children to bed. One of their employees, Curry, was hired after completing a background check, and the Foundation was not aware that he was a pedophile. The Foundation fired Curry after a complaint was investigated against him. Curry was later convicted of nineteen counts of sexual assault, two of which were involving the respondent Bazley. Bazley sued the Foundation claiming they were vicariously liable for the assaults committed against him by Curry. Bazley did not claim that the Foundation had been negligent in hiring Curry or supervising him. The initial lawsuit was for the courts to determine whether or not the Foundation was vicariously liable. The chambers judge and the British Columbia Court of Appeal held that the foundation was vicariously liable, and the Supreme Court of Canada upheld their verdict. Vicarious liability is described as a rule "imposing liability on one party for the actions of another without any need for the former to have been negligent or legally at fault in any way" (Making Someone Pay). In this same way, the church is liable for any sexual misconduct of their pastors regardless of lack of negligence or fault.

The third issue involved in pastoral counselling is confidentiality. Issues impacting confidentiality are laws governing counsellor/patient privileges, and slander laws.

Knowing the provincial laws regulating communication with pastors and counsellors is key. When is overriding this confidence appropriate? Each province has different laws in this area. Pastors need to be extremely familiar with the governing laws. Suspicion of child abuse is generally an example of an appropriate time to break confidentiality (Slaybaugh). Saving a person from harm is another example of a time when breaching confidence is generally permitted; however, knowing the locally accepted confidentiality exceptions is vital. Pastors must never make blanket statements promising to by no means disclose anything communicated in a counselling session. The law may require pastors to disclose confidential information (Gibbs).

Slander is defined as spoken defamation (Smyth 63). Some pastors and churches feel that their duty is to expose any injustices in the congregation. There is an element of accountability and confrontation that culturally influences the way some churches operate, which may sometimes conflict with slander laws. Matthew 18:15-17 is cited as the biblical guidelines for church discipline:

> If your brother sins, go and show him his fault in private; if he listens to you, you have won your brother. But if he does not listen to you, take one or two more with you, so that by the mouth of two or three witnesses every fact may be confirmed. If he refuses to listen to them, tell it to the church; and if he refuses to listen even to the church, let him be to you as a Gentile and a tax collector. (New American Standard Bible – NASB)

Essentially, what Jesus' teachings in this passage of Scripture are interpreted to mean are that if a member of the church does not readily repent of any unconfessed sin, the pastor is not only allowed, but also required to expose that sin in the name of repentance. This act of exposing someone's transgression is dangerously close to the legal term of slander. Churches apply these steps of discipline even if the sin was discovered in a pastoral counselling session.

According to attorney David C. Gibbs, a pastor has a duty to keep any information learned during a counselling session confidential. Any pastor who violates this trust is in danger of being sued for invasion of privacy or slander (Gibbs).

For example, there is one case where a church discovered that a woman in the congregation was having an adulterous affair. They followed the steps found in Matthew 18 and one person confronted her, then a group of three confronted her, and still they saw no repentance, so they brought her indiscretions before the church as a whole. The woman sued for slander claiming she had no idea that this was the church's policy for discipline. Because the church could not prove that she had been informed of this policy, they lost the lawsuit, bankrupting the church and causing them to forfeit their building and property (Walsh).

After this case set the precedent, churches are now becoming much more careful with how they handle church discipline. There is another example of a lawsuit when a woman was caught in an adulterous affair. One person from the church confronted her, then a small group of two or three, and still the church found no repentance in the woman. She sent the church a letter through her lawyer withdrawing her membership from the church threatening a lawsuit if the church went on to tell more people about her actions. The church then consulted their lawyers, and proceeded to inform several people who knew the woman, in hopes that their prayers and support would cause her to be remorseful. The woman sued for slander, but because the church had a signed document stating that she knew that this was the church's policy for discipline, she lost the lawsuit. The only difference between these two lawsuits is that the second church took one extra precautionary step and was then protected from the slander accusations (Walsh).

The final issue involved in pastoral counselling is distinguishing counselling from ministering. Pastoral care and pastoral counselling are two entirely different things. Bill Blackburn, a pastor and contributing writer for the "Handbook for Therapists, Pastors and Counsellors" (Slaybaugh) states that pastoral care encompasses hospital visits, telephone calls and informal, brief conversations about church member's needs. Counselling refers to the times when appointments are scheduled and a church member comes seeking help. Blackburn sets a time limit of four hours per week on his counselling sessions. He also refuses to see people for more than four sessions each. Blackburn also refuses to counsel non-members, except on rare occasions.

While these strict guidelines were not easy for Blackburn to set in place, he finds his support in the Gospels. Jesus did not see every sick person in every village he visited, and he did not heal every sick person he came in contact with. Also, a study found that church members who engage in long-term counselling with their pastors end up leaving their churches because they feel exposed, as if the pastor is singling them out from the pulpit (Slaybaugh). Blackburn keeps his guidelines to protect himself and his church members.

The way that pastors have a desire to do everything in their power to help and serve their congregation is understandable and even admirable; however, the fact remains that pastors who understand that he or she cannot do everything can better serve the people. There are professional associations of counsellors who have professional designation, training and certification. When a pastor is counselling, then he or she is in dangerous territory; providing spiritual guidance, however, is what the pastor is trained for.

The job description of a pastor can be quite blurred and general, essentially stating that the pastor must shepherd the church by preaching the gospel, serving the people, teaching the "Word" and instructing people how to live, and respond and relate to God. This description covers fundamentally all areas of life, and can be interpreted to say that pastors are required to be involved and help in any circumstance. Pastors should not be responsible for a member of their church in all areas. All professionals have their expertise, and a pastor's is to minister, a counsellor's is to counsel. If the pastor and the church have a more concise understanding of what the pastor's job description really is, the pastor will be able to be more productive in areas that he limits himself to, further protecting the church from potential lawsuits.

Negligent counselling, sexual misconduct, confidentiality, and understanding pastoral roles are the most common areas of liability in pastoral counselling. When the pastors and churches familiarise themselves with these specific areas, and take extra precautionary measures to avoid potential lawsuits, their counselling ministry has the potential to be much more effective.

Now that I have discussed the four main risks of pastoral counselling: negligent counselling, sexual misconduct, confidentiality, and confusing counselling with ministering, I will begin discussing what specific preventative measures churches can take in order to protect themselves. According to Patrick Moreland, churches are found negligent when they have failed to take adequate safety precautions or provide proper supervision, thereby making the church liable for damages (Moreland).

To avoid negligence, churches need to take reasonable care when hiring their pastors. Attorney Gibbs describes four simple steps to take reasonable care including contacting previous churches where the candidate has served, contacting former employers of the candidate, request a criminal record check and finally, include a detailed application, interviews, reference and education verifications in the hiring process. One church failed to contact former employers of a candidate for youth pastor, and hired someone who had been dishonourably discharged from the US Navy for sexual molestation (Gibbs).

According to L. Ronald Brushwyler, D. Min., of the Midwest Ministry Development Service in Chicago, another way that pastors can avoid negligence claims is to:

> Refer to [their] activities in 'unambiguously religious,' not professional counselling, terms. Unless [they are] trained and willing to adhere to all of the professional standards of licensed professional counsellors, stay with practices identified as pastoral care. If you hold yourself out as a 'professional' or 'psychological' counsellor, the law will treat [them] you as one. (Slaybaugh)

To avoid false or accurate sexual misconduct claims, pastors and churches should have a detailed screening process for potential pastors, distinct supervisory procedures and a course of action in place when sexual abuse is reported (Moreland).

Experts recommend prohibiting male pastors from private sessions with unaccompanied females. This could mean only allowing women to counsel women, or simply adjust where the sessions take place. Make sure the offices and parking lots are well lit for counselling that takes place in the evening, and install windows in the counsellor's office so all sessions are visible to staff members (Slaybaugh).

Slander lawsuits can be avoided by maintaining confidentiality. In order to do this, pastors should take the duty of confidentiality very seriously. Only under drastic and legally permitted cases is the pastor allowed to breach this confidence, and the pastor is responsible to find out when the laws allow for violating confidentiality (Gibbs). Also, pastors should refrain from promising that they would never tell anything mentioned during the sessions (Slaybaugh).

Churches need to pay close attention to their counselling ministry. If the pastor is found negligent, and the church has not taken the necessary supervisory actions, the church could also be found negligent (Gibbs). Some general guidelines that Gibbs suggests for assisting churches and pastors be more attentive include: setting a limit on how many sessions each individual may receive, refer people with serious health or mental issues to a professional medical or psychiatric counsellor with specialised training, schedule all counselling sessions in writing, keep a secretary aware of the pastor's location at all times, and never counsel a minor without an adult present (Gibbs).

A written pastoral counselling policy should be drafted and signed by both the pastor and the person seeking counselling. The elements that Gibbs addresses that should be included in this policy include:

1. That the counselling provided is biblical not professional.
2. The counselling pastor is not professional in psychological counselling, psychiatric therapy, or marriage and family counselling or therapy, and is not licensed by the state as a counsellor, social worker or therapist.
3. The person seeking counselling agrees not to sue the church for any expenses or damages that result from any of the pastor's counselling services.
4. Agrees that otherwise confidential communications may be disclosed to appropriate state law enforcement authorities where required by law. (Gibbs)

More suggestions that Gibbs has for pastors is that they keep detailed records of counselling sessions including the date, time and location, the names of those present and the reason for their presence, the confidential nature of the session, the problems for which counselling was sought, any unusual incidents or statements that occurred during the session, the spiritual advice given, biblical references shared, specific actions recommended, and actions the counselee was discouraged from taking (Gibbs).

Reacting to a problem swiftly and immediately is essential to the avoidance of lawsuits. A common mistake made by church bodies is to cover up the issue, or attempting to settle the matter quietly. This action only clouds the issue and compounds the churches liability. A common example found in the press currently is the issue of the Catholic Church merely transferring errant priests to another diocese rather than dealing with the root matter. There is currently a case in the Supreme Court of Canada that is dealing with a Catholic priest who committed hundreds of assaults on young boys over a course of thirty years. While the priest has already been convicted and served time in jail, thirty-six of the victims have now sued the Roman Catholic Church for damages rather than only the individual Episcopal corporations. At the moment, victims can sue the offending priest as well as the individual Episcopal corporation that employs him, but not the billion-member world-wide church because the church is not an incorporated body. Bill Sammon, who represents the Canadian Council of Catholic Bishops comments on the dangerous precedent this case could set if the Supreme Court rules that the Catholic church is liable. Sammon is quoted saying, "If you can ascribe liability simply based on faith, then that implicates Charter-protected rights to freedom of conscious and religion, because who will want to belong to a faith where you might be exposed to limitless liability?" This case effectively illustrates the danger of not responding appropriately to a serious issue like an abusive priest, and the dangers of vicarious liability for the entire Catholic Church and the enormous repercussions of the actions of just one priest.

Finally, churches and pastors need to invest in professional liability or counselling insurance. For example, Shield Church Insurance provides services specifically for Canadian churches. Some of their customers include: The Christian and Missionary Alliance in Canada, The Evangelical Fellowship of Canada, Tyndale College and Seminary, Promise Keepers Canada, Focus on the Family, and Youth for Christ (www.churchinsurancecanada.com). Research shows there are very few churches that operate a counselling ministry without adequate counselling insurance.

Churches and pastors need to recognise and safeguard against potential risks. Here are some examples of why this is so important. Legal actions have a vast impact not only on pastors but also their churches and supporting conferences. Lawsuits can be disruptive to a ministry and congregation. The time and energy put into lawsuits inevitably detract from normal functions (Moreland). Some lawsuits are divisive and even if the church survives financially, the congregation will likely split up or lose unity. The pastoral leadership is called into question during a lawsuit, adding to the issue of the divided congregation. The church and pastor is inevitably put into question and could bring shame to the church if brought into a lawsuit. The church can get sued for millions of dollars in damages, forcing the church to shut down. It is even possible, but not common for the pastor or church staff to be sentenced for prison time. (2) Define the range of damages that a church may be liable for.

Lawsuits can be expensive. Whether the claims are factual or false, no church ever comes out a "winner" in a lawsuit. To be liable, or prove you are not liable involves a great deal of costs, including: legal defence costs, court awards for damages, and punitive damages. Punitive damages are damages awarded by a court against a defendant as a deterrent or punishment to redress an egregious wrong perpetrated by the defendant (dictionary.com). A few examples of court awards for damages include pain and suffering and medical expenses. Punitive damages are more common when the injury was caused intentionally or when extreme carelessness was involved (Moreland).

Historically, churches used to be protected from lawsuits. Many years ago churches were protected by what is called "charitable immunity." (Moreland) Their actions were protected because their assets were comparable to a trust fund and could not be used for purposes other than those intended by the donors. Since the donors did not intend for their donations to be used to pay awards in liability lawsuits, churches were immune from paying them (Moreland).

Charitable immunity has disintegrated from society today because courts now recognise that churches need to be accountable and financially responsible for their actions. Moreland states, "Injury that results from church's negligence is no less painful, disabling or financially damaging than injury resulting from any other person's or organisation's negligence. Large court awards against churches attest to their equal status in today's legal arena" (Moreland).

The above reasons are only a few examples of why recognising and guarding against potential legal risks in pastoral counselling is so important.

In reference to the examples given throughout this paper, it is important to note that this paper is meant to cover the topic of pastoral counselling liability in general terms, and the cases references are from all over North America. While the principles of pastoral liability are similar in Canada and the United States, due to the general principles of tort law, there are nevertheless differences in application among the two countries and the specific provinces and states.

In conclusion, pastors and churches need to recognise and safeguard against the legal risks associated with pastoral counselling. A reasonable approach is necessary to take cautionary measures because of the risks associated with pastoral counselling, including: negligent counselling, sexual misconduct, confidentiality, and confusing counselling with ministering. This issue should be taken seriously to protect the church and pastor from lawsuits. The ramifications from church lawsuits are massive, as seen in all of the cases described in this paper. The mistake of just one church worker can lead to years of multimillion-dollar lawsuits, bankruptcy of churches and their conferences, and the devastation of an entire congregation. As Moreland states, injury from church negligence is painful, disabling and damaging. This is not an issue to be taken lightly, or to be overlooked.

After researching of articles, case studies and other materials, the legal liabilities involved in pastoral counselling clearly cannot be ignored. While a pastor's job is to guide and counsel their congregation, pastors must be aware of their limits. Pastors cannot be naïve; they must be fully educated on all of the potential liabilities involved in pastoral counselling. Most importantly they need to take all of the necessary actions and not avoiding facing the hard issues head on. Not only should they be well informed, but also they need to be proactive in taking preventative actions against lawsuits. By taking these preventative measures, the pastors will enable themselves to better serve their congregation.

WORKS CITED

Bourgeois, Donald J. The Law of Charitable and Not-For-Profit Organizations. Markham: Butterworths Canada Ltd., 2002.

British Columbia Statutes. Negligence Act. Victoria: Queen's Printer for British Columbia, 1997.

Brockmann, Jeffery S. "Actions for Sexual Exploitation by a Member of the Clergy." Bassford Remele. Mary Doe v. F.P., Minnesota Court of Appeals. 19 Aug. 2003 <http://www.bassford.com/august22.htm#actions>.

Cart, Terrance and R. Johanna Blom. "Update on Christian Brothers." Charitable Law Bulletin. Jan. 2004 <http://www.carters.ca/pub/bulletin/charity/2003/chylb24.htm>.

"The Court's Jurisdiction in Religious Matters is not over Faith, Doctrine or Morals." Cultural Renewal. Oct. 2003 <http://www.culturalrenewal.ca/lex/lex-2.htm>.

"The Court Claims to Extend its Jurisdiction to Church Matters." Cultural Renewal. Oct. 2003 <http://www.culturalrenewal.ca/lex/lex-52.htm>.

"The Diminution of Freedom of Religion." Cultural Renewal. Oct. 2003 <http://www.culturalrenewal.ca/lex/lex-38.htm>.

Echenberg, Havi, et al. and John McCallum, eds. A Social Charter for Canada? Toronto: C.D. Howe Institute, 1992.

"EFC Pastor/Church Worker Abuse." Evangelical Fellowship of Canada. Oct. 2003 <http://www.evangelicalfellowship.ca/pdf/AbusePastorChurch.pdf>.

Gibbs, David C. Pastoral Counseling: "Safeguard Against Potential Liability." Church Business. 26 Sept. 2003. 20 Oct. 2003 <http://www.churchbusiness.com/hotnews/39h26154458.html>.

Hammar, Richard. Interview. "Law and Disorder." Christianity Today. 47, Issue 5. May 2003: 48.

Jobb, Dean. "Who's Responsible." Canadian Business. Mar. 2003: 39.

Linden, A.M., and L.N. Klar. Canadian Tort Law: Cases, Notes and Materials. Markham: Butterworths Canada Ltd., 1999.

"Making Someone Pay." Cultural Renewal. Oct. 2003 <http:/www.culturalrenewal.ca/lex/lex-32.htm>.

Moreland, Patrick M. "A Guide to Church Liability Risks." Church Business. Oct. 2003 <http://www.churchbusiness.com/articles/9b1Final.html>.

"Rowland et al / Christian Brothers of Ireland In Canada v. Attorney General of British Columbia." The Supreme Court of British Columbia. 29 Mar. 2004 <http://www.courts.gov.bc.ca/jdbtxt/SC/02/08/2002BCSC0848.htm>.

"Sexual Assault: The Defense of Honest but Mistaken Belief in Consent." Cultural Renewal. Oct. 2003 <http://www.culturalrenewal.ca/lex/lex-9.htm>.

Slaybaugh, RaeAnne. "Counseling Can Be Risky, Guarding your good Samaritans is crucial." Church Business: Providing Solutions and Strategies for Today's Churches. Oct. 2003 <http://www.churchbusiness.com/articles/2a1Cover1.html>.

Smith, William L. "Safeguard Your Church, Practical Guidelines for Screening Volunteers." Mar./April 1998, Christianity Today. Oct. 2003 <http://www.christianitytoday.com/yc/8y2/8y2062.html>.

Smyth, Soberman, Easson. The Law and Business Administration in Canada. 10th ed. Pearson/Prentice Hall, 2004.

"Subject Matter Jurisdiction – Separation of Church and State: Odenthal v. Minnesota Conference of Seventh-Day Adventists." Case Law Updates. Jan. 2003 <http://www.bassford.com/january31.htm>.

Terry Nicholas P. "Collapsing Torts." Connecticut Law Review. Spring 1993: 717.

"Top court reserves judgment on Catholic Church liability." CBC News. Jan. 2004 <http://www.cbc.ca/stories/2004/01/15/catholic_reserved040115>.

Walsh, Tony. Personal interview. Nov. 2003.
Oct. 2003 <www.churchinsurancecanada.com>. Nov. 2003 <www.bible.com>. Jan. 2004 <www.dictionary.com>.

"Youth and Human Rights: Justice." Ethnivision, 2001. Videorecording.

Casinos:
Entertainment vs. Social Burden
Chris Meehan

XI

There are frequent stories of respectable people falling victim to the addiction of gambling. In one such case, a Detroit woman lost ten thousand US dollars at the Windsor Casino in Ontario. She then drove home and withdrew the last ten thousand she and her husband had in their savings in an attempt to win back what she had just lost. She failed to do so. This woman is just one face of the multitudes trapped in a life-wrecking addiction to gambling. These individuals are often conveniently turned into faceless numbers, which are then assigned group names such as "minority" or "small percentage." The government downplays the negative impact of gambling on individuals' lives because they receive millions of dollars in revenue from the "charitable" casino industry. This situation is problematic. Current government policies provide significant gambling revenue to government coffers while feeding the appetites of business and gamblers. Consequently, neither party has a reason to articulate any objections to the current policies. However, the existing government policies victimise countless citizens and unarguably cost individuals and society dearly.

My thesis is that casinos stand in opposition to Christian principles and neither the generated revenue for government, nor the positive social benefits, are strong enough to outweigh the negative social consequences inherent in casinos. I will substantiate my thesis through providing a brief history of gambling in Canada to create context, followed by an analysis of casino building requirements and the negative and positive connotations of having a casino in a city. My last point will evaluate casinos from a Christian perspective based on the Bible and the official position of the world wide Pentecostal denomination.

Gambling predates the formation of Canada in 1867. Native American history records primitive gambling which involved throwing painted sticks into the air to determine who would take a wagered lot. Since 1867 the federal government has had an important role in regulating gambling activities. In 1892 a complete ban on all gambling activities was written into the Canadian Criminal Code (Code). In 1900 the Code was amended to allow fundraising raffles which could not exceed fifty dollars to be conducted at religious and charitable bazaars. The Code was amended in 1910 to legalise on-track wagering at race-tracks. This amendment was later suspended in 1917 by the federal Cabinet because the belief was that gambling was not consistent with "the sacrifice necessary during a time of war" (Campbell viii). In 1919 racetrack gambling was once again permitted. The extent of the Code was expanded and clarified in 1922 when it stated that "dice games, shell games, and punch boards" were prohibited. The start of larger changes in gaming in Canada can be traced to 1925 when the Code was amended to permit "games of chance" and "games of mixed chance and skill," to be conducted at agricultural fairs.

Bills begun to surface in the House of Commons in the sixties which sought to legalise lotteries. These bills had the support of the province of Quebec, which had "major financial commitments to the 1967 Montreal World's Fair and the 1976 Olympic Games" (Campbell viii). As a result of this growing provincial support, the Criminal Code Amendment Act was passed into law in May 1969. This Amendment Act was designed to: [A]llow state lotteries at the option of the federal or provincial governments, the broadening of charity gaming along the lines suggested by the Parliamentary Committee in 1954, [and] the continuation of existing exemptions for gambling at agricultural fairs (Campbell ix).

This Amendment Act enabled provincial governments to manage and conduct their own provincial lotteries. The new Act also extended the right to charitable and religious organisations to conduct lottery schemes under an issued provincial license.

In 1985 there was another significant amendment to the Criminal Code pertaining to gambling. The amendment gave provincial governments the option to legalise and administer computer and video gaming devices, which were previously illegal in Canada. This amendment effectively legalised Video Lottery Terminals (VLTs) and slot machines. In short, "VLTs are electronic slot machines with several line-up style games. A gambler will insert a quarter and if the objects in the three windows match one of several possible combinations, the gambler is awarded a prize. Otherwise, no prize is awarded" (Braun). Any new gaming machines would be controlled by the provincial governments, which in turn operate under the regulations and limitations of the Criminal Code.

Gambling in Canada has been synonymous with charity. This could be attributed in part to Canadian's progressive acceptance of gambling as the country has legalised more forms of the activity. As Canadians have gradually moved to accept gambling, the federal government has reduced its involvement in regulating the industry. In 1987 British Columbia lifted a moratorium on new charitable casinos which sparked the beginning of the casino industry in British Columbia.

In summary, over the past one hundred years, sections of the Criminal Code pertaining to gambling have undergone consistent changes to reflect society's views moving from a tolerance to active participation in gaming activities. One author noted, "recent developments, such as increasing legalisation and an improved public image, have more than offset the effect of reform movements and ambivalence. Gambling participation, for all intents, has been legitimised" (Rosecrance 51).

Now that we have examined the evolution of gambling in Canada on a broad scale, I will provide further information on this topic by examining the logistics concerning the development of a casino in a specific municipality. The example selected is the Great Canadian Casino (GCC) with a proposed building site in Richmond, British Columbia. This particular casino location required an extended time period for approval from local and provincial governments. Typically, when the GCC chooses to build a casino it takes about one-to-two years to satisfy government requirements. However, with the new Richmond casino it took approximately five years to pick the site and to satisfy all necessary levels of government (Blank, telephone interview). This delay was due to extensive regulations that had to be met, including city bylaws concerning slot machines within the municipality and rezoning the land at the proposed site.

When selecting a site, the GCC must evaluate a number of important business-related factors vital to the casinos viability. The tourism market in the area is closely examined to determine that the area can support the size of casino being proposed. The site should also be in close proximity to a transportation system. The GCC does not want to locate its building too close to a residential area so zoning requirements are studied to determine a location that is large enough to support the accompanying infrastructure. In this case the casino includes: "a two hundred suite hotel, food services, a six hundred and fifty seat dinner theatre, a conference area, a fitness centre, and a marina (already existing). The site will also accommodate Great Canadian Casino's Head Office" (Lee 2). The GCC feels the site just off Highway 99, a main highway through greater Vancouver, fulfils all of these requirements.

Howard Blank, Director of Media & Public Relations for the GCC, does not think there will be any adverse affects on the residents of Richmond due to the new opening of the GCC. The casino that Richmond already has, located at Sea Island Way, will close its operations as the new location at the former Bridgepoint market opens. As a result of the new opening, Blank estimates traffic will increase in the area by two thousand vehicles a day. This will in turn raise the property value of the local businesses in the area. Another note-worthy item is that the City of Richmond should receive between ten-to-twelve million dollars in direct gaming revenue as a result of hosting a casino in the community. Also, according to Blank, the opening of this new casino and "full entertainment complex" should create upwards of one thousand new jobs.

Beyond business concerns the GCC must comply with many levels of government regulations. Provincial regulations outlined in the Gaming Control Act, Section 19(1)(b) states: "A host municipality must consult with 'each municipality, regional district or first nation that is immediately adjacent or that the lottery corporation considers will be materially affected by the gaming facility or proposed gaming facility and its location, relocation or substantial change, as the case may be'" (Lee 2).

British Columbia gaming regulations describe 'materially affected' as meaning: "An adjacent municipality 'will incur significant new infrastructure or policing costs, experience increased traffic or experience a significant adverse impact on the amenities and character of one or more of its neighbourhoods'" (Section 11, BC Gaming Control Regulations), (Lee 2).

The adjacent municipality in this case is Vancouver. Vancouver city staff reviewed information obtained from the City of Richmond and concluded that "the relocation of the Great Canadian Casino from Number 3 Road to Bridgepoint will not materially affect the City of Vancouver" (Lee 2). The City of Vancouver also solicited the Vancouver Police Department's input. The Department indicated that the new casino will not materially impact the Vancouver Police Department and as such the Department will not incur any new or additional costs.

When I asked Mr. Blank what levels of government have the strictest regulations that GCC must comply with he responded: "We must comply with regulations [outlined by the] B.C Lottery Solicitor General, and the Gaming Policy Enforcement Branch." He continued to state that "British Columbia is one of the strictest places to operate in the world" (Blank).

> The Gaming Branch operates independently from the Gaming Commission; thus, the rules are not enforced by the rule-maker. Thorough background checks are conducted on all persons involved in management and on all owners of casino operations in the province. All staff must pass a security check. Audited statements must be provided to the Commission, and inspectors pay unexpected and frequent visits to casinos. (Campbell 112)

Blank "welcome[s] that scrutiny, because otherwise we (the casino industry) would be like the Wild West" (Blank). Blank also noted that because the GCC is a public company, it is also accountable to its shareholders above and beyond the government's scrutiny.

Chris Wright an Operator of a casino in British Columbia commented, "I can assure you that the members of our [Casino Management] Council work very closely with the Branch and the Commission to ensure that we do not violate rules, regulations, or policies because it is not worth it economically" (Campbell 113).

On May 29 and June 3, 2002 after consulting the public, the Richmond City Council approved a revised casino policy to allow for a casino with slot machines in Richmond. On March 17, 2003 the Richmond City Council held a public hearing to discuss the rezoning for the proposed casino relocation. Local business people supported the proposal with economics in mind. An anti-gambling activist who was in attendance, commented on the proceedings saying, "the province's policy pitted municipalities against each other in the race for gambling revenue. The results can be damaging" (Bryan Casino).

On May 12, 2003 Richmond city council voted five-to-two in favour of adopting the rezoning bylaw for the proposed site at 881/883 River Rd, the former Bridgepoint Market site. Interestingly, Richmond City Mayor Malcom Brodie voted against the rezoning.

At present the casino policy in Richmond is as follows: "Richmond supports: one full service community gaming casino in Richmond which includes slot machines, table games, and poker tables as permitted by Provincial Gaming Legislation and Government Policy, thereby ensuring consistency between the City policy and Provincial regulations on this matter" (Lee 4).

During council meetings the number of slot machines the GCC should be limited to by the city was discussed. As a result, council chose to remove the cap, with regards to the city regulations, as the British Columbia Lottery Corporation (BCLC) would still limit the final number.

Since the process of establishing a casino is very difficult one might reasonably ask why a businessperson would put forth the effort. The single most convincing answer to this question is economics. Casinos generate large amounts of money, both for charities, and for the government. Gaming in British Columbia during 2002 generated approximately two billion dollars; of this, casinos counted for $628 million, after prize payouts. "In 2003/04, the Province of BC will receive an estimated $725 million in net gaming revenue. This includes approximately $414 million from casinos" (Bryan Richmond). The general economic concept can be broken down into several simple arguments.

If British Columbia did not support casinos then residents who wanted to gamble in a casino would travel to the next province or state that provided this entertainment, taking millions of dollars with them. Currently there are hundreds of people in the lower mainland who board buses to Washington State to gamble at the First Nation's casinos less than a two-hour drive away. As casinos are built in British Columbia, this flow of money will be slowed, stopped, or even reversed.

A casino is an asset to tourism. When the Great Canadian Casino builds a casino at the former Bridgepoint Market site, it will also build (for starters) an all-suites hotel, convention space, a spa, nightclub and show lounge. The project is esti-mated to cost between sixty and eighty million dollars. This large amount of money will spur the local economy while attracting out of province tourists, gambling and non-gambling alike. Canadians currently spend an estimated twenty-to-twenty-seven billion dollars on gambling. Building new facilities could increase British Columbia's take of the national pie.

In 1995, net revenue in BC from gambling was $392.3 million or $104 per capita. Thus, gambling generated 1.5% of total provincial revenue that year. Simpli-fied, this means that the tax burden in British Columbia was $104 per person lighter during 1995 due to the proceeds of gambling. The provincial government would have had to raise taxes by $104 per person in the absence of gambling to maintain the same level of government services to British Columbians (Welfare Council 6).

During the same year, gaming revenue was distributed to individuals and community groups in British Columbia as follows (excerpts):

> One hundred thirty six point five million to community organisa-
> tions, $147.3 million to the Health Special Account to support
> health care services and research, $42.3 million to local govern-
> ments that host casinos in their communities, $8.6 million to
> local economic development, four million to problem gambling
> services, and eight million to the Government of Canada, under
> the federal/provincial lottery agreement. (Welfare Council)

In 2003/04 it is estimated that five thousand community organisations will share $166.5 million from gambling revenue.

A unique aspect of casinos in British Columbia is that they provide the highest percentage return to charity in North America. "Charities in BC are assured each and every night, fifty per cent of the gross win of the casino. Government receives ten per cent, leaving the operator forty per cent of the gross win to pay all expenses" (Campbell 111). Due to the low percentage of operator income, in 1994 only half of the eighteen casinos in province operated on a profitable basis. But during the same year they combined to provide thirty-one million to charities, and the government received seven million, for a grand total of thirty-eight million.

Now that I have examined the positive connotations of a casino I will advocate for an acknowledgement of the negative aspects of casinos. Anti-gambling activists argue that gambling is a regressive tax. A regressive tax means that the poorest residents bare the greatest cost and the richest residents the least. The following Illinois case study supports this argument. According to the Illinois Legislative Council, residents of DuPage County earn fourteen thousand dollars per capita and residents of Cook County earn seven thousand dollars per capita. However, residents of DuPage spend an average of thirty-six dollars on lottery tickets while Cook County residents spend an average one hundred and twelve dollars on lottery tickets a year. "People who earn half as much money as their affluent neighbours pump three times as much money into the state's coffers" (Watson 29). A probable explanation for this is that Cook County residents are willing to stake a higher percentage of their income in a desperate bid to 'win it big' and improve their living conditions. Or, perhaps they are less aware of the actual odds of the lottery. Regardless of reason, this case study is a classic example of a regressive tax.

In British Columbia, 'problem gambling' is defined as "gambling behaviours that compromise, disrupt or damage personal, family or vocational pursuits" (B.C Govt. Policy). However, this problem is deemed by the government to be a treatable condition. "Counselling, using a variety of treatment approaches, can provide solutions" (B.C Govt. Policy). Due to the frequency of gaming problems, the province has made many services available to the general public, such as free counselling services and toll-free help lines. To do this, the B.C government supplies four million dollars each year to fund a comprehensive problem gambling program. According to the Gaming Policy and Enforcement Branch, the goal of the program is to:

1. Reduce the incidence of problem gambling
2. Reduce harmful impacts of excessive gambling
3. Ensure the delivery of gambling in a manner that encourages responsible gambling and healthy choices.

Despite the government's best effort, the problems created by casinos do not go away. Richmond City councillor Derek Dang is well aware of this fact. He stated, "I believe we [Richmond] have a family oriented community with values that do not mesh well with the unsavoury elements of the gambling industry and the associated social ills that gambling brings" (Dang). Councillor Dang was one of two city councillors who voted against the new Richmond casino.

Addiction is the strongest argument against a casino; it is the issue at the core of problem gambling. The government takes the following attitude towards addiction:

> For most people gambling is entertainment, enjoyed without adverse consequences. However, a small percentage of people may gamble in ways that harm themselves and their families and may require assistance in seeking information or services to help them. Honourable Rich Coleman, Minister of Public Safety and Solicitor General. (B.C Govt. "Responsible")

This "small percentage" of people in British Columbia is estimated to be between 123,400 and 177,100 people. These numbers represent individuals who according to a Canadian Problem Gambling Index (CPGI) are "moderate problem gamblers." British Columbia is the second lowest province in the total 'problem gamblers' category according to the CPGI study. However, the level of "at risk gamblers" is the highest of any province (which has performed the CPGI study) at 11.1 %.

The CPGI is used to compare British Columbia with other provinces, and also serves as a base line for future research. The South Oaks Gambling Screen (SOGS) allows accurate comparison to previous British Colombian studies in 1993 and 1996. The results between the two tests are not directly comparable because the questions are different.

According to the 2001 CPGI, the typical average spending a month for problem gamblers was $539, moderate risk gamblers $207, low risk $238, and non-problem gamblers only averaged sixty-five dollars. The average age for these groups varied from thirty-seven to forty-four years old. Males were over fifty percent of the group in each category, save the non-problem category in which females comprised fifty five percent of the total.

According to the 2001 SOGS statistics, fifty-one per cent of those polled said that they gambled more than they could afford to lose. Fifty four per cent of those polled said they went back to try to win back lost money, while four-nine per cent needed to gamble more money to experience the same excitement. Finally, sixty-two percent said they tried to cut down but were unable to (Ferris 1). The number of problem gamblers from study to study has slowly increased from 2.6% (1993), to 2.7% (1996), up to 2.8% (2002), (B.C Govt. "Responsible").

Certain segments of the province's population have much higher rates of problem gambling compared to other sections. "Specifically, the prevalence of problem gamblers is higher than average among northern residents (10.2%), young residents (9.8%, 18-24 years old) and lower income residents (6.8%, <30,000)" (B.C Govt. "Responsible"). Studies have shown that teenagers are at an increased risk of developing problem gambling habits in comparison to adults. Gambling at a young age is now considered a risk factor for developing a serious gambling problem as an adult.

Considering the statistics on problem gamblers the question of gambling being strictly 'entertainment' is well warranted, and as such, often debated. Casino representatives, such as Blank see no adverse effects of operating a casino. However, a former casino owner stated: "Casino owners never gamble. We know we'll get our fifteen percent no matter who gets lucky or who folds" (Watson 127). There will always be big winners but the number of people who win is far exceeded by the number of people who lose. Winners often gamble their winnings and eventually lose. Losers often come back to the casino in an attempt to win back what they have lost, only to lose again.

Gambling and casinos go hand in hand; and both phenomena are experiencing unprecedented growth. As such, we as Christians must develop an articulate and clear stance on the issue. The positive economic spin off from casinos are easily identifiable. However, every dollar given to a charity or government from a casino originated from an individual. Often, many of these individuals have gambled more than they can afford. Ask yourself, did each of the individuals who lost money to the casino do so without undue influence? To conclude that they all chose to lose their money would be incorrect. Casinos spend large amounts of money on advertising and promotion. The flashing lights and lure of "big money" are apparent for all to see. Therefore, it is not a stretch to say that not every person in the casino chose to be there. People with weaker will, lower education, and addiction problems among others, are in fact victims of the casino industry.

Christians should find themselves concerned about an industry that relies on "human greed and weakness of will to operate" (Watson 28). Beyond concern, the question for Christians still remains; is gambling a sin? I could walk into the GCC in Richmond and put down a five dollar bet and leave it at that, is that a sin? Could it be that gambling is just a harmless entertainment that occasionally gets out of hand? To understand God's perspective on gambling we must look to the Bible.

In the Bible the casting of lots is mentioned numerous times. However, the mere mention of casting lots in Scripture does not imply Gods approval to our concept of gambling today. In Scripture the casting of lots came in two forms. One form is noted when the soldiers were casting lots for Jesus' clothing. This would be equivalent to today's "drawing straws." The soldiers did not "buy in" with money. They were not gambling. They were simply trying to decide who would receive Jesus' clothing. In most recorded instances in the Bible however, the casting of lots was, in the very action, recognising "the sovereignty of God in all things" (Rogers 59). Proverbs 16:33 reads, "The lot is cast into the lap, but its every decision is from the Lord." Casting lots was used in 1 Samuel 10:20-21 to determine the Israelites next king (Saul). The underlying principle here, as well as many other places in scripture, is that God has an active control of all events. "After Pentecost, the casting of lots was never used again as the means of determining God's will. God had sent the Holy Spirit, and He gave us His written Word as a source of His moral will...The practice of casting lots was no longer needed" (Rogers 59). Therefore the casting of lots can not be used as Scriptural evidence to condone today's practice of gambling.

The Assemblies of God (AG) is a world-wide Pentecostal denomination with approximately forty-one million members and adherents. The AG published a position paper on the topic of gambling. The paper stated four biblical principles that "indicate gambling is an evil to be avoided" (Council). The paper stated "gambling is wrong because...

1. It is a disregard of responsible stewardship.
2. It involves a chance of gain at the expense and suffering of others.
3. It is inconsistent with the work ethic of Scripture.
4. It tends to be habit forming."

These points are addressed and combined with further biblical principles as follows:

> A pertinent biblical concept is that God owns all things (Ps. 24:1; 50:10-12; Matt. 25:14-30; Luke 12:42-48; 1 Cor. 10-26). The money that you or I have does not belong to us. We have been entrusted with money from the Lord and He will hold us accountable for its use. This is the biblical principle of stewardship. When people recognise their stewardship responsibilities they will not consider gambling in any form a proper administration of divinely bestowed resources, time, and ability. Even the ethics of the world will not tolerate those who gamble with resources put in their trust (Council).

Given that casinos provide entertainment for thousands of Canadians, it is important to evaluate the cost at which this entertainment comes. Casinos provide a venue for a person to get rich off the back of his neighbour. This dissection proves that gambling is in defiance of God's Word. The Bible tells us that we must love our neighbours as ourselves (Lev. 19:18, 34; Matt. 19:19; 22:39; Mark 12:31). "Winning at gambling, no matter how distantly removed by the economics of enormous jackpots, always comes at the cost of others. Winners always win less than losers lose" (Rogers 64).

God says, "He who works his land will have abundant food, but he who chases fantasies lacks judgement" (Prov. 12:11). Gambling is an attempt to get something for nothing, the very action of gambling is like chasing a fantasy. Furthermore, by trying to obtain free wealth we are attempting to circumnavigate God's principles. For He said "By the sweat of your brow you will eat your food" (Gen. 3:19). We are, by our created nature, designed to work for our livelihood. Work, biblically, is a command as well as a gift from God (Exod. 20:9; Eph. 4:28; 1 Tim. 5:8). When Paul wrote to the Thessalonians he told them "For even when we were with you, we commanded you this: If anyone will not work, neither shall he eat" (2 Thess. 3:10). Another fitting verse pertaining to gambling is Proverbs 13:11: "Wealth gained by dishonesty will be diminished, but he who gathers by labour will increase." One reasonable conclusion is that money won by chance in the casinos, rather than through hard work, will not last.

The number of lives affected by "problem gambling" can not be reduced to a mere number or statistic. Thousands of people's lives are affected by an addiction to gambling right here in British Columbia. "As in the case of alcoholics and drug addicts, compulsive gamblers are dominated to the extent that they risk not only money, but everything meaningful in life. They have lost control of themselves" (Council). When an individual is controlled by an addiction they are living in defeat, outside of God's principle of living under His control. The Bible teaches that Christians should "not be brought under the power of any[thing]" (1 Cor. 6:12), we are to exhibit self-control (Gal. 5:23).

The Bible has further cautions for mankind pertaining to the love of money and the process of acquiring it. Proverbs 28:20, 22, "A faithful man will abound with blessings, but he who hastens to be rich will not go unpunished. A man with evil eyes hastens after riches, and does not consider that poverty will come upon him." In the casino setting, people are attempting to make money without working for it, ideally they want to get rich fast.

In 1 Timothy 6:9-10 the pursuit of riches is redefined,

> But those who desire to be rich fall into temptation and a snare, and into many foolish and harmful lusts which drown men in destruction and perdition. For the love of money is a root of all kinds of evil, for which some have strayed from the faith in their greediness, and pierced themselves through with many sorrows.

Casinos foster the love for money and according to Scripture the love of money causes many sorrows.

In conclusion, gambling in casinos provides entertainment for thousands of Canadians; however, the price of this amusement on individual's lives is simply too high. For every winner at a casino there is a greater number of losers and thus, operators generate a profit. This is the undisputed principal on which casinos operate. Greed and the love of money are the active principles that transpire everyday in casinos. The economic gain created by a casino is too weak to justify the destruction it inflicts on a person's emotional and spiritual life. So, "while the intrinsic evil of gambling may be debated, the extrinsic effect of gambling may not. Gambling produces negative effects. Bad gambling is redundant. Good gambling is an oxymoron" (Rogers 68).

WORKS CITED

BC's Partnership for Responsible Gambling. Ministry for Public Safety and Solicitor General: Gaming Policy and Enforcement Branch. 2003. 14 Oct. 2003 <http://www.bcresponsiblegambling.ca>.

Blank, Howard. Telephone Interview. 5 Nov. 2003.

Braun, John W. "An Illustration of Bootstrapping Using Video Lottery Terminal Data." Journal of Statistics Education. 1995. 25 Jan. 2004 <http://www.amstat.org/publications/jse/v3n2/datasets.braun.html>.

British Columbia. "What B.C is doing about problem gambling." Gaming Policy and Enforcement Branch. Victoria: Queen's Printer for British Columbia, 2003. 18 Oct. 2003 <http://www.pssg.gov.bc.ca>.

Bryan, Chris. "Casino Moves A Step." Richmond Review. 20 Mar. 2003. 15 Oct. 2003 <http://yourlibrary.ca/community/richmondreview/archive/RR20030320/morenews.html>.

Campbell, Colin S., ed. Gambling in Canada: The Bottom Line. British Columbia: Criminology Research Centre (SFU), 1994.

Cooper, Gerry. "Problem Gambling: A Canadian Perspective." Online Posting. 25 Nov. 2002. 20 Oct. 2003 <http://problemgambling.ca>.

Council of the Assemblies of God. "A Biblical Perspective on Gambling." 10 Aug. 1983. 25 Jan. 2004 < http://ag.org/top/index.cfm>.

Dang, Derek, Richmond City Councillor. Email Interview. 15 Nov. 2003.

Ferris, Jakie, and Harold Wynne. "Canadian Problem Gambling Index: Final Report." Canadian Centre on Substance Abuse. 19 Feb. 2001. 15 Oct. 2003 <http://www.ccsa.ca>.

Gaming Control Act. Gaming Facilities. Victoria: Queen's Printer for British Columbia, 2003. 14 Oct. 2003 <http://www.pssg.gov.bc.ca>.

Lee, Mario. "Casino Relocation in Richmond: Effects on the City of Vancouver."

Vancouver City Council. 12 Sept. 2003. 6 Oct. 2003 <http://www.city.vancouver.bc.ca/ctyclerk/cclerk/20030909/a8.htm>.

Mandal, Perrier V, and Vander Doelen. Chasing Lightning: Gambling in Canada. Toronto: United Church Publishing House, 1999.

McTaggart, Dave, Pastor. Telephone Interview. 6 Nov. 2003.

National Council of Welfare. "Gambling: A Multi-Billion Dollar Industry." Minister of Supply and Services Canada 1996. 21 Oct. 2003 <http://www.ccsa.ca>.

Nelson Study Bible, New King James Version. Nashville: Thomas Nelson, 1997.

"Richmond Antes Up On Slots." Richmond Review. 12 June 2003. 18 Oct. 2003 <http://www.yourlibrary.ca/community/richmondreview/archive/RR20030612/news.html>.

Rogers, Rex. Seducing America: Is Gambling a Good Bet? Michigan: Baker Books, 1997.

Rosecrance, John. Gambling without Guilt: The Legitimation of an American Pastime. Nevada: UP, 2001.

Watson, Tom, Jr. Don't Bet On It. California: Regal Books Publications, 1987.

Bill C-13:
A Failed Attempt for Morality in Stem Cell Research

Aaron Pogue

XII

Imagine the possibilities of medical advancement if one day we could control each and every move of a human cell. Understanding the complex events that take place in cells during their process of growth and development is the main concept, and focus, when considering embryonic stem (ES)[1] cell research. This knowledge would allow us to understand why abnormal cell specialisation occurs, and ultimately cure and prevent most, if not all, abnormalities that take place in humans today. This possibility of genetic engineering has arrived making ES cell research one of the largest and most controversial issues in today's society. One significant aspect of this major uproar is whether we as humans are treating all stages in human life with the utmost respect. This respect of human life is questioned when a human embryo must be destroyed to obtain these stem cells. Issues, such as this, have made it difficult for Christians to support this medical advancement, as well as Canadian law pertaining to ES cell research. This paper will focus on the potential benefits and downfalls of ES cell research. Furthermore, it will analyse Bill C-13, and how it lacks important regulations in the area of ES cell research that would keep traditional Christian ethics rooted in society. Though Bill C-13 regulates many areas of Assisted Human Reproduction that are satisfactory to Christian beliefs, it conversely allows the destruction of human embryos for research which contradicts many of the basic and most sacred beliefs of the Christian faith.

Despite ethical considerations, one needs to comprehend the benefits of ES cell research that are likely to come in the future. This revolutionary technology of transplantation of these stem cells have the potential to be the cure for many of today's diseases and disabilities, such as Parkinson's, Diabetes, Heart Disease, Cancer, Alzheimer's, Multiple Sclerosis, spinal cord injuries, birth defects, and the list goes on. In addition, ES cells could be the key for creating organs. If vital organs could be harvested from ES cells it would mean the end of waiting lists for donor recipients. Researchers have already successfully grown bladders in the laboratory and implanted them into dogs where they were then said to be "functional" (Ruse et al. 87). ES cell research has the potential to help 128.5 million people (Kilner et al. 82). This virtually affects every family and has the potential to better the lives of millions. To deny this therapy from so many individuals seems unreasonable suggesting the deprivation of a healthy and disease free life. After considering these miraculous capabilities it becomes easier to comprehend how society might believe ES cell research is the answer to all their problems thus we should grab a hold of this opportunity and continue ES cell research. However, the ethical concerns have been the underlining reasons for such a long delay in advancement.

These ethical concerns begin with the question of where the ES cells come from, which is the underlining source of the issue. Embryonic stem cells, as the name states, come directly from human embryos. Unfortunately, retrieving these cells from human embryos involves the termination of the embryo. The ethical question arises: Is this embryo considered "a life" at that particular stage of termination? This is the question that has been lingering since the ES cell topic began. For the time being, we know that the embryo is a potential life, just as everyone originated from this stage in his or her development. With this type of perspective, the destruction of an embryo has the same attributes as murder. Can we justify killing potential life for the sole purpose of fixing our imperfections or making our life more enjoyable? One researcher stated, "It is a fact that research is going on, on embryos in this country, and has been explicitly permitted since 1987" (qtd. in Bueckert A7). Canadian Government, started to believe that regulations on ES cell research should be implemented due to the complexity and controversial aspects of this issue.

Over the years, technology in ES cell research has rapidly evolved into reality and become more applicable to human life. As a result, regulating these medical advances and upholding the respect for human life has become increasingly hard for government. Recently, many countries have been making a stand on how they will approach ES cell research. The USA, for example, has banned research on any stem cell lines created after August 9, 2001 (Moran 41). Canada has also been working towards a solution. In 1989the Canadian federal government established the Royal Commission on New Reproductive Technologies. The purpose of this commission was to observe any activities involved in Assisted Human Reproduction (AHR).[2] Their goal was to define and record any regulations that were needed in the area of AHR. In 1993 the Royal Commission created a report called "Proceed with Care" that stressed appropriate regulations in the hope of protecting the interests of all Canadians. This report included 293 recommendations requiring action by the federal government in the area of AHR. The areas of interest included human cloning and the commercialisation of surrogate mothers. In 1995 the Minister of Health put these recommendations on a voluntary moratorium (Health Minister "Bill C-13").

The federal government made giant steps in 1996 when the Advisory Committee on Reproductive and Genetic technologies was established. Soon after, Bill C-13 was established. This Bill was titled Human Reproductive and Genetic Technologies Act, and it would prohibit particular reproductive and genetic practices. Bill C-47was eventually thrown out after the parliament dissolved during 1997 federal election. This demolished all hope that the Canadian government would establish regulations for activities involved in AHR any time soon (Health Minister "Bill C-13...").

A few years later, after the discovery of stem cells in 1998 the Canadian Institute for Health Research (CIHR)[3] made another promising step for the establishment of regulations (Moran 41). On March 4, 2002 CIHR released guidelines that focused on the many areas of AHR. However, these guidelines would only apply to those researchers receiving government funding. The CIHR is currently preparing to distribute this government funding to the many ES cell researchers (Laghi A4). The established guidelines prohibit the creation of embryos solely for research purposes. Other guidelines include the prohibition on the cloning of embryos created during In Vitro Fertilisation (IVF)[4]. In addition, the guidelines stressed that no financial incentives are allowed when donating or creating reproductive material along with required written consent from the donors (Bryngelson et al.). Unfortunately, private organisations are exempt from these guidelines and have no restrictions with what they can do with their money.

The CIHR guidelines paved the way for Bill C-47, Assisted Human Reproduction Act. This Bill was previously known as Bill C-56 drafted under former Health Minister Alan Rock. He urged the House of Commons Standing Committee on Health to evaluate the Proposals for Legislation Governing Assisted Human Reproduction ("Right to Life" 1). After an evaluation by the Health Committee in December 2001 the legislation would be considered as "priority material." Many of the recommendations put forth by the committee would later make up the present Bill C-13 that was introduced to the House of Commons on March 9, 2002 by Anne McLellan, the present Health Minister. Bill C-13 was a collaboration of the Royal Commission's recommendations, the House of Commons Standing Committee on Health, and CIHR guidelines. On October 28, 2003 the House of Commons approved Bill C-13 with a vote of 149 to 109 (Health Minister "Bill C-13"). The final version of Bill C-13 prohibits some activities AHR while only controlling others.

Though the majority of Bill C-13 deals with ES cell research, other areas of interest are worth mentioning. The first is human cloning and how it will be prohibited in all circumstances without exceptions. This includes both reproductive and therapeutic cloning. Germ line alteration is also prohibited. This process involves tampering with the DNA present in human sperm, eggs or embryos. This would potentially eliminate targeted cell modification in the attempt that genetics may not be tampered with. In addition, sex selection is prohibited in all areas except for the preventing, diagnosing, or treating sex related diseases and disorders ("Bill C-13" clause 5).

Another area covered in detail is the commercialisation of surrogacy. This is considered an offence if potential surrogate mothers are offered money. This also includes advertising and any other form of arrangement. Furthermore, any female under twenty one is not allowed to be counselled in or be persuaded to become a surrogate mother (clause 6). Bill C-13 also prohibits the use of any human reproductive material, previously in a non-human, intended for creating a human life. This includes the transplantation of sperm, ovum, embryo or foetus of an animal into a human being. In addition, the transplantation of both chimeras[5] and hybrids[6] into human beings will be prohibited (clause 5). None of these regulations greatly affect ES stem research; however, these regulations show that Bill C-13 is thorough in all areas of AHR.

The following includes the prohibited aspects of the Bill that directly affect stem-cell research especially in the area of accessibility. The Bill will prohibit the creation of in vitro embryos solely for research purposes. Creating an embryo from the cell of another embryo or foetus with the intent of creating human life will also be prohibited. Furthermore, maintaining the embryo outside the female's body for more than fourteen days after its creation would be considered illegal (clause 5).

Financial incentives are also addressed in Bill C-13 regarding in vitro embryos. Under this law it would be illegal to buy, sell, or advertise in vitro embryos (clause 7). Clause eight covers the requirements for written consent of the donor of the in vitro embryo. This would prohibit the use of human reproductive material with the intentions of creating another embryo without first receiving donor's consent. This also prohibits the removal of any reproductive material from the deceased without written consent (clause 8). The Bill stresses that the donor's support is imperative and if the donor feels uncomfortable with their previous decision, they have the right to retract their original consent at anytime.

Bill C-13 offers many controlled activities that affect ES cell research. These activities must be carried out within the regulations and require a license. The manipulation or treatment of any human reproductive material with intentions of creating an embryo would be considered illegal without a license. The same applies for the creation of an in vitro embryo. A license is also required during the handling of in vitro embryos, including the importing and exporting of the embryos (clause 10).

One of the main objectives in Bill C-13 is to provide protection for the families using AHR technologies and also set applicable guidelines that establish ethical principles. With this in mind, an agency called the Assisted Human Reproduction Agency of Canada will be established upon the passing of the Bill. This agency consists of thirteen persons which includes a chairperson and the President of the Agency. The sole purpose of this agency is to regulate the Laws set forth by Bill C-13. This would include upholding the declaration of principles described in Clause two of the Bill. These principles consist mainly of the protection of the children's well being who were born under AHR circumstances, as well as the women who are most deeply impacted by these procedures. Other areas of the declaration stress the preservation of dignity, human individuality and diversity (clause 2). The duties of the agency would consist of issuing licenses to clinics and individuals who are involved in performing any AHR activities. The agency has the right to investigate these clinics or individuals to make sure every action is performed properly under the regulations set forth by Bill C-13. This means that they have the right to take up legal action which includes issuing fines, revoking licenses, as well as enforcing imprisonment (clause 21-27). Ultimately, this agency is the enforcer of Bill C-13 and will do whatever is needed to make sure every part of the Bill is upheld.

One might ask why there is a need for so many laws and regulations, as well an Agency restricting the use of embryos. Understanding the impact and possibilities that embryos have on stem cell research will make things more clear. This involves an understanding of the science behind stem cells.

With all things considered, scientific proof states that every living organism is made of cells. Sexual organisms, such as humans, withhold special types of cells (sperm and the ovum) that fuse together creating a zygote and then continue to divide, forming a more complex organism with every division (Ruse et al. 23). With every division the cells become more specialised, eventually becoming the different types of tissues and organs that are needed for a human to function properly. Stem cells are present in both the earlier stages (ES cells) and the later stages (Adult stem cells) of growth and development. The early stages include the human embryo. Obtaining these embryos is becoming an easier task with the legalisation of abortion and In Vitro Fertilisation (IVF). With every abortion there is the question of what to do with the unused embryo, or foetus. The same questions are asked when it comes to leftover embryos created from IVF, which is the process of creating an embryo outside the mother's womb in a dish for couples who are infertile and can't produce on their own. Within every fertility clinic there are numerous embryos that are conceived but not implanted in the mother. These embryos are commonly called "leftover" embryos and are normally frozen for future use (Antkowiak "Understanding"). Otherwise they are destroyed, donated to couples, or researched upon.

On the surface both ES cells and adult stem cells seem identical. For example, they both have the ability to self-replicate and eventually specialise into specific types of cells. They can both be isolated from other cells and remain non-specialised in a laboratory setting allowing scientists to research more efficiently. Both types of cells will undergo "homing," an attraction of the cells to the injured site of body. A third type of cell, called an embryonic germ cell (EG cell)[7], shares the same characteristics only differing in the area of origin. The foetus of an aborted child is the main source for EG cells ("Stem Cell Research: Part 4"). Though they all share the same purpose and have virtually the same potential, they carry significant differences between them.

ES cells are derived from the "inner cell mass," which makes up about thirty to thirty-four cells that develop into the baby's tissues and organs. To obtain these stem cells they must be extracted from the centre of the embryo in the first week of its life. This, in turn, will kill the embryo, which is where ethical questions arise (Antkowiak "Understanding..."). The advantage of obtaining them so early is that they are pluripotent, meaning they have yet to be specialised and they are easy to identify. In addition, they are the most abundant of the three different types of cells. EG cells share these same qualities only differing in two main areas. The first area, as mentioned earlier, is that they come from an aborted foetus. Secondly, they only double around seventy times where as ES cells double up to three hundred times. One distinct advantage of EG cells is that they pose no chance of forming tumours where ES cells do if they are transplanted in an undifferentiated state ("Stem Cell Research: Part 4"). Unfortunately, it is the diversity of these two types of cells that make them more intriguing to researchers than adult stem cells. It's important to note that to be useful; ES and EG cells must overcome many challenges. Scientists must learn to control these cells. This involves identifying them at every stage of development, making sure they don't over replicate in the body creating tumours, as

well as transforming these cells into the necessary cell types that would be beneficiary to society (Herold 58). This will involve an extensive amount of research which
would destroy many embryos in the process. Fortunately, for Canadian stem cell researchers, Bill C-13 has avoided these concerns and has allowed research to continue
on these embryos.

On the contrary, adult stem cells are considered to be mulitpotent,
meaning that they only have potential to evolve into a limited number of cell types.
Despite the clear disadvantages they do hold a few advantages over ES and EG cells.
First, adult stem cells aren't limited to the developing embryo, but they are present throughout the whole lifetime of the human being. This allows more time for
thorough research. Another advantage is that they would not be rejected by the body
or differentiate into the wrong tissue ("Problems and Promise"). This is because they
are already specialised and can be transplanted back into the same source of where
they came from. However, the downside to this particular advantage is when ES and
EG cells are transplanted into people with different genetics there is a high probability of immune rejection ("Stem Cell Research: Part 4"). The last and most important
advantage is that they do not require the destruction of an embryo.

After analysing both adult stem cells and ES cells it's safe to say that adult
stem cells are still considered the alternative option among most researchers. Researchers find it difficult to deny the fact that the human embryo is the best source of
stem cells (Ali and Wood). Despite the mere convenience of ES cells there is a promising future in adult stem cell research. One of the major breakthroughs in recent
years has been the discovery of stem cells found in the blood of the umbilical cord at
birth. There is said to be a segment of five minutes after the baby is born to retrieve
approximately four to six ounces of blood from the umbilical cord (Ruse et al. 75).
This blood contains stem cells that can be saved for that child in the future. When
this blood is transplanted into an individual it migrates towards the bone marrow ultimately overwhelming the diseased blood and replacing it with healthy blood. This
can potentially repair body tissue and muscle as well as a number of body dysfunc-
tions like nerve, heart, and brain cell damage. This was proven to be a success when
a young boy named Keone Penn was diagnosed with a genetic blood disease called

Sickle Cell Anaemia when he was only six months old. By the time he was fifteen the disease had become unbearable and he decided to take injections of umbilical cord blood, taken from another donor. After three weeks of periodical blood injections Keone's blood type had completely transformed from type O to type B. One year later, doctors declared that his sickle cells had disappeared and was completely cured (75-77). This took place without terminating an embryo.

Not only is there a promising future in umbilical cord stem cells but bone marrow stem cells have also shown promising results. One analyst claimed in an article that the "Ultimate Stem Cell" had been discovered under the extensive research of Catherine Verfaillie ("Ultimate Cell"). This "ultimate cell" has the ability to differentiate into every type of tissue in the body, much like ES cells. The article states that these stem cells are located in the bone marrow of adults and have the replicating characteristics of ES cells ("Ultimate cell"). These new findings, if proven true, mean that ES stem cell research would no longer be necessary.

Such alternative methods like umbilical cord stem cells and bone marrow stem cells make ES cell research hard to justify. These alternatives are why many "pro-lifers" don't understand why Bill C-13 is allowing ES cell research to continue. Some might even argue that ES cell research provokes other controversial procedures. Society looks for reasons to justify certain actions and ES cell research could be the excuse they are looking for. Theoretically, this could provoke more abortions as well as IVF procedures. One writer responded to this issue, "We rightfully fear that if such science and its resulting technology proceed this might encourage couples to fertilise ova for the purposes of sale or donation and that it might encourage abortions for harvesting EG cells" (Peters). Supporters of ES cell research are too transfixed with the apparent benefits and possibilities of ES cell research to actually notice the negative aspects it has on society. One supporter of Bill C-13 states, "We need a comprehensive regulatory scheme that respects and addresses the public unease about technological developments but is flexible enough to accommodate scientific progress and shifting social values" (Caulfield). Supporters of ES cell research have this same mindset, where they consider their own needs first with no respect towards the unborn; this is the case with many abortion and IVF scenarios.

Contributing to the medical field by donating their child's embryo to research is very intriguing to many young women. Louis M. Guenin, and ethical professor at Harvard University Medical school, suggests that donating embryos created by IVF procedures is both "justifiable" and "admirable" (qt. in Montaminy and Neal). Some individuals feel that ES cell research is justifiable because of the medical benefits that it has. Others feel that laws such as Bill C-13 are erasing the values and morals that they have worked so hard to build up. This is the case with many Christians today who feel overwhelmed with the uncertainty of the future in ES cell research.

When evaluating issues pertaining to ES cell research from a Christian perspective there are three underlying principles to consider. One non-supporter of ES cell research has clearly laid out these principles in the hope of sharing some perspective of the heart felt collision between Christianity and ES cell research. The principles evaluated consist of: the sanctity of human life, the beginning of human life, and a universal human sinfulness (Grant). A biblical understanding of these principles will prove ES cell research is not justifiable.

The sanctity of human life, the first principle, illustrates God's respect for all stages of human life. Genesis 1:27 states, "So God created man in his own im- age..." (NIV). We are God's children, a treasure that He values more than anything. It is explained in Colossians 1:16 that everything, including the heavens and the earth, was created by God for His pleasure and purpose, not for ours (NIV). Even when His children turn their backs on Him, He loves them anyway. God's love is unconditional and that resulted in the need for guidelines that protect life here on earth. These guidelines are included amongst the most sacred of laws, the Ten Com- mandments. Commandment six clearly states, "You shall not murder" (NIV Exodus 20:13). When considering ES cell research its important to note that all of the controversy lies on whether or not the human embryo is a life at the time of termina- tion. If the destruction of life were not an issue, there would be few, if any, ethical concerns relating to ES cell research.

The idea of an embryo being considered as a human leads to the second principle, the beginning of a human life. Many people hesitate with the idea of an embryo being alive, and therefore considered a human. The author of an article en-

Perspectives On Christianity, Society & The Law

titled, "When Does Life Begin?," raises the same question, asking, does life begin at conception, birth, or the third trimester? He answers by saying, "In the right to life movement it is axiomatic that life begins at conception." This also is confirmed with scientific evidence (Henderson). The idea of conception is that the sperm fertilises the egg. This would mean that in light of any perspective, including secularism, it would be considered murder to kill an embryo. The respect of unborn is stressed deeply in the Bible. Psalm 139:13-16 illustrates:

> For you created my inmost being; you knit me together in my mother's womb...My frame was not hidden from you when I was in my secret place. When I was woven together in the depths of the earth, your eyes saw my unformed body. All the days ordained for me were written in your book before one of them came to be. (NIV)

While society is worried whether or not life begins at conception, God had already established that He valued our lives before we were even thought of. This idea is expanded, "It's absurd to imagine that a few random chemical reactions kick the process off, without God, and then at some point after fertilisation, God steps in and starts 'knitting'" (Grant 2). Furthermore, the Bible continues to address the issue of respect for the unborn. If an unborn child is killed through the negligent action of another party then the penalty is "life for a life" (Exod. 21: 22-24). By these standards, anyone who takes the life of a human embryo should have their life taken from them as a result. Essentially, Bill C-13 is allowing us to take human life into our own hands, which is not our responsibility.

Lastly, we need to consider the issue of universal human sinfulness. This can be illustrated through the biblical story of Adam and Eve, the first sinners. Despite God's wishes Adam and Eve decided to eat the forbidden fruit only to find themselves in a world of shame and embarrassment (Grant 2). Romans 5:12 reads, "Therefore, just as sin entered the world through one man, and death through sin, and in his way death came to all men, because all have sinned" (NIV). We are all prone to rebel against the law. The passing of Bill C-13 would allow the destruction of these unwanted embryos. Does this make it justifiable since we are under the jurisdictions of the law? The Bible does not support this approach. Romans 3:8 reads, "Why not say—as we are being slanderously reported as saying and as some claim that we may say—'Let us do evil that good may result.' Their condemnation is deserved" (NIV). The wrongful acts that are a result of ES cell research cannot be justified by the benefits they carry. Furthermore, the Bible states, "Cursed is the man who accepts a bribe to kill an innocent person" (Deut. 27: 25). Here, the "innocent person" is the human embryo. It's unfortunate that people are so driven by financial incentives, or fame, that they overlook their sinful actions (Grant). From this perspective, benefiting ourselves through the sacrifice of a human embryo is unethical.

Bill C-13 is definitely a step in the right direction in regulating AHR activities. Conversely, specifically in the area of ES cell research, Bill C-13 lacks necessary regulations that would eliminate any questionable ethical concerns. Embryonic stem cell research should be prohibited all together to retain morality among society. This, in turn, would only leave us with the question of what to do with these spare embryos created through IVF. Christians, as a body of Christ, need to make it known that God is the creator and "sustainor" of life. Nobody knows why God takes life un-expectedly, or why people are born with disabilities. However, it is very important to remember that everything is apart of God's ultimate plan, including infertility. Therefore, the church of Christ should discourage IVF because through it, destruction of life is inevitable and this only encourages ES cell research.

With that said, discouraging all of Bill C-13 would be wrong for Christians. The non-existence of Bill C-13 would mean that research in such areas as reproductive cloning, germ line alteration, and the commercialisation of surrogacy would be legal. Instead, Christians should encourage research in adult stem cells and petition for harsher restrictions on ES cell research.

This paper illustrates the many possibilities and promises of ES cell research as well as the consequences involved. A Christian perspective is provided, which focuses on three biblical principles that are applicable to ES cell research. I have also examined how Canadian law currently regulates ES cell research. This paper, demonstrates how ES cell research is not necessary because of alternative methods such as adult stem cells and the possibilities that they hold. If research is allowed to continue on ES cells it would be for the mere convenience of researchers and society. This would mean that society has chosen itself over other human life, reflecting the ultimate disregard for God's purpose and plan. In a world where social values are withering away rapidly, it is necessary that Christians speak their mind on issues such as ES cell research. It is apparent that Bill C-13 regulates many areas of Assisted Human Reproduction that are satisfactory to Christian beliefs. Unfortunately, Bill C-13 allows the destruction of human embryos for research, which is ultimately contradicting many of the most basic and sacred beliefs of the Christian faith.

Notes

1   Embryonic Stem Cells are commonly referred to as ES cells. They are cells that are taken straight from a fertilised human embryo.

2   Assisted Human Reproduction is also known as AHR.

3   Canadian Institute for Health and Research is commonly referred to as CIHR.

4   In Vitro Fertilisation is the Creation of Embryo outside the mother's womb in a dish and is commonly referred to as IVF.

5   Chimeras are embryos consisting of cells from more than one embryo.

6   Hybrids are a human ovum that has been fertilised by a non-human form.

7   Embryonic germ cells are commonly referred to as EG cells. They are cells that come directly from the aborted fetus.

WORKS CITED

Ali, Amina, and Owen Wood. "Stem Cells." CBC News. April 2001. 3 Nov. 2003 <http://www.cbc.ca/news/indepth/background/stemcells.html>.

Antkowiak, Laura. "Understanding Stem Cell Research." National Right To Life. 2001. 23 Oct. 2003 <http://www.nrlc.org/news/2001/NRL09/laura.html>.

Bryngelson, Dylan, et al. "Stem Cell Technology – Introduction." College of Biotechnology. 2002. 11 Nov. 2003 <http://biotechnology.usask.ca/btech%20400-2002/StemCellTechnology/index.html>.

Bueckert, Dennis. "Embryo Research 'a fact' in Canada." Globe and Mail. 3 Nov. 2003: A7.

Caulfield, Timothy. "Should Stem-Cell Research Be a Crime?" University of Alberta. 2002. 23 Oct. 2003 <http://www.expressnews.ualberta.ca/expressnews/articles/ideas.cfm?p_ID802&s=a>.

Grant, Sandy. "My 'Talking Point' on Embryonic Stem Cell Research." Kurrajong Anglican Church. 2002. 3 Nov 2003 <http://www.kac.asn.au/Other/Stem%20Cell.html>.

Henderson, Charles. "When Does Life Begin?" Christianity – General. 2003. 27 Oct. 2003 <http://christianity.about.com/cs/adultchristianity/a/lifebegins.htm>.

Herold, Eve. "Stem Cells and the Future of Medicine." USA Today Magazine. 131 (2003): 56-8.

Kilner, John F., et al., ed. Cutting-Edge Bioethics. Grand Rapids: William B. Eerdmanns Publishing Company, 2002.

Laghi, Brian. "Ottawa Fears Revolt on Embryo Legislation." Globe and Mail. 27 Aug. 2003: A1.

Life Application Study Bible. New International Version. Zondervan Publishing House, Grand Rapids. 1991.

Minister of Health. "Bill C-13: Assisted Human Reproduction Act." Library Parliament. 28 Oct. 2003. 3 Nov. 2003 <http://www.parl.gc.ca/common/Bills_ls.asp?lang=E&Parl=37&Ses=2&ls=C13&source=Bills_House_Government>.

Montminy, Judith, and Robert Neal. "Stem Cell Research, The Law, Ethics and Common Sense." International Science News. 2001. 22 Oct. 2003 <http://unisci.com/stories/20012/0601016.htm>.

Moran, Jim. "Embryonic Stem Cell Research." Humanist. 63.4 (2003): 41.

Peters, Ted. "Will Stem Cell Research Encourage an Increase in Embryo Destruction and Abortions?" Counterbalance Meta – Library. 2003. 24 Oct. 2003 <http://www.meta-library.net/stemtp/quest1-body.html>.

"Problems and Promise." Northwestern University. 2 April 2002. 27 Oct. 2003 <http://www.northwestern.edu/science-outreach/stemcell/stemcells.html>.

"Right to life." News Canada. Jan. 2003. 3 Nov. 2003 <http://www.rtl-toronto.org/news_archives/winter03.pdf>.

Ruse, Michael, et al, ed. The Stem Cell Controversy: Debating the Issues. Amherst: Prometheus Books, 2003.

"Stem Cell Research: Part 4." Hope. 5 July 2003. 23 Oct. 2003 <http://www.stanford.edu/group/hopes/rltdsci/stemcell/z4.html>.

Westphal, Sylvia P. "Ultimate Stem Cell Discovered." New Scientist. 23 Jan. 2002. 11 Nov. 2003 <http://www.newscientist.com/news/news.jsp?id=ns99991826>.

Thou Shall not Share?
A Christian Approach to Music Duplication in Canada

Jeremy Siegel

XIII

Since 1999, the major record companies have been crying "foul," saying that they are losing business due to rampant unauthorised downloading of music over the Internet. Record companies have brought successful lawsuits against file sharing entities such as Nastier in the past, yet music continues to be widely pirated, as constantly evolving software keeps the sharing masses one step ahead of the law ("Future"). Though overall music sales have decreased in recent years, some studies claim that file sharing is actually encouraging listeners to purchase music. Other studies claim the exact opposite.

In this paper, I will discuss the history of personal music duplication, arguments for the validity of music duplication via peer to peer file sharing, Canada's legal position on the issue, arguments against the legality of music sharing, and finally I will look at the issue from a Christian perspective.

My thesis is that in spite of the wide use of peer-to-peer file sharing networks, we as Christians should avoid downloading copyrighted music by those means with the intention of creating a personal collection of music.

Terms

For the benefit of the reader, I will describe and define some of the terms that I will use throughout the paper, given the technical aspect of the subject matter. First of all, when I discuss online "file sharing," I am referring to a method of duplicating a computer file, by which one computer makes a copy of a file that is taken from a source computer. The computers are linked together by a network or online program. In this paper, "file-sharing" will be used in reference to music files only. "Peer-to-peer" file sharing occurs when one computer shares, or "uploads," a file copy directly to the acquiring computer, which "downloads" the file. Early file sharing programs, such as Napster, displayed the audio files that existed on users' computers using Napster's servers; anyone wishing to download the files from each other could do so without charge. Users would simply enter keywords into Napster's search engine, and a list of songs would be generated. To obtain a song, the users simply had to click on the link, and the file could be downloaded from another user, by way of Napster's servers. More advanced versions of file sharing software, such as the Kazaa program, which can be obtained at Kazaa.com, connect users directly without using intermediary servers. In other words, users can engage in "peer-to-peer" file sharing, rather than downloading from one central source.

The History of Personal Music Duplication

The original method of duplicating music has existed for over two decades, and can still be implemented today. Cassette tapes can be used to copy music from a variety of media. Music played from an LP record, compact disc, another cassette tape, or even an MP3 player can be connected to a tape deck and recorded onto a cassette. Though this method of music duplication is no longer in vogue, it serves as a case study of how unauthorised duplication once affected the music industry. The record companies worried that the introduction of cassette technology would deal a tremendous blow to music sales, assuming that rampant copying of copyrighted work would ensue. However, the record companies survived, and would later emerge more profitable than ever.

Here are some possible reasons why cassette tape copying did not impact the record industry in a negative way. For one, a loss of audio fidelity, or quality, is experienced when recording onto a tape because it is analog in nature; in other words, it does not make an exact replication, unlike some digital methods. Secondly, the record industries were able to successfully introduce a new technology which effectively replaced the cassette tapes; namely, compact discs. Thirdly, tape copying, or "tape trading," as it was called, allowed some previously unknown musical acts to develop an underground fan base in a short amount of time. For example, heavy metal groups such as Metallica gained popularity in the early eighties because of tape trading, and that popularity would soon translate into millions of legitimate record sales (Alderman, 113). In this case, initial unauthorised duplication of music eventually helped Elektra Entertainment sell more music than it otherwise would have, because the duplication served as an unintentional marketing tool.

The next stage of personal music duplication began with the introduction of the CD-Burning drive in the nineties. Using a variety of possible software programs, the drive reads the compact disc and stores the information on the computer, typically as a Wav file. Then, the drive writes the information on to a blank recordable CD (or CD-R). This marked the first time that music could be copied digitally, preserving audio fidelity. In other words, you could make an exact copy of the musical work, which makes a "burned" CD a markedly more desirable object than a recorded cassette tape. It was in response to this advance in technology that the Copyright Board of Canada addressed the issue of personal music replication, by updating the Copyright Act of Canada. I will expound upon this action of the Board later in the paper, but it needs to be pointed out at this juncture that Part VIII of the Act was enacted before the widespread use of file sharing programs began.

A major development in technology that would eventually lead to unauthorised duplication on a grand scale was the introduction of the ISO-MPEG Audio Layer-3 computer file, or as it would later be known, the MP3 (27). The MP3 was originally invented in 1987 by German scientists working for the Fraunhofer research company. Their intention was to develop a method of converting large audio-video files by compressing them into a playable format, since the computers at the time could not handle large files. The audio portion of the algorithm became the MP3. Since MP3s are much smaller audio files than Wav files, MP3s became the audio file of choice to download and upload on the Internet. Seven years after the MP3 was invented, Real Network's Real Player and Gnutella's Winamp helped to change the way people perceived their computer. A computer could now be an all-purpose music station.

The first time that music was posted on the Internet, and made available for public access, was in 1993 by the Internet Underground Music Archive, or IUMA. IUMA used MP2 technology, the predecessor to MP3, in a day when home use of the Internet was rare. Bands without record contracts would send in samples of their music to IUMA, to be made available to the public as a way of promoting the band. The next phase in the evolution of online file sharing saw individuals distributing copyrighted music over their own personal hobby websites. Oftentimes, it would be university students, who had access to a school's wide bandwidth, who would post some of their favourite songs onto their own music sites, and run them off of their own computer. One figure of importance at this stage was David Weekly, whose MP3 Audio Consortium site, was at one point occupying eighty percent of Stanford's broadband in 1997 (29). This got the attention of not only the school administration, but also Geffen Records, a key record label within the Universal Music Group, and a subsidiary of Vivendi Universal, who had the site shut down.

The most important innovation in the distribution of MP3s was Napster, which was launched in June 1999. The program allowed users to duplicate and share their songs with each other by linking users' computers together over the Internet. Shawn Fanning's creation became immensely popular, and allowed for mass pirating of copyrighted music. Napster was a direct challenge to the essence of copyright law. Though Napster eventually landed in legal trouble in the US, and was forced to shut down, it opened the floodgates for similar programs to take its place and assist the file sharing public to acquire music for free. "Shareware" programs such as Audiogalaxy (audiogalaxy.com), Morpheus (morpheussoftware.net), and Kazaa soon followed; and while recent lawsuits are threatening the existence of Kazaa, a new program called Bit Torrent (bitconjurer.org), waits in the wings. In other words, there will always be a way to download music for free on the Internet. Laws can be put into place to curtail the copyright infringement, but realistically, enforceability of these laws is nearly impossible. The best the record companies can hope to do is make an example of a handful of file sharers by taking them to court, and in the process, hope that they scare the masses from further sharing. However we cannot, in good conscience, dismiss the law as meaningless. So, in an effort to justify music file sharing, many are arguing for its legality.

Perspectives On Christianity, Society & The Law

Much of the file sharing public sees the Recording Industry Association of America (RIAA) as a cartel. Although it appears that there are multitudes of competing record labels, in actuality there are only a handful of media companies, such as Sony BMG, who control the industry through their various subsidiary record labels. Uniform pricing, identical methods of distribution, and similar product formats serve as rationale for this outlook on the RIAA. In addition, the record companies have not met the demands of the market for MP3s. During the Internet's development stage, the music industry did not participate in adapting to the changing environment; rather, they seemed content to rely on the profitability of compact discs for as long as they could. That lack of foresight has backfired, as the online community has created their own methods of online music distribution, effectively beating the record companies to the punch. File sharers often justify their actions by sighting the industry for its inflexibility in regards to media format. In an attempt to remedy this situation, there are now sites, such as Apple Computer's iTunes, where copyrighted MP3s can be legally purchased. But, as of yet, these sites don't offer as wide a selection of music as the file sharing community can offer. Others justify file sharing by arguing that the music is priced unreasonably high. Over the last few years, CD price increases have far exceeded the normal inflation rate. Recently, in an attempt to win back the hearts of the public, Universal Music Group announced that it would implement a thirty percent price cut on CDs, bringing the cost down to about thirteen dollars (US) per compact disc ("Universal Cuts," CNN). Universal's CDs had previously cost approximately eighteen dollars (US). Some enthusiasts believe that file sharing will not have any real impact on the music industry. They feel that the record companies will survive; just as they did, after the introduction of the cassette tape.

Another aspect of the argument for the legality of peer-to-peer file sharing has to do with the sampling of music. By engaging in peer-to-peer sharing, a listener could potentially be exposed to new music, and new artists that they would not have learned about otherwise. This may actually encourage the listener to purchase the artist's music. In fact, a study carried out by Jupiter Research in 2001 says that thirty-four percent of file sharers who have had at least six months of file sharing experience, are now spending more money on music than they did before they began to download music (Borland). This study directly challenges record company claims that file sharing has been the reason for a drop in music sales.

Some recording artists see peer-to-peer file sharing as an ideal way to sample music. Courtney Love has said that she is happy to let anyone sample her work and decide if it is something that they want to make a part of their lives, because music is, after all a "service" (Alderman, 125). Arguing for the legality of file sharing on the grounds of sampling does seem reasonable, but the problem lies in defining the difference between "sampling," and "consuming." In other words, at what point in the file sharing process does sampling end and consumption begin? For some people, sampling becomes consumption once they have recorded the downloaded music onto to a CD. On the other hand, others now use MP3s as their media of choice when listening to music.

File sharing might also encourage the purchasing of music by acting as a promotional tool for bands. On sites such as MP3.com or Cornerband.com, unsigned bands can post MP3s for anyone to download for free. They hope that through file sharing, they will be able to develop a fan base just as cassette tape trading did for some bands in the past. Ironically, the aforementioned Metallica, whose fan base was developed due in large part to the early form of "sharing," was the first band to directly challenge Napster, and Internet file sharing in general. Other artists, such as Moby, are on the other side of the spectrum in regards to file sharing. It seems that the majority of artists fit somewhere in between the two opposing views, with only a few vehemently in opposition to it (Strauss). They want their music to be accessible to today's changing market, but at what cost? Veteran rapper Ice-T expressed this mixed outlook on file sharing: "There's a point where you cross the line and you are robbing people who are counting on this stuff for their life savings...It's very touchy. Just put it out there for free? Food should be free then right?...But when your record is on the radio it's free. It's really hard to break it down the middle (125)."

In 1997 the Copyright Board of Canada made an important amendment to the Copyright Act, as Part VIII, entitled 'Private Copying' was added. It became law in March 1998. For all intents and purposes, it makes CD-Burning legal in Canada. The board found that it is not a violation of copyright to reproduce all or any substantial part of:

(a) a musical work embodied in a sound recording,

(b) a performer's performance of a musical work embodied in a sound recording, or

(c) a sound recording in which a musical work, or a performer's performance of a musical work, is embodied onto an audio recording medium for the private use of the person who makes the copy does not constitute an infringement of the copyright in the musical work, the performer's performance or the sound recording.

(Copyright Board of Canada Part VIII section eighty),

provided that someone does not act with the intention of,

(a) selling or renting out, or by way of trade exposing or offering for sale or rental;

(b) distributing, whether or not for the purpose of trade;

(c) communicating to the public by telecommunication; or

(d) performing, or causing to be performed, in public" the media in question. (Section eighty limitations)

In order to give compensation to the artists and record companies, a levy was put on blank media used in the copying process. The most important forms of blank media, as it relates to our topic, are the CD-R, and CD-RW. A levy of ¢5.2 per unit is charged on each CD-R and CD-RW (Copyright Board's Decision: Private Copying.) How does this affect consumers? When people purchase CD-Rs, it costs them between $3.50 and $10.00 per spindle more than what they would have paid previously before the levy, depending on the amount of CD-Rs purchased.

The implications of Part VIII of the Copyright Act on current situations in music copying are debatable. Peer-to-peer users see Section Eighty of the Act as the green light to engage in as much file sharing as they like. This fact makes the enforcement of law in other countries more difficult to impose. For example, the Recording Industry Association of America is fighting a war in the courts to make illegal peer-to-peer sharing more enforceable in the U.S., but peer-to-peer networks go beyond national borders. If Canadian file sharers feel that they are free from prosecution, they will continue to share with confidence, and will supply American sharers with files that would be considered "illegal" in the U.S. Ironically; it was because of Canadian record company lobbyists that the blank media levy was enacted in the first place. Today, their American parent record companies are regretting that the Copyright Board of Canada acted as it did. Canada's legal position on the issue is now a primary argument for the American sharers, who support the legality of file sharing. In principle, the idea of an imposed levy on blank media seems like the ideal solution to sharing enthusiasts. But in actuality, the levy was not intended to be a remedy for file sharing.

Arguments against the legality of music duplication via peer to peer file sharing

A major argument against peer-to-peer file sharing in Canada is that there has been, in my opinion, a gross misinterpretation of what Section VIII of the Copyright Act is actually saying. We must remember that Section VIII was originally written in 1997, a full year before the peer-to-peer initiator, Napster, was launched. The issue that Part VIII is truly addressing is private CD-burning, not mass file sharing. In the limitations section of Section Eighty of the Act, we learn that it is indeed an illegal copyright infringement when a party is "distributing, whether or not for the purpose of trade; or communicating to the public by telecommunication," copyrighted media (Part VIII, Section Eighty, limitations). When someone shares a music file, this is exactly what they are doing; they are implicitly distributing the file to the public. If anyone in the public forum wants a given music file, the person from whom they are receiving the files has made the file available to be distributed.

In a modern peer-to-peer program, such as Kazaa, party A, who wishes to obtain a file, must download it from party B. This is accomplished by party A using the Kazaa program to search the computers of other users so that he can download the desired file. In order for A to see the files that B is sharing, B must voluntarily have those files placed in his 'shared folder.' B knows that by keeping files in his shared folder, other Kazaa users can and will obtain copies of those files. When A decides to download a file from B; the file is simultaneously uploaded from B's computer, and subsequently downloaded onto A's computer. A's computer will automatically put the newly obtained file into A's "shared folder" for others to access. This is how a file is transferred.

In my estimation, party B has broken Canadian law because he or she has made his copy of the file available for public distribution. However, party A has not infringed upon copyright law because in Section 80 of the Act, he has a right to engage in the "reproducing of all or any substantial part of a musical work embodied in a sound recording" (Part VIII Section 80). In other words, downloading music files in Canada is legal, provided that you then do not distribute your copy to the public, because only private copying is protected under the Act. So party A would simply need to remove the file from his shared folder once the download has been completed in order to make his newly acquired file legitimate.

Although it is technically legal to download music via peer-to-peer methods in Canada, in order for someone to download a file, someone else must upload the file in order for a download to take place. The implication of this fact is that every time a peer-to-peer download occurs in Canada, a law is being broken because someone is uploading a file, i.e. distributing it to the public. Therefore, the question of downloading is not a legal one, it is an ethical one.

The root of the problem is that the Copyright Board of Canada did not foresee the concept of peer-to-peer file sharing. Unfortunately, laws that were enacted to protect the musicians and record companies at one time are currently being used as an excuse for mass file sharing. I feel that the Board's ruling was very appropriate in its original context, as it addressed music duplication in the form of private CD-burning, right as CD-burners were becoming more commonplace. It will be interesting to see if further amendments will be made by the Board to specifically address peer-to-peer file sharing, so as to dispel the confusion surrounding the legality of the issue.

A CHRISTIAN PERSPECTIVE

In Romans chapter thirteen, the Apostle Paul informs the church in Rome that God has placed the authority figures over them, and they were to obey the law of the land. In the case of Canadian Law and file sharing, the law is quite murky. It is possible to draw out various conclusions depending on which side of the debate you favour. Nevertheless, I believe that Part VIII of the Copyright Act does not make file sharing legal because in the peer-to-peer process, copyrighted files are being made available to public distribution. Therefore, knowingly uploading copyrighted music is a violation of the law of the land.

We also should consider showing due respect for the rights and property of the musicians themselves. It is easy to depersonalise file sharing, but in reality, we are dealing with someone else's property. The possible wealth or fame a given musician is immaterial; we can not in good conscience justify unethical activity on the grounds of someone's status in society.

The debate over the use of peer-to-peer file sharing comes down to a question of intent. For what purpose are you downloading music? Knowing that the odds of facing any form of prosecution are minimal at best, the issue becomes one of personal conscience. I believe that downloading for the purpose of sampling a given artist or song is a just motivation. I also feel that if you already own the music in another form, downloading an MP3 version is completely acceptable. For example, if you owned a LP vinyl record of a certain band, you might want to be able to listen to it in MP3 form as well. However, if you download a copyrighted song with the intention of adding it your music collection, I argue that you have infringed upon copyright law. There is a fine line between sampling and collecting music over the Internet, and this is precisely the situation in which the individual must make a personal ethical decision, based on good conscience.

In conclusion, I have discussed the history of personal music duplication, examined arguments for the legality of music duplication via peer-to-peer file sharing, shown Canada's legal position on the issue, and have offered some arguments against the legality of music duplication from both a legal and Christian perspective. The peer-to-peer file sharing phenomenon is an example of what happens when the law seems to disagree with the masses. As US Senator Norm Coleman puts it; "law, technology and ethics are not in sync right now" (Harmon 1). In Canada, this imbalance is even more evident than in the US, since the law pertaining to private music copying was enacted before peer-to-peer networks came into being. In spite of this ethical uncertainty, I believe that as Christians, we should refrain from downloading copyrighted music, with the intention of adding that music to our personal collection.

WORKS CITED

Alderman, John. Sonic Boom: Napster, MP3, and the New Pioneers of Music. Cambridge: Perseus, 2001.

Associated Press. "File-Sharing Software Company Sues Record Industry." Fox News Online. 24 Sept. 2003. 24. Sept. 2003 <http://www.foxnews.com/ story/0,2933,982100,00.html>.

Associated Press. "Future of on-line file-sharing debated." The Globe and Mail. 19 Sept. 2003. 25 Sept. 2003 <http://www.globetechnolgy.com/servlet/ story/RTGAM.20030910.wxmecdcd10/BNStory/Technology/>.

Associated Press. "Universal cuts CD prices." CNN Money. 4 Sept. 2003. 24 Jan. 2004 <http://money.cnn.com/2003/09/04/news/international/universal_ cds/>.

Black, Jane. "Will Cable Unplug the File Swappers?" Business Week Online. 12 June 2002. 24 Sept. 2003 <http://www.businessweek.com/technology/con tent/ jun2002/tc20020612_1108.htm>.

Blackwell, Richard. "Murky laws make piracy suits less likely in Canada than US." The Globe and Mail. 10 Sept. 2003. 25 Sept. 2003 <http://www.globetechnol-ogy.com/ servlet/story/RTGAM.20030910.wxmecdcd10/BNStory/Technol-ogy/>.

Borland, John. "Apple unveils music store." CNET News.com. 28 April 2003. 24 Jan. 2004 <http://news.com.com/2100-1027-998590.html>.

Borland, John. "Study: File sharing boosts music sales." CNET News.com. 3 May 2002. 24 Sept. 2003 <http://news.com.com/2100-1023-898813.html>.

Canada. Copyright Board. Annual Report 2001-2002.

Canada. Economic Council of Canada. Report on Intellectual and Industrial Property. Ottawa: Crown, 1971.

Canadian Intellectual Property Office. "A Guide to Copyrights: Copyright Protection." 31 Dec. 2002. 22 Sept. 2003 <http://strategis.ic.gc.ca/sc_ mrksv/cipo/cp/copy_gd_protect-e.html>.

Communication Canada. "Copyright on the Internet." Canadian Government Publishing. 4 July 2002. 21 Sept. 2003
<http://cgp-egp.gc.ca/copyright/ internet-e.html>.

Copyright Board of Canada. "Copyright Board's Decision, Private Copying 1999-2000." 17 Dec. 1999. 21 Sept. 2003
<http://www.cbcda.gc.ca/news/c1999 2000fs-e.html>.

Currie, Jay. "Blame Canada." Tech Central Station. 18 Aug. 2003. 23 Sept. 2003
<http://techcentralstation.com/081803C.html>.

Department of Justice Canada. "Copyright Act." 1997
<http://laws.justice.gc.ca/en/C-42/index.html>.

Harmon, Amy. "Music File Sharers Keep Sharing," New York Times Online. 19
Sept. 2003. 24 Sept. 2003 <http://www.nytimes.com/2003/09/19/technology/
19TUNE.html?ex+1064548800&en+8aad3c48c94e7fa9&ei+5062>.

Lessig, Lawrence. The Future of Ideas: The Fate of the Commons in a Connected
World. New York: Random House, 2001.

Metz, Cade. "The Changing Face of Online Music." PC Magazine Online. 24 Sept.
2003. 24 Sept. 2003 <www.pcmag.com/article2/0,419,1298685,00. asp>.

Nelson, Chris. "Upstart Labels See File Sharing as Ally, Not Foe." New York Times
Online. 22 Sept.2003. 24 Sept. 2003 <http://www.nytimes.com/ 2003/09/22/
business/media/22INDY.html?ffa+y>.

Rodgers, Michael. "Why the Record Companies Have to Play Hardball." Newsweek. (By way of MSNBC News Online.) 23 Sept. 2003. 23 Sept. 2003
<http://www.msnbc.com/news/970644.asp>.

Sanderson, Paul. Musicians and the Law in Canada. Toronto: Carswell, 1985.

Strauss, Neil. "File-Sharing battle leaves musicians caught in the middle." NY
Times. 14 Sept. 2003. 24 Jan. 2004 <http://www.nytimes.com/2003/09/
14/technology/14MUSI.html?ex =1378872000 &en=2832300 e467debbe &ei=5
007&partner=USERLAND>.

White, Mervin. F. "Copyright Law in Canada." Carter & Associates, 1997. 19 Sept. 2003 <http://www.carters.ca/copyrigt/Copyright.html>.

Beyond Rendering to Caesar:
A Justification of Civil Disobedience in a Christian Context

Braden Spotts

XIV

Throughout the course of history the issue of civil disobedience has proven to be complicated for both practical and philosophical reasons. Many individuals, both wise and foolish, have often felt that certain laws are not in the best interest of themselves, groups they associate with, or even mankind as a whole. Merriam Webster's Dictionary defines civil disobedience as a "refusal to obey governmental demands or commands especially as a non-violent and usually collective means of forcing concessions from the government." This definition very accurately characterizes the process and motivations of the act on a basic level, but quite obviously disregards the more difficult and complex aspects of the issue. Further complications arise when religion is drawn into the picture, because the practice of any religion requires that a certain authority be granted to a deity held to be greater than any human (or, by connection, any human institution). If supreme authority is granted to a deity, then what sort of credibility, if any, should be given to the laws of the land put in place by a human ruler? This issue is partly dealt with in Christianity by several passages in both the New and Old Testament of the Bible, but as with many other issues dealt with by the Bible there often seems to be conflicting evidence that requires careful interpretation to be understood correctly. Some of the more relevant biblical writings on the subject include Daniel in the Old Testament, as well as Paul (ROM.), Luke (Acts), Peter (1 Peter), and the life and teachings of Jesus in the Gospels. Also, there are a number of non-biblical writers, whether writing from a Christian perspective or not, who have made significant contributions to the case for civil disobedience. Henry

David Thoreau, John Rawls, St. Augustine, and Rev. Martin Luther King, Jr. are each owed a great deal of credibility on the subject (even within a purely Christian context) because of the significance of their actions and the lasting value of their insights on the nature of justice. Most importantly, the current reality in a society such as the United States or Canada where the laws and policies are becoming further separated from the values of any religious system is that citizens are often faced with a choice as to whom they should render their utmost allegiance. On the one hand, part of a Christian's biblical mandate is to respect instituted authority and uphold the established laws of the land. But, on the other hand, biblical teachings also indicate that a separation between obedience of man's earthly authority and submission to God's sovereignty must be maintained (Redekop). My thesis is that as a result of this necessary separation Christians should be prepared to resist established laws that are contradictory to their collective beliefs in a manner consistent with biblical teachings so that the credibility and relevance of the Christian voice on political and social matters is protected.

In order to develop this thesis, first I will present the biblical arguments in favour of civil disobedience, along with the relevant scriptural support for each individual argument. Second, I will present important practical details that should be observed when civil disobedience is carried out, some of which are taken directly from scripture, while others are merely implied. Finally, I will present some modern examples of civil disobedience practiced in a Christian context, which should serve to tie each of the previously presented arguments together through demonstration.

Before developing the arguments in favour of my thesis, a few distinctions and definitions must be made in relation to the nuances of the topic, as well as clarifications as to which portions of the subject are relevant to this particular discussion. Primarily, there is the matter of direct and indirect disobedience. Indirect disobedience involves the practice of disobeying a law that is largely unrelated to the injustice in question with the intent of gaining the attention and sympathy of the public or the government (Redekop 8). An example of this would be blocking traffic with a demonstration to raise awareness of specific environmental concerns. The key assumption operating within this method is that the injustice is seen to be of such a nature that if only the greater community was aware of such an unjust policy it never would have existed in the first place. On the other hand, direct disobedience involves the breaking of a law in order to get that particular law changed, or to seek an exemption so that the conscience of the disobedient can be relieved of any guilt caused by perpetrating what in their mind would be an injustice (Rawls 365).

This raises the idea of the next distinction that must be made, which is between a civil disobedient and a conscientious objector. The goal of a conscientious objector is always to gain an exemption (Redekop 8). One example of this would be a nurse requesting to not participate in abortions during the course of employment based on personal moral beliefs. Since such a request does little to have an arguably immoral policy or practice changed she must be kept separate from a civil disobedient, whose goal is always change (Redekop 9). An example of this within the same issue is a pro-life activist who undertakes direct or indirect acts of disobedience with the aim of physically preventing abortions from occurring. The distinction can be further clarified by understanding conscientious objection as a private solution, and as a means of simply publicizing one's moral or religious convictions that they might be known, but not necessarily adopted (Rawls 380). The exemption sought in such a case is primarily for the benefit of the objector, whereas in the case of civil disobedience, the protest is meant to put a stop to an injustice regarded as morally wrong for all (Rawls 366). For the purposes of this essay, conscientious objection and its related terms are not as relevant as the issue of civil disobedience itself. Since most people would not contest the right of an individual to seek an exemption to a law on a singular basis, this particular subtopic will not constitute a significant part of the discussion beyond this point, although further distinctions will be raised regarding specific issues.

The final distinction to be made is between an individual whose acts are based upon Christian convictions, and the individual whose acts are simply based upon a secular yet well informed interpretation of the principles of justice, (Rawls refers to this second type of person as the "High Moral Character"). Civil disobedience is frequently rooted in Christian or otherwise religious beliefs and is an important part of the Christian way of life in a society that does not always recognize the sovereignty of God, but it need not be based on a Christian perspective. The concept of the "High Moral Character" is widely accepted under the pretense that some individuals, regardless of their belief about the existence or nature of a holy being, may wish to participate in the formation of public policy in a way that goes beyond the ballot box. Thoreau brings this to light when he writes in his famous essay "Resistance to Civil Government": "Cast your whole vote, not a strip of paper merely, but your whole influence" (235). So while the issue can clearly be supported from many perspectives with many different motivations, this discussion will primarily be concerned with the issues as they relate to the Christian perspective; although secular writers will be used at times to help foster a sense of acceptance and credibility within any reader not inclined to recognize the authority of the Bible alone.

There are two separate types of passages that will be presented in support of the case for civil disobedience as a viable part of a Christian's lifestyle. The first group consists of verses that do not require clarification, while the second group of verses will need to be looked at more in depth in order to be used in support of civil disobedience. Additionally, the first group of verses is intended to display specific biblical examples of civil disobedience so that patterns may be examined in order to help establish standards for a Christian who disobeys the law in a modern context. Another item of note is that the passages presented in the second group are often cited as evidence that the Bible does not support defiance of the law under any circumstances. The first two passages presented from the first group are both found in the Old Testament Book of Daniel:

> 3:15-18 – Now when you hear the sound of the horn, flute, zither, lyre, harp, pipes and all other kinds of music, if you are ready to fall down and worship the image I made, very good. But if you do not worship it, you will be thrown into a blazing furnace. Then what god will be able to rescue you from my hand? Shadrach, Meshach and Abednego replied to the king, "O Nebuchadnezzar, we do not need to defend ourselves before you in this matter. If we are thrown into the blazing furnace, the god we serve is able to save us from it, and he will rescue us from your hand, O king. But even if he does not, we want you

to know, O king, that we will not serve your gods or worship
the image of gold that you have set up.

6:10 –Now when Daniel learned that the decree had been published, he went home to his upstairs room where the windows
opened toward Jerusalem. Three times a day he got down on
his knees and prayed, giving thanks to his God, just as he had
done before.

There are many other verses in the Old Testament that depict disobedience of authority, but these particular passages are especially noteworthy because of
the parallel elements of the two stories which serve as a good introduction to three
important ideas on civil disobedience within a Christian context. In neither case is
the defiance of the established law secretive, nor is it violent in nature. Also, in both
cases the punishment is readily accepted as a better alternative to ignoring their own
personal concepts of justice. Each of these items will be addressed more in depth later.

The next passage presented is found in the second part of Luke's letter to
Theophilus, in Acts 5:27-30. The text reads:

Having brought the apostles, they made them appear before
the Sanhedrin to be questioned by the high priest. 'We gave
you strict orders not to teach in this name,' he said. 'Yet you
have filled Jerusalem with your teaching and are determined to
make us guilty of this man's blood.' Peter and the other apostles
replied, 'We must obey God rather than men! The God of our
fathers raised Jesus from the dead—whom you had killed by
hanging him on a tree.'

Testifying to what they had seen of Jesus was in direct defiance of orders from
the Sanhedrin, but such defiance was a holy obligation in light of what Jesus had
required of them just before his ascension when he told them to "go and preach
the good news to all of creation."[1] In light of this, Peter's statement serves as a clear
reminder that authority need not be obeyed in a circumstance where doing so would
prevent them from spreading the gospel.

Romans 13:1-2 is the first passage from the second group, and is actually one of the primary passages used as a biblical argument against civil disobedience. But upon more careful examination it becomes apparent that the intent of the writer was not to condemn disobedience of the law. The verse reads as follows:

Everyone must submit himself to the governing authorities, for there is no authority except that which God has established. The authorities that exist have been established by God. Consequently, he who rebels against the authority is rebelling against what God has instituted, and those who do so will bring judgment on themselves. With these two verses Paul likely meant to reinforce the idea that the law is necessary even when imposed by pagans because it provides a necessary structure to society. The evidence behind this lies at least partially in Paul's word use. The Greek word "hypotassomai" means "to obey" or "to be subject to," indicating that Paul's intent was not to encourage Christians to obey every law in every situation, but to encourage them to submit themselves to the authorities. This idea further reinforces the lessons learned from the lion's den and the fiery furnace in Daniel; the law may be disobeyed but punishment for illegal deeds must be readily accepted. Had Paul meant to suggest that all laws must be obeyed at all times either of the Greek verbs hypokouo or peiphomai would have better served his purposes (Redekop 12). It seems that Paul's main intent, in view of the greater context of the book, was to encourage the people of the early church in Rome to view obedience to the state as part of their overall righteousness. If the members of the early church had treated the pagan laws as a separate institution to which no allegiance was owed, then their credibility within that society, and therefore their ability to spread the gospel, would be seriously restricted.

The next verse to be clarified is 1 Peter 2:13-15, which reads:

Submit yourselves for the Lords sake to every authority instituted among men: whether to the king as the supreme authority, or to governors, who are sent by him to punish those who do wrong and commend those who do right.

Again this is a verse that is often cited as evidence that the Bible does not support civil disobedience, yet in light of what was learned by investigating the intent behind the passage in Romans, discerning the true intent of this verse is not difficult by any means. Again, this verse reinforces the idea that the institution of government is to be respected. The mention of governors sent by the king to "punish those who do wrong and commend those who do right" further reinforces the established idea that acceptance of punishment for disobedience of the law is mandatory. As in Romans, submission to authority is once again placed amidst encouragement to the early Christians to live righteously amongst the pagans so that God might be glorified by their actions, instead of slandered by their lawlessness. In a similar spirit, Matthew 5:14 says to "let your light shine before men, that they might see your good works, and glorify your father which is in heaven" (Tactics).

These passages clearly support the idea that the instituted government should be respected by Christians, yet at the same time each one carefully leaves room for disobedience of laws that do not align with the commandments of God. Simultaneously, these verses (as well as some others that were not discussed) have established a few common precepts that should be considered by those who feel that disobedience of the law is their only remaining opportunity to avoid becoming an agent of injustice to another person. First, civil disobedience should not ordinarily be done in a secretive fashion. In Daniel, Shadrach, Meshach and Abednego openly told the king they would not serve his gods nor would they bow down and worship any god except their own. So rather than pretend to worship the golden image or find some way to avoid the confrontation, the three stood up and defied the king even though they might have been killed for their defiance. In the second passage, Daniel continued to pray just as he had before King Darius had issued the decree, three times a day with the windows open, even though he knew that the king's administrators would be waiting for him to disobey the decree. Likewise, Peter's forthright statement to the Sanhedrin as to whom he must obey in the Book of Acts serves as yet another example of open disobedience of authority. Beyond these examples there still may be some circumstances where covert action is more desirable than blatant defiance. In such a circumstance John Rawls suggests that a separate term such as conscientious evasion be used, since such an action would be fundamentally different (364). Rawls goes on to say that civil disobedience should be seen as a form of public address (366), comparable to a speech or message, and as being "the final appeal of one's case" (376). This concept clearly fits with the already established definition of the term as well as the biblical concept of civil disobedience that has been put forth.

Second, civil disobedience is by its very nature non-violent. To infringe upon the rights of another in the act of expressing one's case against a particular injustice would certainly weaken the message. In the three cases of biblical disobedience that are presented, each is dealt with in a similar fashion: clear and calculated use of words and actions which are contrary to the instructions of the authority. This is done in a way that establishes a purpose for the disobedience, as well as expresses a rational argument about the unjust nature of the law or request (Redekop). The story of Daniel in the lion's den may not seem to fit with this on a superficial level since there is no specific statement made to the authority figure, but the book very clearly describes the king's overwhelming amount of sympathy toward Daniel, indicating that the king did not need to hear a man as righteous as Daniel speak to realize the injustice of the situation.

The third common element of the stories is that the punishment was readily accepted. In Daniel, both the lion's den and the blazing furnace were readily acknowledged as a better alternative to worshiping a something other than the one true God. The passage in Acts as presented states no specific acceptance of punishment, but later in verse 5:41 it says that the Apostles celebrated after their confrontation with the Sanhedrin because they had been counted worthy of suffering in the name of the Lord. Persecution was a major issue in the early church as the established governments and religious leaders of the day saw the teachings and authority of Jesus as a direct threat to their own power. Many early Christians spent time in jail or were martyred as punishment for spreading the gospel (Blank). Ironically, a significant portion of what would later become the New Testament was written by the apostles during their time spent in prison. Another relevant fact is that all twelve of the apostles were eventually martyred for the sake of Christ, with the possible exception of John (Blank).[2] In light of this evidence, it would be safe to assume that the Apostles would have accepted any real punishment meted out in Acts 5 if any had been given, since such persecution would have been endured for the sake of Christ.

The above passages clearly indicate that the acceptance of punishment is the key factor for justification of the practice of Christian disobedience for several reasons. As mentioned previously, the acceptance of punishment is what maintains the biblical mandate of respecting the institution of government. Civil disobedience should not be associated with criminal behaviour where the perpetrator seeks to evade the law, but rather should be seen as an entirely different category of illegal activity. Additionally, the acceptance of punishment for an action that does not warrant such a harsh penalty will often do at least as much to gain public support as the disobedient act alone. Once again, this is related to Rawls' concept of civil disobedience as a form of public address. He indicates that the sympathy of the public is obtained because within a reasonably just society there will be a common sense of justice (which may not always be represented in the actual law of the land) that will weaken the society's capacity to defend an unjust position (387).

Beyond the concepts of how civil disobedience should be practiced in light of the biblical examples provided, there are several additional items that require consideration before civil disobedience from a Christian standpoint can be effective. Most of these characteristics are not directly stated by the biblical examples of civil disobedience, but each are mutually agreed upon by Christians as important not only for the protection of the individual, but also for the protection of the interests of the Christian community as well. In other words, the following precepts as to what constitutes effective tactics have been developed by men in light of rational decision-making as well as biblical teachings, as opposed to those in the previous group, which are purely based on biblical example. First, an act of civil disobedience should presumably be conducted with the goal of benefiting the greater community (Redekop). The individual must not stand to gain from this action more than anyone else, although he or she may certainly be a member of the community that stands to benefit from the deed. If one were to be the primary benefactor of any results achieved by the resistance, the act would be better classified as conscientious objection.

Second, a precept that naturally follows is that if an action is to benefit the larger community such as a church or particular denomination, then any action undertaken should be done so in direct consultation with that group. There are actually numerous reasons for this particular requirement. Primarily, a singular conscience is frequently not nearly as rational or as informed as the collective conscience in reference to morality (or anything else for that matter) (Redekop). Although the collective conscience may be seen as too conservative at times, it is important to remember that the proper role for the singular voice is to motivate the church or community to collective action, not to take the entire matter into his or her own hands (Redekop). A singular objector is often unable to be sufficiently heard within the larger realm of society. This is often why individuals are forced to seek an exemption through the means of conscientious objection, since they cannot hope to arouse the necessary attention to effect social change on a large scale on their own. Those who would challenge this thought may be quick to point out that there have been many singular voices throughout history that have brought about change to unjust circumstances. A leading example of such a case would be Rosa Parks and her famous refusal to move to the back of the bus during the fight against segregation in the American south.[3] It may be easy to then suggest in light of this case that without her willingness to disobey on a singular basis the change brought about by her actions could not have occurred. This is a valid assertion, and it should be noted that this essay does not intend to suggest that what Parks did was wrong, or that there is no situation where singular action is appropriate. However the reality of the situation is that the subsequent mobilization of the Black community through the leadership of Rev. King, Jr. during the Montgomery bus boycotts is what made Parks' refusal to move to the back of the bus effective. Furthermore, it is important to remember that none of these precepts about civil disobedience in a Christian context are being presented as absolutes, but rather as guidelines on how civil disobedience ought to be practiced in order to bring the greatest benefit to the Christian community.

The third principle is derived from a subject briefly discussed earlier in relation to the biblical examples as well as the writings of Rawls, which is that a particular aim for the disobedient actions should be established on a public level

(366). If civil disobedience is to be viewed as a legitimate form of public address then those who use it must make every effort to ensure that the audience grasps the intentions of the act. This is especially important in cases of indirect disobedience where the laws that are broken are not directly related to the changes sought. This may include a tactic such as explaining the objective of the protest in a written format for the purpose of distribution, or ensuring that all participants are well informed about the goals of the action, and ready to discuss them with anyone at a moments notice. Not only does this give the onlookers a chance at gaining a deeper perception of the traffic jam that made them late for work, but more importantly it gives the media a chance to portray the event as accurately as possible. The media can be a powerful tool for the distribution of a message if the opportunity is properly managed, which serves as one more reason why secrecy in civil disobedience is rarely desirable. If the media is alerted beforehand about the location and nature of a protest, an accurate portrayal of the group as well as the message is far more likely to occur. These brief guidelines are meant to serve as an introduction to the most important considerations to be made regarding the use of resistance tactics, as well as a reminder that disobedient endeavours are not to be undertaken light-heartedly (Stevick 106).

There are many noteworthy examples of civil disobedience and conscientious objection that are taking place in the modern church. A prime example are the so-called "historic peace churches," such as the Mennonites and other Anabaptist denominations. Some of these denominations refuse to pay taxes that support military activity as well as repudiate military conscription orders. Some church members have chosen to break the law in these circumstances and have received jail sentences as a result (Redekop 32). This issue is relevant because it illustrates how a government may be influenced to change policies because of their perceived unjust nature. Imprisonment of a person for not paying taxes or refusing a government order would not ordinarily come into question, but in a circumstance where the person is clearly doing so with unselfish motives; can the punishment still be justified? As a response to this question, Canada introduced the Conscience Canada Peace Tax Fund, as well as what are known as Conscientious Objector Camps (Redekop). On a basic level, each one is a means of allowing a citizen who holds pacifistic beliefs to maintain his obligation to pay taxes or be conscripted into the war effort without becoming an agent of injustice to any other fellow human. In this case has the government created a mutually beneficial situation? Or rather has it simply avoided the issue by taking would be disobedients who might expose injustice, and turned them into mere objectors who will instead be content with an illusion of justice? This idea in turn raises questions concerning the potential inadequacy of the position of a conscientious objector. Conscientious objection has been established as a practice similar to an expression of personal beliefs to others, not as a means of arousing the corporate conscience and calling others to action. On the other hand, if resistance is taken too far and others are harmed (regardless of any injustice caused by compliance to a supposedly unjust law), is this not worse than doing nothing at all? The importance of these questions becomes clear in the issues surrounding the pro-life movement during the last fifty years. Nurses and hospital employees have been known to request that they not take part in abortion operations. On the opposite end of the spectrum within the pro-life community are those who have been committing acts of violence on abortion doctors and abortion clinics alike since the seventies (Robinson). One side of the spectrum can be criticized for not doing enough, while the opposite side is clearly doing far too much. These opposite poles within the same stream of thought are prime reasons why this essay has focused on the virtues of civil disobedience, which if applied appropriately does neither too little, nor too much.

In the fifties and sixties in the southern United States the battle for civil rights was at its peak. In 1953 the landmark case of Plessy vs. Ferguson, which had established the constitutionality of segregated facilities in 1896, was overruled by the Supreme Court (Buzzard and Campbell 105). In spite of this ruling however, there were certain loopholes that allowed the state of Alabama to maintain their segregation laws on the public buses (Buzzard and Campbell 106). On December 1, 1955 Parks made her famous refusal to move further back on the Montgomery city bus she was riding once the section designated for Caucasians had become full (Buzzard and Campbell 108). Guided by prayer and careful consideration the Black community of Alabama, under the leadership of Rev. King, Jr., decided to boycott the bus system as a means of non-violent protest against an unjust situation until

Perspectives On Christianity, Society & The Law

more fair treatment could be guaranteed (Buzzard and Campbell 110). For about six months the Caucasian community enforced every possible law on the Black boycotters hoping to coerce them to end the boycott, which was causing the bus company serious economic trouble (Buzzard and Campbell 110). Then on June 4, 1955 the federal district courts ruled that bus segregation was unconstitutional, which was confirmed by the Supreme Court in November of that same year. The Montgomery bus boycott did more than mark a great accomplishment for the Black community; it also helped establish the use of non-violent resistance as a viable force in causing large-scale social and political change in America (Buzzard and Campbell 111). King immediately recognized the power of such public actions to focus the consciousness of America on the plight of the Black community and the racial inequalities of the south in the United States at that time.

This case is especially relevant to this discussion because it exhibits many of the previous established principles of civil disobedience in action. First, the illegal actions taken by Rev. King, Jr. and the rest of the Black community were not what forced the city to act, but rather the public outcry after witnessing the unjust treatment is what likely caused the city to acquiesce. Second, while the action was begun by one person, it was the corporate will to overcome the oppression which had the ultimate effect. Third, the decision to act was only made after careful consideration and consultation with God and with men, and the actions were then undertaken with great seriousness. And last but certainly not least, the injustice and oppression imposed by the Caucasian majority was met with non-violence and even sentiments of love from the Black minority. Rev King, Jr. was very adamant that those who followed his leadership in the battle for civil rights adhere to the commandment issued by Jesus to love ones neighbour, and to show kindness to one's enemies.

In conclusion, the ultimate question for those faced with a conflict of interest between the requests of their government and the requirements of their religion is not "should disobedience be justified?" But rather, "can anyone be justified in feeling as if their civic duty has been satisfied entirely by their actions in the ballot box?" At a core level, Christians are "children of God" and followers of Christ; ultimately the most important thing we can do is to have our actions reflect this on an everyday basis, not just on the day the ballots are cast. A Christian's awareness of this concept is key, but equally important is that the duty is not undertaken lightly. As one commentator points out, "breaking the law of the land is serious, but as we have seen, it is not always wrong" (Redekop). Perhaps the most compelling source of practical guidance on the subject is Rev. King's, Jr. in light of his experiences as well as the vast wisdom displayed in his words. Rev. King's, Jr. view on civil disobedience was rooted in the message of Romans 14:19 which states "let us therefore do whatever leads to peace and mutual edification." When imprisoned in 1963 for directly disobeying a court order, Rev. King, Jr. wrote his famous "Letter from a Birmingham" Jail to a group of clergymen who were upset with his illegal deeds. Truly, it is the words of Rev King, Jr. himself in this letter that provide possibly the most cogent and accurate portrayal of the spirit of Christian civil disobedience. In this letter Rev King, Jr. wrote the following:

> An individual who breaks a law that his conscience tells him
> is unjust, and willingly accepts the penalty by staying in jail to
> arouse the conscience of the community over its injustice, is in
> reality expressing the very highest respect for the law.

NOTES

1   Mark 16:15

2   This includes Matthias, who was chosen by the remaining 11 to replace Judas Iscariot who had hung himself after betraying Jesus.

3   In this instance "the south" refers to the states that were part of the confederacy during the U.S. Civil War, and were a centre of major racial prejudice as well.

WORKS CITED

Bennett, John C. Christians and the State. New York: Charles Scribner's Sons, 1958.

Blank, Wayne. What Happened to the Apostles. Daily Bible Study. 18 Mar. 2004
<http://www.keyway.ca/htm2002/whatapos.htm>.

Buzzard, Lynn, and Paula Campbell. Holy Resistance. Ann Arbor: Servant Books,
1984.

Childress, James F. Civil Disobedience and Political Obligation. New Haven: Yale
UP, 1971.

King, Martin L. Letter from Birmingham Jail. Dr. Martin Luther King Jr. Memorial
Foundation. 18 Mar. 2004
<http://www.mlkfdn.org/letter_from_birming ham_jail.htm>.

Redekop, John H. The Christian & Civil Disobedience. Winnipeg: Kindred Press
1990.

Redekop, John H. Christians and Civil Disobedience. 20 Jan. 2004 <http://www.
evangelicalfellowship.ca/resources/resource_viewer.asp?Resource_ID=106>.

Robinson, B A. Violence at U.S. Abortion Clinics. 15 Mar. 2004. 20 Mar. 2004
<http://www.religioustolerance.org/abo_viol.htm>.

Stevick, Daniel B. Civil Disobedience and the Christian. New York: The Seabury P,
1969.

Tactics of Christian Resistance: A Symposium. Ed. Gary North. Tyler: Geneva
Divinity School, 1983.

The NIV Study Bible. Ed. Kenneth Barker. 2nd ed. Grand Rapids: Zondervan
House, 1995.

Thoreau, Henry D. Walden and Resistance to Civil Government. Ed. William
Rossi. 2nd ed. New York: W.W. Norton & Company, 1992.

PROTECTING FREEDOMS FROM HATE LAW

Jeremy Vallerand

XV

In September 2003 the much-debated and highly-controversial Bill C-250 was passed in The House of Commons by a vote of 141 to 110. The Bill seeks to amend the "hate propaganda sections of the Criminal Code to expand the current definition of protected groups that now includes "colour, race, religion, or ethnic origin" to also include 'sexual orientation'"("Vote Results on C-250"). My thesis is that Bill C-250 poses a direct threat to the freedom of religion and one's ability to express the beliefs of that religion. With these threats in mind, the religious community must understand and consider the implications of Bill C-250 in order to ensure that freedoms are preserved and protected.

In order to clearly present the issue and adequately support my thesis, I will discuss the topic in the following manner. First, I will present a brief legal background of hate propaganda, which will provide a general understanding of what hate crime is and how it has traditionally been defined and understood. Secondly, with this framework in place, I will continue by discussing the history of Bill C-250, considering how and why the Bill came into being in order to develop an understanding of the purpose and motivation behind the Bill, as well as the reason the Bill encountered so much criticism and debate. Thirdly, I will discuss the threat, whether real or perceived, of the Bill and whether those threats have the potential to infringe upon the freedoms of religious groups. Fourthly, after considering the possible threats that Bill C-250 presents, I will then present a Christian response to the Bill and discuss what measures can be taken in order to protect certain freedoms.

In order to effectively engage and interact with the issues surrounding Bill C-250, it is essential to first develop a brief understanding of hate propaganda as a part of Canada's Criminal Code. Hate propaganda is a significant aspect of the Criminal Code, covered in sections 318–320. The hate propaganda sections are in place to protect groups from the "public incitement of hatred" which is defined as "communicating statements in any public place" in a manner that "incites hatred against any identifiable group where such incitement is likely to lead to a breach of the peace" (319 [1]). According to the Criminal Code "'statements' includes words spoken or written or recorded electronically or electro-magnetically or otherwise, and gestures, signs or other visible representations" (319[7]).

The terms, definitions, and explanations regarding hate law in the criminal code are quite extensive. Though some areas are very detailed and may be difficult to understand due to the ambiguity of terms, the code strives to define very clearly, in section 318, the potential punishment for those advocating or promoting genocide. The criminal code states that those found guilty of an indictable offence may be punished by a prison sentence of up to five years. The sentences given by judges, however, can cover an extremely large range, varying from the maximum prison sentence to a small fine.

Within the Criminal Code there is an important statement that is repeated as a subsection of sections 318-320: the statement declares that there can be no proceeding for an offence without the consent of the Attorney General. In other words, for any criminal case dealing with a hate law violation there must first, before there can be any proceedings, be approval by the Attorney General. This statement is designed to serve as a safeguard to ensure that certain rights are preserved as well as to prevent proceedings based on perceived violations that are the result of a misinterpretation of the Criminal Code.

Another significant safeguard within the code, which is designed to protect religious groups, is the statement from section 319, subsection 2b, which states that no person can be convicted "if, in good faith, he expressed or attempted to establish by argument an opinion on a religious subject." This safeguard is designed to protect religious groups who may wish to express certain beliefs held by their religion which may be seen as controversial or even hateful. There is, however, significant debate over the meaning and interpretation of the words "in good faith" and as a result many feel that there is very little that is actually protected by this statement.

In order to understand the Bill and the reason for much of the debate over the issues presented by the Bill, it is important develop a brief understanding of who the key figures are in the political debate. The two primary figures are Svend Robinson and Vic Toews. Bill C-250 was created by MP Robinson with the intent of adding "sexual orientation" to those considered an "identifiable group" in section 318 of the criminal code. Robinson was first elected in 1979 to the House of Commons and now represents the Burnaby-Douglas constituency of British Columbia. At one time, after being nominated at the age of twenty-five , he served as the youngest member of the federal New Democratic Party caucus. Robinson is now British Columbia's senior MP, having been elected and e-elected seven times.

Since his completion of his graduate studies at the London School in Economics in England, Robinson has become an influential and respected political figure. Robinson has also received numerous awards some of which include the Edith Adamson Award for Leadership in Issues of Conscience and the National Kurdish Human Rights Award. Robinson is also known for being the first Member of Parliament who is openly gay (Biography of Svend J. Robinson MP).

Toews, the Chief Opposition Justice Critic for the Canadian Alliance, has been one of the most significant opponents of Bill C-250. Toews has served as a Legal Counsel to numerous departments of government as well as Crown Prosecutor in Brandon, Manitoba. After his appointment as the Director of Constitutional Law for the province of Manitoba and a Queen's Counsel, Toews received much of the experience he needed to eventually become the Attorney General and Minister of Justice for the Province of Manitoba (Personal Profile of Vic Toews).

In a speech made to the members of Parliament, Toews condemned Bill C-250 and spoke directly of his opponent, MP Robinson. In the same speech he also stated the views of the Canadian Alliance party and expressed his concerns with the proposed Bill:

I want to make it clear that the Canadian Alliance rejects hatred
directed at any group in Canada. We have heard the kind of
vitriolic statements made by the member for Burnaby—Douglas [Svend Robinson] against certain groups in our society. Even
if he does not share their religious beliefs, a little more respect
toward those religious groups would be in order. Our party
does not choose and pick favourites. We reject hatred directed
at any group in Canada. In that context we have consistently
expressed concern about Bill C-250 on the basis that it raises
serious concerns for fundamental freedoms.

While this bill may be motivated by good intentions,
and I give the member the benefit of that doubt because I have
no reason to doubt his word as an [honourable] member, good
intentions however often have unintended consequences. When
those intentions and unintended consequences form a part of
our laws, the impact can significantly interfere with the ability
of people to communicate or to adhere to essential matters of
personal belief, religious or otherwise. (Speaking Out on C-
250)

This quote, in many ways, represents the majority of those who are opposed to the

Bill, especially at a political level. Many of those opposed to the Bill, have taken great

care to ensure that Canadians do not equate opposition of the Bill with the support

of hatred. Members of the Canadian Alliance continually emphasise that they do not

seek to promote hatred by opposing this Bill, but rather to protect freedom. They ar-

gue that though Bill C-250 may seem to protect some Canadians, it threatens many

more and jeopardises their fundamental freedoms.

In the "Frequently Asked Questions" section of his website, Robinson spe-

cifically addresses the question "Will the new Hate Crimes Legislation (Bill C-250,

formerly C-415) interfere with Canadians' freedom of religious expression?" In his

response to this question Robinson states:

It is important to note that C-250 in no way limits or threatens the freedom of religious expression or religious texts. The
Criminal Code expressly protects this freedom in subsection
319(3), which states:

No person shall be convicted of an offence...if, in good faith, he
expressed or attempted to establish by argument an opinion on
a religious subject.

There is an additional protection in that no criminal
proceeding under section 318 and 319 of the criminal code may
be instituted without the consent of the Attorney General. This
will prevent frivolous and trivial prosecutions.

Though Robinson offers an accurate description of what preventative measures
presently exist within the Criminal Code, those who disagree with Bill C-250 insist
that these measures are not enough. This fundamental disagreement between the
two sides, as to whether or not freedoms are being compromised, is what has kept
Robinson and Toews in heated debate over the issue.

It is extremely evident that there are drastically different views as to the
impact and implications that Bill C-250 will have, so it is important to develop a
thorough and informed perspective on the issues presented by this Bill. To do so we
must consider why Robinson sees this Bill as an important step for Canada to take
towards the protection of homosexuals from hatred. We must also, however, consider
the reasons for the opposition. To what degree does the Bill pose a threat to the
freedoms of Canadians, and what freedoms could be threatened? With these ideas in
mind we will now consider the issues surrounding this controversial Bill and how it
will affect Canadians and the freedoms they value.

Catherine Cookson writes that "during periods of panic, society may
select a nondominant segment and an activity identified with that segment, and
imagine itself to be seriously threatened by that Otherness" (113). She then goes on
to quote from Stanley Cohen's, "Folk Devils and Moral Panics" which states:

Societies appear to be subject, every now and then, to periods
of moral panic. A condition, episode, person, or group of
persons emerges to become defined as a threat to societal values
and interests; its nature is presented in a stylised and stereotypi-
cal fashion by the mass media; the moral barricades are manned
by editors, bishops, politicians, and other right-thinking people.
(Cohen 9)

In some ways this seems to be descriptive of much of the controversy surrounding Bill C-250. Much of the year leading up to September of 2003, when Bill C-250 was passed by the House of Commons, could have been characterised by a state of fear and panic, as those who opposed the Bill made every effort to prevent it from becoming law. During this time religious groups, politicians, and many others were making desperate attempts to defeat the Bill by sending out urgent messages in church bulletins, distributing information pamphlets, emailing newsletters and taking countless other measures. At the same time, and in the time leading up to this, the creator of the Bill, Robinson, was also driven by a strong sense of urgency to get the Bill through the House. One of the major driving forces motivating Robinson, an openly gay member of parliament, was a strong sense of conviction and determination to protect the citizens of Canada from the hateful activity of people like. Fred Phelps, pastor of Westboro Baptist Church in Topeka, Kansas.

The Westboro Baptist Church, under the direction of Phelps runs the controversial website www.godhatesfags.com and is responsible for picketing hundreds of schools, churches, funerals and other events with signs saying things such as "Fags burn in hell," "AIDS cures fags," "Fags can't repent," "Fags are beasts," and "Fags are worthy of death." Groups of protesters affiliated with the Westboro Baptist Church have stirred up controversy all across the United States, especially in their attendance at funerals. In response to a question about why the church picketed funerals, Phelps stated, "[w]hen people go to funerals, they have thoughts of mortality, heaven, hell, eternity, etc., on their minds. It's the perfect time to warn them of things to come. Is it mean, hateful, uncompassionate, etc.? I'm sure it is..." ("Why Do You Picket Funerals").

One of the biggest scandals surrounding the Westboro Baptist Church and its anti-homosexual movement has been the monument that it is attempting to erect in a park in Casper, Wyoming. The monument is to be dedicated to Matthew Shepard, a young man who was killed for being homosexual, and says "MATTHEW SHEPARD, Entered Hell October 12, 1998, in Defiance of God's Warning: 'Thou shalt not lie with mankind as with womankind; it is abomination.' Leviticus 18:22" ("Letter to the City Council"). In addition to these controversial activities, Pastor

Phelps has expressed a desire to bring his anti-homosexual movement to Canada, exactly the kind of thing Mr. Robinson is striving to prevent. Both politicians and law enforcement figures have expressed concerns that without the passing of Bill C-250, there is little that could be done to prevent Phelps from spreading his hatred in Canada. Though the Bill may prevent people like Phelps from promoting hatred, many believe that such prevention comes at too high a price and that the Bill threatens too many freedoms, namely those dealing with religion and speech.

In order to consider the extent to which Bill C-250 threatens religious freedom and the freedom to express the beliefs of that religion, it is important to briefly consider what it means to have freedom of speech and freedom of religion. Nicholas Wolfson states, "free speech, liberally interpreted, permits the flowering of the human mind" (48). Shortly after this he states that "the model of a free market of ideas limited to bloodless, cerebral cogitation is too limited to encompass the reality of discourse. Hence, to complain about racial and sexist speech because it is emotionally charged and low in ideational content is not very convincing." In other words, by limiting the extent of the freedom of speech to what is pleasant the very flowering of the human mind is stunted. Wolfson goes on to say that "we address the contention that hate speech causes emotional, societal, and psychological harm and therefore should be censored. We argue that the purpose of free speech protection is to safeguard speech that the government views as harmful. Any other approach would permit the government to be the arbiter of what ideas are safe." According to this argument the very purpose of the laws protecting freedom of speech is to prevent the government from determining what is appropriate and what is not, therefore to allow the government to do so is to defeat the purpose altogether.

The freedom of religion is, in many ways, linked very closely to the freedom of speech. In his commentary on the Constitutional Law of Canada Peter Hogg states, concerning religious freedom, that "it must include the right to hold any religious belief and to profess it openly" (Hogg 711). He then goes on to quote the International Covenant on Civil and Political Rights, which "provides that freedom of religion includes the right to manifest [one's] religion or belief in worship, observance, practice or teaching." If the ability to express and teach the beliefs held by a religion is hindered or even prevented, then the freedom of religion itself is compromised. It is therefore impossible to threaten the ability to express certain controversial religious beliefs, without inherently threatening the freedom of religion itself.

In 1945 there was a motion in the House of Commons by MP Alistair Stewart that "there should be incorporated in the constitution a Bill of rights protecting minority rights, civil and religious liberties, freedom of speech and freedom of assembly; establishing equal treatment before the law of all citizens, irrespective of race, nationality or religious or political beliefs" (Romanow 221). The protections of rights and freedoms that MP Alistair Stewart envisioned over fifty years ago, many believe, are now being threatened by Bill C-250. On September 17, 2003 when the Bill was passed in the House of Commons, Toews called it "a dangerous Bill that will toss fundamental Canadian freedoms out the window" ("Free Speech in Jeopardy") and stated that "it raises serious concerns for freedom of expression and religion in Canada" ("Alliance Amendments to C-250 Strengthen Freedom").

One of the major issues in discussion is the threat that Bill C-250 poses to the freedom of speech. There has been much debate over the legitimacy of the fears that this Bill will threaten the freedom of speech (as many proponents of the Bill claim). Those in favour of the Bill argue that it will not infringe upon freedom of expression nor threaten the abilities of religious groups to express their moral beliefs. They claim that "while Bill C-250 may appear to authorise criminal prohibitions against the expression of moral concerns about homosexual activity, this new law would never be used in that way because a prosecution requires the consent of the provincial Attorney General" (Bill C-250 – An Attack on Free Speech). In other words, those who support the Bill claim that there is a sufficient safeguard in place to ensure that the Bill does not violate the freedom of speech. This safeguard, they say, lies in the fact that before there can be prosecution, a case must be approved by the Attorney General, who will ensure that inappropriate cases are not admitted to trial and thus prevent the misuse or abuse of the Bill.

Those who oppose the Bill, however, disagree with this point because the consent of the Attorney General is not required for either civil or non-criminal pro-

Perspectives On Christianity, Society & The Law

ceedings. They state that the above argument "fails to recognise that these provisions can and will be used by private interest groups as a basis for civil lawsuits and other non-criminal proceedings in order to restrict free speech and religious freedom" (Bill C-250 – An Attack on Free Speech). The application of the Bill in civil and non-criminal cases could be widespread. Such application would include the ability of Canada Customs to prevent both materials and visitors from entering the country should they express moral concerns about sexual orientation. The Bill could also threaten the charitable tax status of religious organisations or religious educational institutions that express those same moral concerns about sexual orientation (Bill C-250 – An Attack on Free Speech). In short, the protection offered by the Attorney General clause is believed by many to be insufficient to provide adequate protection of the freedom of speech or the freedom of religion.

Many opponents of the Bill also have expressed fear about the loose drafting of the Bill. Brian Rushfeldt, executive director of the Canada Family Action Coalition, says that the most dangerous aspect of the Bill is that "hate" and "hate propaganda" lack a concrete definition. In addition to this, "Prime Minister Jean Chretien, when he was justice minister, told a constitutional parliamentary committee in 1981 that 'sexual orientation' should not be in the Canadian constitution because it is too 'difficult to interpret, to define'" (Moore). Many Canadians share the belief that the loose drafting of the Bill is what threatens freedoms the most. There are numerous concerns, from both religious and non-religious groups, that there is not an adequate number of safeguards within the Bill to ensure that freedoms are protected. Toews stated that "while no one should express hatred against homosexuals, this law is so loosely drafted that it would make it an offence to criticise homosexual conduct" (Concern Over Bill C-250 continues to Grow). Toews is not alone in his belief that this Bill could criminalise mere criticism of homosexuality, a topic of particular interest to religious groups whose religious texts speak directly against homosexual practices.

In October of 2002, the Canada Family Action Coalition distributed an "action alert" that contained a list of possible consequences should the Bill become law in Canada. The list was as follows:

- The Bible, at least certain portions of the Bible, may be declared "hate literature."

- Churches will not be able to mention certain Scriptures.

- Clergy may be subjected to criminal charges if they refuse to marry homosexuals.

- Parents may be subjected to criminal charges if they refuse to allow their children to attend classes that teach about and promote homosexual behaviour.

- Expressing disagreement with homosexual behaviour or the homosexual agenda, either verbally or in writing, would be considered hate propaganda.

- Educators, including those at private religious schools, will not be able to refuse to teach homosexual curriculum.

- Religious institutions will not be allowed to teach anything non-supportive of homosexual sex.

- Canadian Blood Services will not be allowed to screen risk-behaviour donors.

- Governments (including local municipalities) will be prevented from passing (even debating) sex standards laws. (World Net Daily)

Some advocates of the Bill argue that the above list is merely an attempt to strike fear into the hearts of Canadian citizens in order to raise up a strong opposition to the Bill. Many, however, feel that such outcomes are not only possible but may be inevitable should the Bill become law.

In response to the question, are the freedoms of religion, speech and expression at risk in Canada today? The answer is a resounding yes. Even prior to Bill C-250 being passed into law, these freedoms were being threatened. A example of this threat is the federal court ruling from December of 2002, in Saskatchewan, which determined that "the Bible amounted to hate literature" (Plowman). The case involved an advertisement run in the Saskatoon Star Phoenix on Gay Pride day by Hugh Owens. The add, run in 1997, featured references to four biblical passages condemning homosexuality, followed by an equal sign, and then a red circle with a slash through it (similar to a no smoking sign) over two stick men holding hands. In response to questioning about the add, Owens stated that he wanted to draw attention to the biblical teachings on homosexuality. Shortly after the article was run, Owens was sued by three homosexuals. Eventually, the judge ruled in favour of the homosexuals and Owens was forced to pay each man fifteen thousand dollars. According to the judge Owens was in violation of the provincial human-rights code which "forbids publication of text and symbols that would expose people to hatred, ridicule, or 'affront of dignity' on account of their sexual orientation" (Plowman). In other words, the use of those biblical passages, within that context, was determined to be a violation of the provincial code.

Cases like this are already establishing a precedent within the legal system, and it is safe to assume that such cases will only increase if their cause is strengthened by the passing of Bill C-250. With this in mind, Christians need to be informed and educated about the issues at hand and active in voicing their concerns about them. As the issues surrounding Bill C-250 become increasingly apparent throughout Canada, the Christian community should not merely assess the present state of society but rather engage the issues in a manner that will facilitate action and invoke change.

I recently sent an email to. Vic Toews to inquire about how Canadians can continue to express opposition to this Bill in a relevant and effective manner. In response to the email Toews' Legislative Assistant, Tara Baran, said "Most likely, when Parliament resumes in January, Robinson will re-introduce Bill C-250 and it will automatically be referred to the Senate. For this reason, we are continuing to encourage people to write to senators, in particular the senators who sit on the Standing Senate Committee for Legal and Constitutional Affairs." In addition to this information, she also referred me to the website of the Evangelical Fellowship of Canada. The EFC, in response to the Bill, encourages Canadians to:

- Pray for the Senators as they deliberate on this Bill. Pray particularly that they will hold full public hearings on the Bill. This was not done at the House of Commons, partly because it was a private member's Bill.

- Pray for the EFC and others who are responding to this issue.

- Letters of concern can also be sent to Senators. Due to the urgency of this issue, letters should be sent by e-mail or by fax. (Hate Literature, Bill C-250)

There is a variety of other information available from the Evangelical Fellowship of Canada which can be accessed on their website (www.evangelicalfellowship.ca), including a sample letter for those interested in contacting a senator.

In order to protect the freedoms jeopardised by this Bill, the Christian community must join together in a politically effective and culturally relevant manner. Toews has made continual efforts to do so by proposing a variety of amendments to the Bill that would greatly limit its ability to infringe upon religious freedoms. Unfortunately, however, none of his amendments have been accepted and in January the Bill will most likely go to the Senate in its original form. This does not, however, mean that the Christian community should abandon the cause. Instead, they should continue to stand upon their rights, taking every precaution to ensure that their freedoms are protected. The threat is real, the opposition is strong, but hope is not lost. The Christian community must emphasise that their intent is not to exploit their freedoms like Fred Phelps of the Westboro Baptist Church has done, but simply to protect them. British author George Orwell stated in regards to liberty and free speech that "If liberty means anything at all, it means the right to tell people what they do not want to hear" (Orwell). The goal is not to promote a democratic freedom to hate, but rather to protect the freedom and liberty of all Canadians by guarding the right to tell people what they do not want to hear.

In conclusion, I believe that Bill C-250 poses a direct threat to the freedom of religion and one's ability to express the beliefs of their religion. After considering the intentions and the implications of the Bill, I believe it becomes evident that the Bill is a threat to Canadians and their freedoms. As a Christian community it is essential that we stand in opposition to the Bill in order to protect freedom of religion and expression. We must move forward in unity, educated on the issues at hand, sensitive to the culture around, and grounded in the values we hold, so that together we can guard the freedoms of Canadians.

WORKS CITED

"Alliance Amendments to C-250 Strengthen Freedom of Expression, Religion." 6 June 2003. 17 Oct. 2003 <http://www.victoews.com/c_250/Report%20Stage%20Amendments_press.pdf>.

"Bill C-250 An Attack on Free Speech." 9 Oct. 2003 <http://www.victoews.com/c_250/Bill%20C-250%20%20An%20Attack%20on%20Free%20Speech.pdf>.

Biography of Svend J. Robinson MP. 18 Oct.2003 <http://www.svendrobinson.ca/bio/>.

Cohen, Stanley. Folk Devils and Moral Panics: The Creation of Mods and the Rockers. London: MacGibbon & Kee, 1972.

"Concern Over Bill C-250 continues to Grow." 28 Jan. 2003. 10 Oct. 2003 <http: //www.victoews.com/c_250/c250_grows.pdf>.

Cookson, Catherine. Regulating Religion: The Courts and the Free Exercise Clause. New York: Oxford UP, 2001.

Criminal Code. Aug. 2003. 10 Oct. 2003 <http://laws.jus tice.gc.ca/en/c46/41491. html>.

"Hate Literature, Bill C-250." 15 Oct. 2003 <http://www.evangelicalfellowship.ca/social/initiatives.asp#Bill_C_250>.

Hogg, Peter W. Constitutional Law of Canada. Toronto: Carswell Company Ltd, 1985.

"Free Speech in Jeopardy After Liberals Pass 'Dangerous' Law." 17 Sept. 2003. 11 Oct. 2003 < http://www.victoews.com/c250/freespeech.pdf>.

"Letter to City Council of Casper, Wyoming." Online Posting. 3 Oct. 2003. 15 Oct. 2003 <http://www.godhatesfags.com/fliers/oct2003/Matthew_Shepard_Monument_10-2-2003.pdf>.

Moore, Art. "The Law of The Land: The Bible As 'Hate Literature'?" World Net Daily. 21 Oct. 2002.16 Oct. 2003 < http://www.worldnetdaily.com/news/article.as p?ARTICLE_ID=29328>.

Orwell, George. "Speech Quotes." 28 Jan. 2004 <http://quotes.telemanage.ca/quotes.nsf/quotesByCat?ReadForm&Start=1&Count=1000&ExpandView&restrictToCategory=Speech>.

Personal Profile of Vic Toews. MP. Online Posting. 18 Oct. 2003 <http://www.victoews.com/bio.asp>.

Plowman, Edward E. "Silenced in Saskatchewan." World Magazine 1 Mar. 2003: Vol.18, No.8.

Romanow, Roy. John Whyte, and Howard Leeson. Canada... Not Withstanding: The Making Of the Constitution 1976-1982. Toronto: Carswell/Methuen, 1984.

"Vote Results on C-250." Online Posting. 17 Oct. 2003 <http://www.victoews.com/c_250/index.asp>.

"Why Do You Picket Funerals." Online Posting. 12 Nov. 2003 <http://www.godhatesfags.com/main/faq.html#Funeral>.

Wolfson, Nicholas. Hate Speech, Sex Speech, Free Speech. Connecticut: Praeger Publishers, 1997.

ABOUT THE SCHOOL OF BUSINESS

Established in 1975 and located in Langley, British Columbia, the School of Business at Trinity Western University aims to equip students with what they need to face the ethical and moral issues they'll encounter in today's complex marketplace.

With an enrolment of over 500 students, our business program is values-based and experiential. Our expert faculty bring a carefully thought-out Christian faith perspective to the classroom. Students are challenged to evaluate the theories, practices and problems of modern business in light of biblical principles. In the context of an overall Trinity Western liberal arts education, students discover business in an integrated framework—enabling them to approach issues with an informed, critical mind.

Our graduates have gone on to start their own businesses, work with national and multi-national companies, establish careers with non-profit organizations, and attend graduate schools across the country in the fields of business and law.

Our leading program is the Bachelor of Business Administration (BBA). Within the BBA we offer seven specializations: accounting; finance; marketing; human resource management; entrepreneurship; international business; and leadership and management. For flexibility, we also offer a Bachelor of Arts with a major in Business Administration (BA).

For more information, visit us on the web at www.twu.ca/business